Poetry and Personality

Steven Van Zoeren

Poetry and Personality

READING, EXEGESIS, AND HERMENEUTICS IN TRADITIONAL CHINA

STANFORD UNIVERSITY PRESS

Stanford, California   1991

Stanford University Press
Stanford, California
© 1991 by the Board of Trustees
of the Leland Stanford Junior University
Printed in the United States of America

CIP data appear at the end of the book

The House Was Quiet and the World Was Calm

The house was quiet and the world was calm.
The reader became the book; and summer night

Was like the conscious being of the book.
The house was quiet and the world was calm.

The words were spoken as if there was no book,
Except that the reader leaned above the page,

Wanted to lean, wanted much most to be
The scholar to whom his book is true, to whom

The summer night is like a perfection of thought.
The house was quiet because it had to be.

The quiet was part of the meaning, part of the mind:
The access of perfection to the page.

And the world was calm. The truth in a calm world,
In which there is no other meaning, itself

Is calm, itself is summer and night, itself
Is the reader leaning late and reading there.
                                    —Wallace Stevens

I shall read very carefully (or try to read, since they may be
partly obliterated, or in a foreign language) the inscriptions
already there. Then I shall adapt my own compositions, in
order that they may not conflict with those written by the
prisoner before me. The voice of a new inmate will be no-
ticeable, but there will be no contradictions or criticisms of
what has already been laid down, rather a "commentary."
. . . My "works" . . . will be brief, suggestive, anguished,
but full of the lights of revelation. And no small part of the
joy these writings will give me will be to think of the person
coming after me—the legacy of thoughts I shall leave him,
like an old bundle tossed carelessly into a corner!
                                    —Elizabeth Bishop, "In Prison"

The Odes have no perfect interpretation.
                                    —Dong Zhongshu

Acknowledgments

In writing about an approach that constantly reverts to questions concerning earlier texts, authorities, and teachers, one is led to reflect on the sources of one's own ideas and concerns. Most of these sources are, I hope, documented at the end of this volume, but there are a few individuals whose contributions cannot be summed up in the confines of an endnote. In my first years at Harvard, I profited from the teaching of Professors James Robert Hightower, Patrick Hanan, and Ronald C. Egan. To the last I am indebted for many insights concerning the *Analects* and the *Zuo Tradition*. Roberto Mangabeira Unger of the Harvard Law School inspired me with the example of his intellect and his commitment; moreover, he first suggested to me the idea of working on exegetical tradition. Professor Benjamin Schwartz introduced me to the study of Chinese thought and was a supportive and insightful reader of the dissertation from which this study grew. Stephen Owen was a friend when I needed a friend and a teacher when I needed a teacher; without him this study would surely never have been completed.

Philip J. Ivanhoe, Richard John Lynn, John McRae, and Lothar von Falkenhausen all read the manuscript in its entirety and offered many useful corrections and suggestions, as did the anonymous reader for the Stanford University Press. Michael Fuller offered cogent criticisms of my discussion of Ouyang Xiu. At the Stanford University Press, I must thank my editor, Helen Tartar, as well as John Ziemer, who, in addition to offering many useful suggestions, saved me from many embarrassing errors. For those that remain, of course, neither he nor any of the people mentioned above should be held responsible.

Two institutions have been important for the writing of this study. The Society of Fellows at Harvard gave me time, office space, and good conversation. My colleagues at the Department of Asian Languages at Stanford, especially Albert Dien, John Wang, and Chuang Yin, have provided both moral support and answers to the questions with which I plagued them.

Finally, I must thank my wife, Pei-shan, for her support and for her willingness to take time away from her own busy schedule to write characters, discuss interpretations, and generally hold my hand. As for my children, Allie and Nick, I should thank them for adding, in the words of Joseph Levenson, "years to the writing, and joy to the years."

S. V. Z.

Contents

Poetry and Personality

CHAPTER ONE

Introduction

This is a history of the hermeneutics of China's earliest classic, the *Odes*. Neither a reading of the *Odes* as such, nor yet a history of their interpretation, this study attempts, rather, to trace the principles that guided the interpretation of the *Odes* over some two thousand years of Chinese history. In particular, it focuses on the style of reading associated with the Mao school of *Odes* scholarship, an approach that became orthodox in the early imperial period, informed the influential general hermeneutic of the Song Neoconfucians, and affected the understanding and composition of literary texts, painting, and music. This hermeneutic had a long and complex history, and it differs in some interesting and important ways from the dominant hermeneutic traditions of the West.

A consideration of hermeneutic context has been largely absent from most studies of Chinese thought; but it was not, for all that, unimportant. Perhaps more than any of its historical counterparts, China's civilization was preoccupied with problems of interpretation. The earliest Chinese thought and religion were mantic: the world was alive with portents and omens, of which the signs on the oracle bones of the Shang kings are only the most famous examples.[1] Moreover, for much of its history Chinese civilization focused upon and revered the study of the canonical texts of the past. Adherents of all the great "teachings" (*jiao*) of China—Confucianism, Daoism, and Buddhism—closely studied their various classics (*jing*) and exegetical traditions (*zhuan*), and the interpretation and exegesis of canonical texts were occasions for normative, political, and speculative teaching and thinking. In this respect, Confucianism, Daoism, and Buddhism more nearly resembled the doctrinal cultures that grew up among "the peoples of the Book"—Jews, Christians, and Moslems— than they did what we call philosophy in the West,[2] and their concerns and controversies are often impossible to understand apart from their hermeneutic context.

The hermeneutic disposition also shaped the political, social, and cultural institutions of traditional China. The study of the classics was seen as one of the central tasks—indeed often *the* central task—of one engaged in the Confucian, Daoist, or Buddhist project. The imperial patronage of Confucianism (and, more rarely, Daoism and Buddhism) and especially the examination system in which candidates for state office were tested on their knowledge of the canon made questions concerning the interpretation of the canon prominent in public as well as in private life. The court debates over the content of the orthodox canon and its correct interpretation, the great scholarly projects by which the state attempted to specify doctrinal orthodoxy, and the perceived links between doctrinal and political iconoclasm testify to the importance of hermeneutics. The study of texts and their authoritative commentaries—"classics study" (*jingxue*), as it came to be called in the case of Confucianism—permeated the intellectual and religious life of China, from the most public uses of state power to what may have been the paradigmatic instance of a private, internal (*nei*) activity: silent, individual reading.[3]

The reconstruction of the hermeneutics of traditional China thus has an inherent historical interest, but the project attracts our attention for other reasons as well. Recent literary criticism and theory have shown a deepening appreciation of the fact that reading is not a simple or passive process, that it is, rather, one in which the reader plays an active and constructive role.[4] What is more, it has become apparent that the codes readers use to construct meaning are social, learned phenomena that are, their apparent inevitability notwithstanding, provisional and historically specific.[5] The study of Chinese hermeneutics offers a perspective from which we may learn to understand the codes by which traditional Chinese texts were written and read. We may thus learn to read them better—to understand them in ways that remove their obscurities and allow them to speak again. We may hope, moreover, that an understanding of traditional Chinese hermeneutics will highlight and make more available our own deeply ingrained assumptions concerning texts, meanings, and minds.

So far, I have spoken of hermeneutics as if it were a simple and readily identifiable phenomenon. In fact, as many writers on the subject have noted, the term "hermeneutics" is and has been applied in the Western tradition in a wide and somewhat confusing variety of ways.[6] We can distinguish several types. In the first case, we may speak of a kind of "textual" hermeneutics. In this, perhaps the earliest sense of the term, "hermeneutics" is used to refer to the rules or principles that guide the interpretation of texts (as opposed to interpretation or exegesis itself). Such hermeneutics were present from an early date in the exegesis of both sacred and secular texts in the ancient and medieval West, as they were also in China.[7] Although they were only rarely explicitly stated, their tacit rules and principles can be reconstructed; indeed, in much of what follows, I give just such a reconstruction of the hermeneutics of the Odes.

Or "hermeneutics" may be used to refer to a theory or body of teachings concerning interpretation, either descriptive or (more commonly) normative. Although there were relatively early obiter dicta concerning interpretation in China and the West, it was not until relatively late in both traditions that systematic and comprehensive attempts were made to specify the principles which should govern reading. In the Western case, hermeneutic theory arose from a reaction on the part of Reformation theologians against the Catholic church's claim that scripture could not be understood apart from the church's teaching; in response, Flacius and others like him attempted to specify the principles by which any reader could interpret and understand the scriptures.[8] In the Chinese case as well, the general hermeneutics developed by the Song Neoconfucians was both a response and an incitement to the breakdown of exegetical authority. The development of this Song general hermeneutic is the subject of the second half of the present work.

In still another sense, "hermeneutics" refers to a methodology, program, or approach in the human sciences. In its various forms, this kind of "programmatic" hermeneutics has been advocated as the privileged method of historiography, literary study, philosophy, and social science.[9] There is no single set of criteria common to all versions of programmatic hermeneutics, but we can distinguish a number of shared concerns: an emphasis on the recovery of the animating intentions behind literary and other cultural texts; the idea that such a recovery is made possible by some bond of common experience and sympathy between the interpreter and those whose works are being interpreted; and the rejection or discounting of methods and approaches that fail, by their devotion to a scientistic methodology, to do justice to the complexities of human experience.[10]

Finally, at the most general level, we can speak of the philosophical hermeneutics of Martin Heidegger and Hans-Georg Gadamer. Paul Ricouer has pointed out how the notion of hermeneutics has shown a tendency to become progressively more general and universal in its application.[11] In the thought of Heidegger, this tendency is taken to its extreme: for the German thinker, humanity's very Being (*Dasein*) is hermeneutical, for it always possesses and seeks to expand upon what Heidegger calls a "preontological" understanding of Being.[12] Moreover, since this preontological understanding cannot simply be taken over into ontology, the phenomenology of Dasein must itself be hermeneutical, since it seeks to restore and expand upon Dasein's preontological understanding.[13] Thus both the content and the method of philosophy are hermeneutical for Heidegger.

In the thought of Gadamer, hermeneutics is concerned once again with historical understanding. In this sense, Gadamer's work is in the spirit of programmatic hermeneuticians like Wilhelm Dilthey, but with the crucial difference that in contrast to, say, Friedrich Schleiermacher, who hoped to overcome or efface historical distance through understanding, Gadamer points to the ineluctably historical nature of understanding. For Gadamer, the interpreter no less than the text studied is also a product of what he calls "effective history" (*Wirkungsgeschichte*) and, as such, is necessarily always within a hermeneutic horizon. Indeed, the "prejudices" that are the result of effective history are not just an unfortunate obstacle to understanding, but rather its very preconditions. At the same time, interpreters are not hermetically sealed within these horizons, but enjoy the possibility of expanding and transforming their horizon through what Gadamer calls a "fusion" with that of the work studied.[14] Although Gadamer writes from a Eurocentric perspective, his work has rich implications for those engaged in the study of culturally or historically remote works, and this study has been influenced and in a sense inspired by his insights.

In this study I use the term "hermeneutics" in a sense narrower than any of those described above. We can say that hermeneutics comes into play when certain texts become authoritative within a culture and are treated as the privileged loci in which value is inscribed. Such texts become the centerpieces of their tradition, and they provide an ultimate justification and foundation for normative argument within that tradition. Studied, memorized, and explicated, their reading and interpretation are not of simply instrumental or historical interest, but rather are consequential both for the interpreter and for society.[15] It is when certain texts become authoritative in this way that the peculiarly intense and careful reading that I call "hermeneutical" comes into being.

Hermeneutics thus defined clearly was a prominent feature of traditional Chinese civilization. What is perhaps less obvious, or perhaps so obvious as to be commonly overlooked, is the extent to which our own culture is likewise hermeneutical and text-centered. The authority and prestige once associated exclusively with sacred texts have not disappeared from the contemporary world but are now shared by literature and the arts, which have for many moderns become a kind of secular scripture. Within the university the close study of texts remains the privileged method of humanistic education, and one of the few assumptions uniting deconstructive theorists and their conservative opponents is the conviction that certain texts can pronounce authoritatively on the nature of the world, social life, or language.[16] Even critics of the orthodox canons take as their preferred method the close reading of those texts they intend either to criticize or to promote. To study a hermeneutic culture like traditional China's is therefore not only to undertake research into something remote, but also to learn about ourselves.

The Odes

The *Odes* (*Shi*), or, as it later came to be known, the *Classic of Odes* (*Shijing*),* is on most modern accounts a collection of early songs and hymns, perhaps representing the repertoire of Zhou court musicians in the sixth or seventh century B.C.E. From an early date, it has been one of the centerpieces of the Confucian tradition and, at least since the time of Xunzi in the third century B.C.E., dignified with the title of "classic" (*jing*).[17] We cannot be sure when most of the pieces that make up the collection were composed; some, most scholars agree, must go back to the earliest years of the Zhou (ca. twelfth century B.C.E.), whereas the composition of others may predate the compilation of the collection by only a few decades.[18] As for the collection of the Odes into a canon, references in the *Analects* and other early texts suggest that the process had already begun in Confucius's day, as does the use during the Spring and Autumn period (722–481 B.C.E.) of the Odes in the "recitation of the Odes" (*fushi*) practice (see Chapter 3). The sixth century B.C.E. seems a likely date for the fixing of the collection in more or less its present form.

The materials collected in the *Odes* are heterogeneous in nature. The "Lauds" (the "Song," the last of the four major sections into which the Odes are divided in the received text) are mostly dynastic hymns and ceremonial pieces, possibly connected with, if not actually performed at, the ancestral sacrifices of the royal houses of Zhou, Lu, and Song.[19] The second

---

*I italicize "Odes" when referring to the *Odes* as an integral text and cite them simply as "the Odes" when it is the poems themselves that are intended. Of course, traditional Chinese texts did not make this distinction, and in practice it is often difficult to say whether a passage in them refers to the Odes themselves or to their collection into a classic.

and third sections, the "Greater Elegantiae" and "Lesser Elegantiae" ("Daya" and "Xiaoya") contain more dynastic pieces, as well as hunting and banquet songs and some political complaints and satires.[20] These songs were quite likely composed at the Zhou court.[21]

The Odes collected in the first section of the *Classic*, the "Airs of the States" ("Guofeng"), hold the greatest interest for the history of hermeneutics as well as for that of literature. These pieces, some one hundred and sixty in number, derive ultimately from the folk songs, spells, and omen-sayings of early China; they include songs of community life, farming, feasting, and, above all, love.[22] Although these songs were modified during their career at the Zhou court, they retain a remarkable and beautiful freshness, songs, it has well been said, from the morning of the world.[23]

A good deal of the charm and also of the historical interest of the Airs derives from the fact that they preserve something of a society which was as yet largely "pre-Confucian," if I may use such a term. They present a world of seasonal festivals, assignations, and infatuations that was, if not untouched by the concerns and strictures which were to coalesce into the system of values we call "Confucianism," at least not totally controlled by it.[24] Take, for instance, the first Ode in Arthur Waley's 1937 translation, *The Book of Songs*, traditionally entitled "Ye you mancao" (Mao #94):*

> Out in the bushlands a creeper grows,
> The falling dew lies thick upon it.
> There was man so lovely,
> Clear brow well rounded.
> By chance I came across him,
> And he let me have my will.
>
> Out in the bushlands a creeper grows,
> The falling dew lies heavy on it.

---

*Scholars identify the 305 Odes by their numerical order in the received "Mao text" of the *Odes* (my "Mao #").

There was a man so lovely,
Well rounded his clear brow.
By chance I came upon him:
'Oh Sir, to be with you is good.'[25]

The structural symmetry of the two verses, along with the
repetition of whole lines and of formulas, suggest the song
origins of this Ode. As Bernhard Karlgren comments in a note
to his translation, it is difficult if not impossible to specify
whether the "person" of the third line is male or female and
to which sex the poem's speaker must belong.[26] In any case,
however, although the liaison may seem to us pastoral and innocent, for later interpreters it posed a thorny problem, for it
articulated an attitude and suggested circumstances uncon-
fined by and even subversive of conventional Confucian morality. Rather like the *Song of Songs* in the Bible, this Ode and
others like it seemed out of place in a work endowed with an
aura of sacrality and antiquity, and as with that work, they
tested the ingenuity of later interpreters.[27] It was out of the
apologetic exegesis of these pieces that the traditional hermeneutic of the Odes developed.

In the chapters that follow, I trace among other themes
some of the ways in which later exegetes accounted for these
Odes. Still, given their "subversive" character, we may wonder how they were collected and why they were in the repertoire of Zhou court musicians. We can, I think, distinguish
three possibilities. First, it would be a mistake to project back
onto Spring and Autumn society the more schematic and puritanical morality advocated and even occasionally enforced
by later Confucians upon princes. Not only the Zhou kings,
but monarchs throughout Chinese history, sought in music
and dance pleasures that could not be accommodated within
the relatively austere ethos of Confucianism. If, as we suppose, the *Odes* represents a "snapshot" of the repertoire of the
Zhou court musicians in the sixth or seventh century B.C.E.,
we should not be surprised to find there the words to songs

that seem incompatible with the sacred character later ascribed to the collection as a whole.[28]

Moreover, at the Zhou court the Odes were first and foremost music, not texts; indeed I argue in Chapter 2 that the historical Confucius, insofar as we can reconstruct his teachings from the *Analects*, was still primarily concerned with the Odes as the musical adjuncts to ritual rather than as texts.[29] It may well be the case that the words of the Odes were a relatively unimportant element of their musical performance or even that they were preserved simply as a mnemonic device. It was only when the music of the Odes had been largely displaced by newer, more seductive sounds that the words became prominent, and an embarrassment to the Confucian ritualists in charge of their teaching.

Finally, certain songs in the present text of the *Odes* suggest that there was already at work in the age while the Odes were being created and altered an accommodating hermeneutic that served to naturalize and defuse the most subversive implications of the Odes. This hermeneutic, which may be reflected in the later practice of recitation of the Odes, seems clearly presupposed by certain of the Elegantiae. The Ode "Gufeng" (Mao #201), for instance, which by its placement among other more manifestly "political" complaints suggests the manner in which it is to be read, is in the form of the plaint of a discarded lover. It is likely that others of the Airs employing the language and imagery of disappointed love were either composed by members of the Zhou court or performed by them as indirect and tactful complaints or remonstrances.[30] It may well be the case that in their life at the Zhou court the Odes had already begun to accrue the associations that would eventually be canonized and mythologized in the Mao school interpretations.

In fact these explanations are not incompatible. There are numerous examples from later Chinese literary history of texts whose supposed didactic character served to justify or allow the pleasure of their reading. James Robert Hightower has suggested, for example, that the Han dynasty *Exoteric Commentary on Han's Odes* (*Hanshi waizhuan*) may have survived because "it was an acceptable anthology of extracts from early literature" whose "pervading moral tone, combined with a nominal association with a Classic, kept the book from the suspicion of frivolity."[31] And David Knechtges has shown in his study of the Han rhapsody (*fu*) how in that form sensual beauty and didactic instruction coexisted in an uneasy alliance.[32] It is entirely possible that associated with the Odes from an early date were two "readings": one proper and apologetic; the other secret, pleasurable, and dangerous.

At any rate, whether because the words of the Odes were considered irrelevant to their function as music or because there already existed during their career as court music interpretive conventions that denied (and yet permitted) the dangerous pleasure of such songs, these Odes were allowed to remain in the canon. The fact that as songs they were memorized verbatim ensured that they would not be prey to the kind of incremental reformulation that shaped and reshaped most doctrinal materials in the pretextual era,[33] and so these Odes survived to trouble and to attract later generations with a unique and disquieting strangeness. This was a remarkable and, I think, very nearly unique event in the history of Chinese literature and thought.[34] It was the need to come to grips with the *Odes* that provided the first occasion for study, hermeneutics, and hermeneutical reflection in China.

The Hermeneutic of the Odes

Doubtless there were a number of different ways of reading the Odes in early China. In the event, however, the reading that was to exert a lasting influence over the history of Chinese hermeneutics was the one summed up by the phrase "The Odes articulate aims" (*shi yan zhi*). Although much of what follows is intended to tease out the complexities of the history (and prehistory) of this claim, it may be useful to begin here with an ahistorical presentation of some of its meanings.

The phrase is a paronomastic definition of the type so common in early Chinese doctrinal teaching. In this formula, the Odes were defined by analyzing the graph for "Ode," *shi*, into its constituent elements, *yan* ("articulate") and *zhi* ("aim, project"): "The Odes articulate *zhi*." The key element in this definition, *zhi*, was a complex term that appeared in a wide variety of contexts in early literature. Variously translated as "aim," "intention," "will," or "purpose," *zhi* perhaps originally meant "goal" or "target."[35] In early texts like the *Zuo Tradition* (*Zuo zhuan*), it has the sense of "ambition"; whereas in the *Analects* the *zhi* was a guiding preoccupation or orientation, rather like the Heideggerian "projection."[36] In later texts like the *Mencius*, the *zhi* became an element of the philosophical anthropology of the day, standing for something like the will.

In dealing with such a protean term, it is well to heed the warnings frequently voiced by Chinese interpreters that words do not necessarily have one single core meaning valid for all contexts.[37] If nevertheless we insist upon such an all-embracing sense for *zhi*, we can perhaps revert to another example of paronomastic definition and explicate the graph for *zhi* in terms of its constituent elements, "heart" (*xin*) and "go" (*zhi*). The *zhi* is where the heart goes: it is the heart in motion toward an as yet unrealized goal.[38]

From the very outset there was a doubleness to the term *zhi*. As with many of the English terms, like "ambition" or "intention," with which we might translate it, *zhi* referred at once to an unrealized but desired state of affairs in the world and to that desire itself as a feature of someone's personality: to both the content of the wish and to the wishing itself. We can employ this distinction to develop some of the complexities of the hermeneutic that focused upon the *zhi*. On the one hand was an interest prominent in the *Analects* stories about "stating (articulating) the aim" (*yan zhi*) and in certain of the *Zuo Tradition* narratives that mention recitation of the Odes. This tradition focused on the internal dimension of *zhi*, taking its articulation to be important because it exemplified something about the person who made it. In this metonymic hermeneutic, the *zhi* revealed or articulated in the Ode was connected to or exemplary of the personality of its author. (This notion of the "connection" between the *zhi* and the personality as a whole was given a quite literal and concrete expression in certain late Zhou texts, notably the *Mencius*.)[39] To reveal the *zhi* was to reveal one's deepest and most compelling hopes and dreams. These dreams—these *zhi*—were by definition unrealized and thus not manifest in the overt text of one's behavior or social role. The revelation of the *zhi* was an assertion that one had depths as yet unplumbed, ambitions as yet unrealized, complexities and value and abilities as yet unperceived and unappreciated.

Then there was the family of approaches to the Odes that stressed the "external" dimension of *zhi* "aim." This view of the Odes, their composition, and their recitation tended to understand the Odes as addressed by an inferior to a superior: from an abandoned wife to her husband, from a minister to his prince. In such readings, by articulating the *zhi*, the Ode's author said what was longed for, whether the reconciliation to be effected was between two lovers or between the prince and the Way. Because for reasons of propriety or prudence such wishes could not always be frankly stated, these *zhi* were indirectly expressed via the Ode. The Odes, in the more schematic versions of this view, were "remonstrances" (*jian*), which "encouraged" (*quan*) the ruler, either by "praising" (*mei*), or, more commonly, "goading" or "satirizing" (*ci*) him. The function of the making or the recitation of the Ode (the two were often not clearly distinguished) was persuasion: by presenting a criticism of things as they were or by presenting a vision of a remade social world, the Ode was to move and to change the other.

This way of looking at the function of the composition or recitation of the Odes had deep roots. In their earliest use, the Odes were closely linked with word magic: with spells, charms, and omen sayings. In the Spring and Autumn and the Warring States (480–222 B.C.E.) periods, it was believed that the Odes could help one to "speak" (*yan*); this view was interested in not only the elegant language of the Odes but also the suasive power that the ancient Chinese no less than the ancient Greeks found so striking in music and poetry. (The *Zuo Tradition* abounds in portrayals of the magically efficacious recitation or quotation of the Odes.) By the Han, if not before, the idea that the Odes could serve as persuasions was given a new twist: the promulgation of the Odes was claimed to be one of the privileged means by which the moral transformation of the empire could be achieved. Moreover, the Odes could be used not only to persuade others but to persuade oneself. Their close study, especially their memorization, recitation, and internalization, became a central element in the Confucian program for personal moral transformation. Like the music with which they were associated, the Odes were thought to elicit in a particularly direct, unmediated way in the student the feelings and impulses that originally gave rise to their composition; they thereby provided a privileged means to the project of mobilizing the emotions in the service of Confucian norms. The Odes became "super-texts" that overcame some of the most intractable difficulties in the Confucian tradition.

Although the notion that the Odes articulated the *zhi* could thus be given a variety of emphases with differing consequences for the meaning and significance of the *Odes*, in practice the two views were connected, and the distinctions between them effaced rather than highlighted. Self-revelation was never disinterested; it was always addressed to another or to others, no matter how vehemently that might be denied. And the particular vision enunciated in the composition or recitation of an Ode was always understood to have social and political consequences. On the other hand, it was precisely the revelation of the self and its inscription in the Odes that were thought to give the Odes their peculiar power.

This account and the hermeneutic associated with it were to be enormously influential in traditional China. When in the eleventh and twelfth centuries C.E. the Song Neoconfucians formulated their new general hermeneutic of the classics, it was the hermeneutic of the Odes that provided the structure if not the vocabulary. And the influence of this method of interpretation was not limited to classics studies. We can list some of the assumptions, first articulated in connection with the Odes, that figured in the poetics of the *shi* "lyric," which took shape as a literary genre in the first, second, and third centuries C.E.[40] Poetry was occasional: it was the product of and indeed "about" certain concrete and typically specifiable situations. It was also self-revelation, the means by which the poet showed to his peers and to posterity those features of his own personality and of his moral vision that were not exhausted by social reality; the reading of poetry was thus often conceived in terms of a process of coming to know the poet as a person. Finally, the poet's concerns were often claimed to be representative of the concerns of society as a whole; he spoke with moral authority. Although such assumptions were by no means uniform throughout the lyric tradition, they did provide the basic context in which much *shi* poetry was composed and read.[41] Variously modified, they also played an important role in the rhetoric of the visual arts and of music.[42]

The history of the reading of the Odes thus provides a unique vantage from which to trace the history of hermeneutics in China. In what follows I attempt to trace that history, or at least part of it. The study falls naturally into two parts. In the next four chapters, I trace the rise and development of

what I call the "medieval" reading of the Odes, as it was ex-
emplifed by the teachings of the Mao school, especially the
"Great Preface." Chapter 2 provides the pre-Han background
to that hermeneutic, describing the change in the status of the
Odes as it can be traced in the *Analects* of Confucius. Chapter
3 discusses the genesis of the particular hermeneutic associated
with the Odes. Chapter 4 focuses upon the *Preface to Mao's
Odes*, especially the "Great Preface," and Chapter 5 treats the
most ambitious development of the medieval tradition, the
great *Correct Significance of the Five Classics* commentary.

In the second half of the book I turn to the Song reformation of classics studies. The subject of Chapter 6, Ouyang Xiu
(1007–72), was a key figure in the history of the critique of
the received exegetical tradition. Chapter 7 treats Cheng Yi
(1033–1107), the great eleventh-century Neoconfucian clas-
sicist and teacher in whose teachings the new general hermeneutic was first adumbrated. Finally, in Chapter 8 I discuss the
"great synthesis" of Zhu Xi (1130–1200), who gave to both
the critique of the exegetical tradition and the new general hermeneutic influential formulations that dominated later
Chinese history.

To ask about hermeneutics is to pose a special kind of question in that it inquires about the very activity in which it is
engaged. We come to the study of China out of a hermeneutical interest, hoping to be surpised or even shaken in our assumptions about people or texts or history, and yet at the same
time striving to make our own that which formerly was remote or incomprehensible. In seeking neither to impose our
own assumptions and categories uncritically upon the texts
with which we engage, nor yet to allow those texts and the
concerns they imply to remain utterly outside our understanding, we are always confronted with the practical dimension of
the hermeneutic problem: How shall we read so as to really
understand, and what are the consequences of such understanding? The texts treated in this study attempt to answer
these very questions.

CHAPTER TWO

The Discovery of the Text
in Ancient China

The most difficult initial problem in the history of literacy
is appreciating what preceded it.
—M. T. Clanchy, *From Memory to Written Record*

From folk songs and court music, the Odes became in time a classic, a canonized and revered
text thought to repay the most careful study and
reflection. In most accounts, the author of this
transformation was the great ritualist teacher
Confucius (Kong Qiu, traditional dates 551–479
B.C.E.). Confucius is supposed to have edited the
classics or at least to have advocated their close
study and, in particular, to have promoted or initiated the reading of the Odes later enshrined in
the Mao school orthodoxy. This view is based
largely upon the *Analects* (*Lunyu*), the traditional
source for the deeds and sayings of Confucius
and his disciples.

But as scholars have long realized, the *Analects*
is a heterogeneous text, with a complex and
problematic relationship to the teachings and
deeds of the historical Confucius. When the character of the *Analects* is taken into account, a
somewhat more intricate picture emerges. Not
only does the kind of reading of the Odes depicted in the *Analects* differ in some important

ways from that of the later orthodoxy, but a careful reading suggests that far from advocating close study of the *Odes* and other received texts, the historical Confucius probably lived and worked in a largely oral, pretextual doctrinal culture.

Pretextual Doctrinal Culture in Early Confucianism

Although pretextual doctrinal cultures are by their nature less well documented than those that focus upon and generate texts, they form an important stage in the development of many traditions. Perhaps the best-known and best-studied example of the recovery of a pretextual doctrinal tradition from its later redactions is the history of the materials that eventuated in the so-called synoptic gospels of the Christian New Testament: that is, those three books, Matthew, Mark, and Luke, that offer varying versions of the life and career of Jesus of Nazareth.

In the late nineteenth century, biblical scholars concerned with determining which of the synoptics presented the most accurate picture of Jesus engaged in a careful study of those texts, comparing their similarities and differences in order to establish their relative priorities. Although the debate is by no means over, these scholars, who were engaged in what has come to be called source criticism,[1] succeeded in decomposing the gospels into their putative sources. In one well-known version, for example, they posited that both Matthew and Luke relied upon Mark and upon certain materials they shared in common (commonly referred to as "Q," for German *Quelle* "source"), as well as upon others unique to each.[2] In the field of Old Testament studies, similar results were realized by Karl Graf and Julius Wellhausen, who argued that the Pentateuch derived from the conflation of two documents, one of which habitually employed the term "Yahweh" for the Hebrew deity, the other of which used "Elohim."[3]

The next stage of the historical criticism of the Bible employed the method known as form criticism (German *Form-geschichte*), perhaps the most influential single movement in biblical criticism in the twentieth century.[4] Led by Martin Dibelius and Rudolf Bultmann, form criticism attempted to push back the frontiers established by source criticism of the Bible, seeking to recover the sources of the literary documents combined by the redactors of the biblical books. Searching for the sources of these constituent documents, form critics discovered not other, more primitive writings, but rather oral traditions stemming from a doctrinal culture in which scriptural accounts of the life and teachings of Jesus had played only a limited role. These interpreters argued that the early Christian communities, inspired as they were by the expectation of the imminent return of Jesus and frequently blessed by the gifts of prophecy and visions, had no need for a fixed, canonical scripture; rather, doctrine developed in the practical context, or *Sitz-im-leben*, of the preaching or proclamation by the early Christian churches concerning Jesus (the *kerygma*). Working in a circular procedure (it is no coincidence that Bultmann was an early associate of Heidegger, the exegete of the hermeneutic circle), they constructed partly from external sources but mostly from the gospels themselves a picture of the concerns and activities of the early church in which the gospels took shape and then applied these insights to the understanding of the gospels.[5]

The virtue of the form-critical approach is to illustrate what we might call the generic character of the materials that made up the gospels. By showing that these materials were worked up or developed in the course of practical activity—specifically, of preaching—this approach shows that they did not belong in any sense to the genre of history or historical recollection but were pervasively structured and motivated by the concerns of the early churches. In the same way, I believe, once we grasp the possibility that a text like the *Analects* developed in the course of practical doctrinal activity, it can be seen that it was pervasively structured—"determined"—by the interests and nature of those activities and that it has only a problematical and tangential relation to the historical Confucius.

What was the practical context in which the traditions of early Confucianism developed? Doubtless a number of contexts called for the exposition and development of Confucian doctrine; we can distinguish at least three. Controversial activity was certainly an important impetus to the development of doctrine; the famous vitality and variety of the late Zhou intellectual world, as well as the schisms that occurred with the various schools, provided many opportunities for debate and polemics.[6] Much of the material preserved in the *Mencius*, for instance, was clearly developed in the context of polemical discussion; this material includes disagreements (some fictionalized or heavily edited) with critics of Confucianism like Xu Xing[7] and discussions of very particular points of Confucian doctrine and mythology that probably reflect disagreements within the Confucian school.

Closely related to doctrinal controversy, and indeed sometimes presented in the form of stylized controversy, was doctrinal exposition. Exposition probably took place in a variety of venues, but the type about which we know the most—the type most fully documented in the historical record and most evident in doctrinal writings—are those given at court by great teachers like Mencius. These could take the form of a lecture by an eminent teacher or, just as often, an interview between the master and the prince, his potential patron. The constant reversion of these early works to the perspective and concerns of the ruler suggests that much of their material developed either in the course of such doctrinal exposition before the prince or with an eye to such use.

Finally, and most important, doctrine was developed in the course of teaching; the first and greatest work in the tradition we are discussing, the *Analects*, emerged from just such a matrix. Not only did Confucius himself give expression to his ideas in the course of teaching, but the *Analects* itself was formed and written down within the Confucian schools. Teaching was perhaps *the* characteristic Confucian doctrinal activity (comparable in this respect to preaching and evangelical activity in the formation of Christian doctrine and the gospels). As such, it tended to spill over into, and to provide the rhetorical form for, other doctrinal activities such as exposition (as, for example, when the emperors of the Northern and Southern Dynasties "lectured" on the Confucian classics).[8] Teaching took place both in state-sponsored academies and under private teachers. It was addressed not only to children of the elite, who were being given a humanistic polish to qualify them for bureaucratic office, but also to mature and committed students who attached themselves to some great teacher. It was the great medium in which Confucian doctrine developed and was transmitted.

A pervasive aspect of the doctrinal culture that prevailed in the early Confucian schools was traditionalism. By "traditionalism" I mean the quality, in a doctrinal tradition, of valuing above all else (and indeed of making the central test of authority) the characteristic of having been received—of being associated with and received from the authoritative teachers of the past. Traditionalism in Confucianism, however, by no means entailed a reverence for texts as such. The Confucian teachers who developed the teachings that eventuated in the *Analects* and *Zuo Tradition* were supremely confident in their participation in the original vision of their teachers. Unlike their descendants in the Han and thereafter, they were not troubled by the possibility that they did not possess the substantive vision of the Master or that they did not belong to the same universe of discourse as he. In a profoundly ahistorical way, they felt free to articulate the truths in which they participated in terms appropriate to their situation, revising and expanding what they had been taught as the occasion demanded. They attended not to the form but rather to the substance of a vision that they assumed they understood. We might say that they engaged in the indirect rather than the direct quotation of what they had been taught.

The continual reformulation and incremental modification of doctrine were facilitated by its transmission through oral teaching rather than written texts. Certainly written texts existed in the late Spring and Autumn and early Warring States periods. People had been writing things down on bones and bronzes for many centuries, and the very term for "cultivation," *wen*, suggests a link with reading and writing. But generally speaking, things were written down when they had to be—because they were in danger of being lost—and the notion that the revered and living truths of the tradition might be lost unless they were written down was, I believe, a relatively late development. Even if the traditions that led to the *Zuo Tradition* and *Analects* were periodically written in some form, as indeed we must suppose if we are to account for the received versions of those texts, those redactions did not exert the sort of limiting force over doctrinal exposition—they did not have the *authority*—of later texts.

Materials transmitted in the context that I have described—that is, in the context of oral teaching, by interpreters confident of their participation in the vision of the traditional materials—tend to have certain characteristics. First, they typically become narratively more elaborate as they are transmitted. In the synoptic gospels, for example, there is general agreement that the oldest materials, around which the gospel narratives grew and which are occasionally preserved in those narratives, were collections of sayings of Jesus. These were expanded by the provision first of narrative and explanatory contexts and then of connecting passages that tied the resulting anecdotes into the relatively coherent narrative of the gospels. Similarly, in the *Analects*, there is a strong correlation between narrative elaboration and linguistic or contextual markers of lateness. Those sections of the *Analects* generally thought to be earliest are characterized by sayings with no narrative context at all or relatively simple contexts. In those chapters generally thought to be late, on the other hand, we find narratives of complexity and sophistication.[9] It is also possible to distingish in the *Zuo Tradition* narratives that are relatively simple, sometimes fragmentary, from those that are richly developed, either narratively or in their exposition of doctrine. Examples of the latter are marked by their frequent anachronistic predictions and obviously "motivated" character as relatively late.[10]

The essential fluidity of these texts also made possible another of the distinctive characteristics of the late materials in these traditions, the introduction and accommodation of the concerns of succeeding generations, largely although by no means exclusively the concerns of the schools that transmitted the materials. Thus, in the case of the gospels, Jesus is made to address the relation of the early church to contemporary Judaism and to the political authority of the day, as well as the problem of his own martyrdom. Indeed, so pervasive was the modification or creation of material in the light of later concerns that form critics of the gospels generally agree that one of the few markers which can be supposed to guarantee that an authentic saying of Jesus has been preserved is that of incongruity or dissimilarity. If a statement attributed to Jesus is incongruous with the concerns of the early church, it has a prima facie claim to authenticity, since it cannot otherwise be accounted for and indeed would probably have been expunged or altered had it not some special aura of authority.[11]

So too in the *Analects*, we see in the materials that are agreed to be late signs of the concerns of the later Confucian schools. Indeed, as in the case of the synoptic materials, it is precisely these materials that are our richest source of information about those schools and their concerns. Such materials are often a response to some controversy. In the case of the *Analects* we can distinguish two types: controversy with the adherents of other traditions, such as Daoist or proto-Daoist critics of Confucianism, and controversies within the Confucian school. A particularly important controversy among Confucians concerned the conflicting claims of Confucius's disciples and their followers to possess the real, authentic teachings of the Master. As we shall see, the Odes were a particular bone of contention in this respect.

Such a pretextual doctrinal culture stands in vivid contrast to one that has become centered on texts. In a pretextual doctrinal culture, the nuclear teachings of the school are relatively fluid, modifying themselves as it were insensibly in the process of their transmission. In the case of a doctrinal culture based on a text or texts, on the other hand, this process must come to a halt; the text is, by definition, reiterable, fixed. Confronted with such an object, the necessary process of accommodating doctrine to new concerns and questions must be displaced from expansion and reformulation to interpretation. Texts have a certain flinty resistance to the mind's tendency to constantly remake the world, and as time passes, they begin to acquire a quality of alterity that is the source of both their difficulty and their fascination.

How do texts arise in an oral doctrinal culture? First and most typically, early texts are redactions of hitherto oral traditions, redactions that then may themselves undergo extensive "literary" reworking. This is the process that generated the synoptic gospels of the New Testament and the *Analects* and *Zuo Tradition*. Although there may be a number of impetuses to such a specification of authoritative teaching, the most important is doctrinal controversy. When disagreements arise concerning the content of the founder's vision, disciples and followers find it necessary to specify in a reiterable, defensible form what he really said. In the generations after the death of Confucius, various of his disciples became the heads of traditions and schools that claimed to represent the authentic and orthodox Confucian tradition; each presented a version of Confucius's teachings that emphasized and expanded upon certain aspects of his teaching and discounted or ignored others. As the competition between such schools for the mantle of the orthodox representative of Confucianism grew more intense, it became imperative for them to specify what did indeed count as Confucius's teaching (and, perhaps more important, by excluding their rivals' most distasteful claims, to specify what did not). It was probably this impulse to rule out competing versions of the Confucian vision that led to the redaction of the largely oral doctrinal tradition into a fixed text.

The history of the Odes represents an alternative process of text generation. In the case of redaction, an authoritative but non-textual doctrine is fixed into a text—it "becomes textual." In the case of the Odes, on the other hand, a text that had not previously been considered doctrinally authoritative was made so. To explain this process, let me make a distinction between a "text in the weak sense"—a stable, reiterable discourse, usually although by no means always written—and a "text in the strong sense"—a stable text that has become central to a doctrinal culture and thus the object of exegetical exposition and study. It is in this latter intensive, often reverent engagement that we first discern an attitude which may properly be termed "hermeneutic," and it is in connection with this sort of study that the hermeneutic theory develops. The story of the canonization of the Odes is the story of how a text in the weak sense became the first object of hermeneutic attention and reflection—the first text in the strong sense—in China.[12]

The Odes in the *Analects*

The early history of the Odes is illustrated in the *Analects*, the collection of traditions about Confucius and his disciples that is one of the centerpieces of the Confucian tradition. Representing not a literary work composed by a single author, still less the transcription or reportage of the events it purports to relate, the *Analects* was, rather, the product of the redaction of various late Warring States traditions, and its later elements probably assumed substantially their present form sometime around the third century B.C.E.[13] Or perhaps more accurately, it is a collection of a number of such redactions, some relatively early, some later. It is this heterogeneous character of the work that makes it possible to use it as a source—a difficult and problematical source, but a source just the same—for the development of the reading of the Odes as strong texts.

Students of the *Analects* generally agree that the present text gathers together several earlier collections and that it is possible to distinguish several distinct strata of individual "sections" (*zhang*; sometimes called "chapters") that make up the book. As the great Qing scholar Cui Shu (1740–1816) showed, certain of the book's twenty chapters (*pian*; literally "rolls [of silk]"; often rendered in translations of the *Analects* as "books") were brought together at a relatively early date, and others are clearly later.[14] We can distinguish four strata. First, a group of five "core chapters" composed of chapters 3–7 is probably the earliest material.[15] Second, four chapters—1, 2, 8, and 9—seem to have been added at a later date around the core chapters but contain many early materials. Chapters 10 through 15 seem to constitute another, still later layer, and the last five chapters, 16 through 20, are marked by linguistic criteria as latest of all.

Although scholars speak of "early" and "late" chapters, it must be borne in mind that since even the earliest chapters were probably not compiled until several generations after Confucius's death, the individual sections within them are not all of the same age, and the "late" chapters may occasionally contain sections representing relatively early traditions. Moreover, the sections at the end (and, to a lesser extent, at the beginning) of chapters are often later than the rest (the ends of a roll of silk being a convenient spot for editors to note down a new or variant tradition).

When the various sections are examined according to their presumptive dating, it becomes apparent that certain formal and ideological features are closely associated with relative earliness or lateness. Sections from the earliest contexts—from the central portions of early chapters—tend to be narratively simple, most commonly relatively brief comments prefaced only by "The Master said . . ."; for instance, *Analects* 3.20: "The Master said, 'The "Guanju"—joyful, but not abandoned; sorrowful, but not harmfully so!' "

Later passages, on the other hand, are often narratively more elaborate. Take, for example, 14.39, admittedly an extreme example, from the end of a late chapter:

The Master was playing the stone chimes in Wei. A man who passed in front of the door, carrying a basket, said, "The way he plays the stone chimes is fraught with [frustrated] purpose." Presently he added, "How vulgar! How petty! If no one understands him, then he should give up, that is all.

> When the water is deep, go across
> by wading;
> When it is shallow, lift your hem
> and cross."

The Master said, "That would be resolute indeed. Against such resoluteness there can be no argument."[16]

The original nucleus of this story was, I believe, an anti-Confucian story circulated by Daoist or proto-Daoist critics; in this earlier version, the story probably ended before or just after the quotation of the Ode by the basket-carrier.[17] Such stories must have been embarrassing and irritating for Confucius's partisans, and they would have sought ways to disarm and refute them. The most effective way would have been not to deny a story that had already achieved currency, but rather to present a revised version—the "true story." In the case of

Analects 14.39, this was achieved by giving Confucius the last word, a sarcastic comment that disarms the original criticism. It is easy to imagine the triumphant certitude with which the Confucians would have retailed their version of the obnoxious tradition.[18]

Analects 3.20, on the other hand, does not address the concerns of or serve the apologetic interests of the Confucian schools in any obvious way; in fact it must have been somewhat anomalous in its emphasis on the musical rather than the hermeneutic significance of the Odes (see below). Such passages, which, in addition to an early context and a relatively simple form, meet the criterion of dissimilarity, must have the strongest claim to be considered relatively early and relatively close to the actual teachings of Confucius.

I do not mean to minimize the difficulties of this method or to imply that it can "prove" that one passage is earlier than another. The criterion of dissimilarity, for instance, tends to systematically discount the continuities in a tradition, perhaps unfairly. Most of what we assume about the institutional context of the text derives from inferences based on the text itself. And we cannot assume that even if we succeed in isolating the earliest elements in the tradition, we have reached the words and deeds of the historical Confucius. Finally we must acknowledge that, in questions of dating, form-critical analysis must always bow before linguistic, textual, or archaeological evidence. Still, such analysis is indispensable if we are to move beyond naive readings of these texts. Moreover, as I hope to show below, the internal consistency of these arguments can be persuasive.

The Earliest Passages: The Odes as Music

The Ru—the ritual specialists and wise men we commonly refer to as "Confucians"—were famous for their devotion to the musical performance of the Odes. As the *Mozi* puts it,

"They recite the three hundred Odes, play the three hundred on strings, sing the three hundred, and dance to the three hundred."[19] In Chapters 3–7 of the *Analects*, agreed by most students of the text to be relatively early, are four passages that concern the Odes: 3.2, 3.8, 3.20, and 7.18. Of these, I think 3.8 probably reflects the concerns of the later Confucian schools; the other three may reflect, if not the teachings of the historical Confucius, at least relatively early traditions concerning him. Two of these three plausibly early sections, and several of the possibly early sections from the next layer of chapters as well, are concerned with the Odes as the musical accompaniment to ritual.

Take, for instance, *Analects* 3.2: "The Three Families used the 'Yong' Ode at the clearing away of the sacrifices. The Master said, ' "By rulers and lords attended, / The Son of Heaven, mysterious."[20] What use has this [Ode] in the halls of the Three Families?' "

In Confucius's day, three great clans (the Zhongsun, Shusun, and Jisun) had largely usurped the power of the legitimate ducal house of Lu. They had not only taken control of the state but also openly arrogated the regalia of ranks not their own, going so far in this instance as to employ in their family sacrifices the "Yong" Ode (Mao #282) originally sung at the rituals of the royal Zhou house. This kind of lèse majesté was anathema to Confucius, not only because it symbolized the debasement of politics in his day, but also because it was a corruption of the beloved ritual (*li*), which Confucius believed could reconstitute the natural order of society.

In this passage, Confucius is portrayed as protesting against the ritual misuse of the "Yong" Ode. Although he mentions the words of the Ode, it is clear that his intention is not to explicate a text; nor is there any implication that the Ode was a source of teaching. Rather, the concern is entirely with the propriety of the musical performance of the "Yong" at the sacrifices of the great families. This is the same distress that

Confucius felt when he saw one of these families use a ritual reserved for the Zhou kings.[21]

The concern with ritual is also reflected in a passage from the second stratum of chapters, which may nevertheless reflect an early tradition: "The Master said, 'It was only after I returned to Lu from Wei that the music was put aright, the Elegantiae and Lauds being given their proper places'" (*Analects* 9.15).

This famous passage is the probable source—certainly the only mention in the *Analects* that can be so construed—of the tradition that Confucius edited the Odes.[22] But as He Dingsheng has pointed out, by "giving the Elegantiae and Lauds their proper places" Confucius meant something quite different from the selection and arrangement of the Odes into a text. Surely the Elegantiae and the Lauds were "given their proper places" (*de qi suo*) only by Confucius's making clear in the course of his teaching just where and when they were to be ritually performed.[23] The reform of the music that Confucius mentions and the specification of the "places" of the Odes were not two different things but different aspects of the same task.

Although Confucius's concern with the Odes was clearly connected to his more general concern to preserve and maintain the correct ritual norms, it was not exclusively so; he seems also to have been able to appreciate the music of the Odes in a way we would call "aesthetic." This interest is evident in another passage from the earliest stratum of materials. This passage, mentioned above, which contains Confucius's comment concerning the "Guanju" Ode (Mao #1), was to play an important role in the later history of the reading of the Odes: "The Master said, 'The "Guanju"—joyful, but not abandoned; sorrowful, but not harmfully so!'" (*Analects* 3.20)

If I understand this passage correctly, Confucius was concerned with the musical qualities rather than with the language of the "Guanju." The phrasing of 3.20 is somewhat ambiguous; Confucius's comment could refer to the words of the Ode, and of course that is exactly how later exegetes in the Mao tradition understood this passage.[24] There are, however, two reasons why I think that is not so. First, whenever, as in this case, the *Analects* refers to an Ode by its title, it is either the musical performance of the Ode or its musical qualities that is intended. *Analects* 3.2 is one example; another is at 8.15, an arguably early passage from a second-layer chapter: "The Master said, 'The beginning by Music Master Zhi, the coda of the "Guanju"—how floodlike do they fill the ear!' "[25]

We also saw that 9.15, in which Confucius refers to the Elegantiae and the Lauds, is also concerned with the Odes as music; as are the two possible references in the *Analects* (15.11, 17.18) to the Airs (*feng*) of the state of Zheng.[26] When, on the other hand, Confucius or someone else is portrayed as engaging in the quotation of an Ode or its exegesis, the title is never mentioned.[27]

Second, the language of personality and moral accomplishment in which Confucius characterizes the "Guanju" in *Analects* 3.20 is typically associated with music rather than with the Odes as texts. *Analects* 3.25 is an example: "The Master deemed the Shao [music] perfectly beautiful and perfectly good; and he deemed the Wu [music] perfectly beautiful but not perfectly good."

Indeed, there is a close link in the *Analects* between music and the ideal of the perfection of the personality, especially as that perfection is conceived as deriving from an education of the emotions.[28] In the Han, as evidenced in the *Preface to Mao's Odes*, this powerful and seductive promise that the Odes could remake the emotional nature would become prominent again. For the Han, however, it was the language of the Odes—the texts of the Odes—that had this power; for the historical Confucius insofar as we can discern him in the earliest stratum of the *Analects*, it was, I believe, the Odes as music, in their ritual setting.

There are two possible exceptions. *Analects* 7.18, although a comment about Confucius rather than a saying attributed to him, may well reflect an authentic tradition concerning the Master: "As for the Master's use of the standard pronunciations [*ya yan*]—with the Odes, with the Documents [*shu*], in the practice of ritual: in these he used the standard pronunciations." As Arthur Waley says, *ya* here must be equivalent to "the ethnic term Hsia [Xia], the common name of the Chinese, as opposed to the barbarians."[29] Thus Confucius used the standard, old pronunciations instead of those of his native Lu dialect in certain situations concerning the Odes. But what were those situations? Was Confucius reciting the Odes, as the reference to the Documents might seem to imply, or performing them, as is suggested by the association with ritual, or both? In any case, there is no implication that he was engaging in their exegesis.

One section from chapter 3 certainly does portray Confucius as concerned with the texts of the Odes. In *Analects* 3.8, Zixia, one of Confucius's most famous disciples, asks about Ode #57:

> Zixia asked, "What about
> Oh the sweet smile dimpling,
> The lovely eyes so black and white!
> Plain silk that you would take for colored stuff."[30]

The Master said, "The painting goes on after the plain [groundwork]."
[Zixia] said, "Then ritual comes after?"
The Master said, "It is Shang [i.e., Zixia] who picks me up! Now we can talk about the Odes!"[31]

It is a puzzling passage. There is some difficulty about the meaning of Confucius's first comment, which seems to be an abstract moral truth expressed in metaphorical and concrete terms; Zixia must make it clear by referring it to a practical question—"Then ritual comes later?"—whose consequences in terms of Confucius's thought as a whole remain unclear. Moreover, whatever the meaning of Confucius's interpretation, it seems to have little in common with the sort of hermeneutic that came to be associated with the Odes in the Mao tradition. The anomalous character of this passage, its roughness, and its difficulty all seem to argue for a relatively early date, according to the criterion of dissimilarity.[32]

On the other hand, however, the passage can be explained in terms of the concerns of the later Confucian schools. After Confucius's death, various of his disciples including Zixia established schools of their own or gathered followers about them; perhaps more to the point, subsequent schools tended to identify themselves with one or another of Confucius's disciples. Among such schools competition was inevitable, and the question of which school possessed and taught the authentic version of Confucius's teachings must have been a particular issue of contention.[33] If, as I argue below, these schools increasingly came to emphasize the study and exposition of the Odes, the question of which disciple's interpretations of the Odes had been certified by the Master would have become a particularly urgent and hotly disputed one. It is not hard to see how this passage may reflect the interest of the disciples of Zixia in showing that it was their master who was capable of passing on to his students the real meaning of the Odes.[34]

The story may have served another function as well. Many of the stories concerning Confucius and his disciples have an illustrative character. In such stories, the disciples represent attitudes or personality types upon which Confucius comments (as, for instance, the many stories about the impetuous and unreflective Zilu). In *Analects* 3.8, Zixia is an exemplary reader, able to grasp not only the meaning of the Ode but also of Confucius's comment. Such stories would have had a particular interest in an environment in which the interpretation of texts was becoming of central importance.

The thesis that *Analects* 3.8 grew out of an interest on the part of the later schools in promoting the status either of a founder or of exemplary students is lent support by a passage from the second layer of chapters, 1.15, which presents another version of the story. In this passage, Confucius is conversing with another disciple, Zigong.

Zigong said, " 'Poor and yet not indulging in flattery; rich and yet not arrogant'—how about that?"
The Master said, "That will do, but it is not so good as 'Poor and yet happy; rich and yet devoted to courtesy [*li*].' "
Zigong said, "The Ode says,

> As thing cut, as thing filed,
> As thing chiseled, as thing polished.[35]

I suppose that refers to [what you just said]."
The Master said, "Si [i.e., Zigong]! Now we can talk about the Odes! If I give you one half, you come back at me with the other!"

This passage is as smooth and glib as 3.8 is rough and confusing. Zigong and Confucius trade maxims and glosses with a cultivated and urbane ease, culminating in Confucius's approving comment, which adds to the earlier passage's "Now we can talk about the Odes" a further certification of Zigong's skill as a student.

What is the relationship between the two stories? It is perhaps not inherently impossible that Confucius might have had two conversations so close in structure and wording. Or 3.8 might represent the original version of the story and 1.15 an imitation. In fact, 3.8 may well be older than 1.15; both its context and its relatively primitive form argue for that. In the final analysis, however, I believe that it is more parsimonious to see these passages not as historical nucleus and subsequent imitation, but rather as two alternative outcomes of the same impulses—here, to bolster the authority of a school by illustrating a disciple's exemplary ability to grasp the implications of the Master's teachings. It is unlikely that either reproduces a historical reality. The relatively rough and unsophisticated character of 3.8 may reflect a relatively early stage in the development of the topos, but not, I think, the words of the historical Confucius; rather, it is the product of impulses realized with greater skill in 1.15, which are for that reason more apparent there.

The "Middle" Passages: The Odes as Pretexts

The act of quoting the Odes illustrated in 3.8 is anomalous in the context of the earliest stratum of the *Analects*, but it fits well into the hermeneutic milieu of the second and third strata of that text—that is, chapters 1, 2, 8, and 9; and chapters 10–15. In these sections, Confucius and his disciples are typically portrayed as concerned not with the musical qualities of the Odes or with their role as the musical accompaniments to ritual, but with their words, which they use to ornament polite conversation or to make a didactic point.[36] In this practice, the Odes were not invested with stable, historically defined meanings or inherent moral significance; rather, lines could be and were quoted out of context and used to illustrate points quite remote from their original meaning in the Ode as a whole. Although the focus of attention had shifted from the musical qualities of the Odes to their wording, the Odes were not yet texts in the strong sense, but what we might call "pretexts."[37]

We have discussed a number of these passages already. Take, for instance, Zigong's conversation with Confucius at 1.15 and the anecdote concerning Confucius and the basket-carrier at 14.39. In 1.15, Zigong shows that he has understood Confucius's comment by quoting two lines from Ode #55:

> As thing cut, as thing filed,
> As thing chiseled, as thing polished.

In their original context, the lines refer to the beauty and cultivation of an aristocratic lover; they have little to do with the unremitting moral striving Zigong understands Confucius to enjoin. Although Confucius says "Now I can discuss the Odes with you!" it is Zigong's apt quotation of the Ode rather than any exegesis of it that excites Confucius's admiration.

The lines from Ode #34 quoted by the basket-carrier in 14.39 are used in a similar fashion:

> When the water is deep, go across
> by wading;
> When it is shallow, lift your hem
> and cross.

In the Ode, these lines urge resolution and determination on someone hesitant to cross a river; in the story at hand, they serve to advise Confucius to "Take the world as you find it."[38] Once again, Confucius's ironic reply has to do not with any claim concerning the meaning of the Ode, but rather with sentiments expressed by its quotation in the particular circumstances.

The question of the status of the moral lessons or truths expressed by this sort of quotation of the Odes is relevant to two famous passages from the middle chapters of the *Analects*. *Analects* 8.8 is one of the earliest statements in the *Analects* concerning the role of the Odes in moral education: "The Master said, 'Be stimulated [*xing*] by the Odes, established by ritual, and perfected by music.'"

The problem of deciding what is meant by *xing* in this passage is complicated by the long subsequent history of the term. It reappears again in *Analects* 17.9 and in the *Mao Commentary*, where it seems to be a kind of technical term for one of the characteristic tropes of the Odes.[39] Much of the subsequent discussion of *xing* has been muddied by the attempt to relate the technical use of the term to its uses in the *Analects*. In fact, there may be a tangential sort of relation, in the sense that *xing yu shi* ("Be stimulated by the Odes") may have been a paronomastic definition of the same type as *shi yan zhi* ("The Odes articulate aims"); that is, Confucius may have seized on the existence of a technical term already associated with the Odes, *xing*, in formulating his definition of the function of the Odes.

In this passage, however, as elsewhere in the *Analects*, *xing* seems to mean "to stimulate or be stimulated by."[40] The striking and apposite quotation of a few lines of the Odes was intended to stimulate the hearer, thereby initiating the process of moral cultivation that was consolidated by ritual and perfected by music. Confucius must surely be referring here to the practice we have just been discussing, whereby the Odes were to help to stimulate the understanding (without themselves embodying moral teachings). As the other *Analects* passage that mentions *xing* in connection with the Odes (17.9) indicates, this was one of several uses that could be made of the Odes.

The other "theoretical" passage in this stratum of the *Analects* is 2.2: "The Master said, 'As for the three hundred Odes: if one saying can cover them, it would be *si wu xie*.'"

In this passage Confucius is portrayed as summing up the teaching of the Odes with a maxim from that collection. The phrase appears in the "Jiong" Ode (Mao #297), the first of the Lauds of Confucius's own state of Lu. In this Ode, which praises the fine horses of a duke of that state, the first word of the line, *si*, is commonly agreed by modern scholars to be a meaningless particle or exclamation, a particle that was, however, written with a graph commonly used in the *Analects* and elsewhere to mean "thought" or "to think." About the second and third characters of the line Confucius quotes there is no controversy; *wu xie* refers to the way in which the horses run, "without swerving."

The difficulty then is with the first word of the line, which Confucius has quoted as characterizing or, more literally, "covering" the Odes as a collection. One possibility is to suppose that Confucius intended by the line something very like its original meaning; on this reading, *si* is meaningless, and Confucius says that the Odes can be summed up by the expression "no swerving"—from the Way, as we should understand. Another possibility, endorsed by many traditional interpreters, is to take Confucius's meaning to be "no swerving in the thoughts." Among those who subscribe to this view, there has been disagreement whether these "thoughts" were those of the authors of the Odes or those of their readers; and if the latter, whether it meant that the reader was to approach the Odes (especially the "depraved Odes") with no "twisty thoughts," as Ezra Pound put it, or whether the Odes were to create this effect within the reader.[41]

A third possibility, however, seems to me most likely to reflect the original sense of this passage. This is the interpretation found in the commentary of Huang Kan (488–544). In this view, Confucius did intend *si* as "thoughts" or "to think," but was not for all that making any claim about the nature of the Odes. Rather, he selected out from the Odes a single line to "cover" all the other lines one might select and quote from the Odes (rather like saying "The best line in the Odes is . . ."). The phrase meant something like "as for thoughts: no swerving," in the sense of either "think always of not swerving" or "as for your thoughts [your focus]: let there be no swerving." This interpretation has the advantage of harmonizing with the other uses of the term *si* in the *Analects*, which, as Arthur Waley pointed out, have more to do with the focus of the attention than with reflection or cognition as such.[42] Whatever particular nuance Confucius attached to this phrase, it was not in my opinion a claim about the thoughts of the authors of the Odes (like the Han claim that all the Odes inscribed *zhi*, or aims, that were paradigmatically normative), or indeed "about" the Odes at all. Rather, Confucius used the phrase as a *xing*, or "stimulus," employing it as the vehicle by which a moral truth (on the order of "ritual comes after" in 3.8) could be articulated, but without claiming or implying that the Odes themselves embodied this particular quality.[43]

The assumptions underlying the *xing* practice portrayed in the *Analects* can be clarified by examining another body of materials, the narratives concerning the recitation of the Odes (*fushi*) in the *Zuo Tradition*.[44] As depicted there, the Odes were chanted by various figures—princes, ministers, a palace lady—as a means to elegant or persuasive expression. Very likely the practice was associated with banquets and diplomatic missions; it may have served a function roughly analogous to the toasts or speeches made at diplomatic functions today. As with toasts and speeches generally, the messages delivered by the recitation of the Odes would have tended toward polite compliments and expressions of hospitality and solidarity, although there was room for the subtly veiled threat as well. As in the *Zuo Tradition* generally, the narratives concerned with the recitation of the Odes were shaped and structured by a desire to show the workings of Confucian morality in the lives and doings of human beings. Although they are marked by certain features that show that they cannot be taken (as they often are) as completely accurate depictions of the reality of the seventh through fifth centuries B.C.E., still there are reasons to believe that the stories do reflect in some oblique way the uses made of the Odes during the Spring and Autumn period.

The following is a typical *Zuo Tradition* narrative dealing with the recitation of the Odes. It is part of the story of Prince Chonger, later to become the famous hegemon Duke Wen of Jin. When young, he was forced into exile from Jin as a result of a power struggle within his own family and traveled with his loyal retinue for a number of years among the other small states that competed in north and central China during the seventh century B.C.E. After many trials and adventures, he at last visited the state of Qin, which was to sponsor his return to power in Jin.

One day the duke feasted Chonger. [Before the feast] Zifan [one of Chonger's advisers] said, "I am not so cultured [*wen*] as [Zhao] Cui [another adviser]; please have him accompany you."

[At the feast] Chonger recited the "Heshui" Ode, and the duke recited the "Liuyue" Ode. Zhao Cui said, "Chonger, make a bow!" Chonger descended the platform and bowed to the ground, and the duke came down a step to decline [the honor]. Zhao Cui said [to the duke], "When you charge Chonger to 'assist the Son of Heaven' [a line in the 'Liuyue' Ode], dare he not bow?"[45]

The banquet setting of this narrative is typical; it may be that the recitation of the Odes derived from or was somehow linked to the musical performance of the Odes at banquets or at the rituals they often followed. But "reciting" (*fu*) an Ode was not the same thing as singing or giving a musical performance of it; that was usually left to musicians in attendance, whereas the recitation of the Odes seems to have been done by the principals themselves. Neither were the Odes recited in ordinary speech; rather, they were crooned or chanted in a rhythmic, singsong fashion.[46]

Most of the titles mentioned in these narratives appear in the received text of the *Odes*. Usually not the whole Ode, but only a stanza or two were recited. Occasionally the stanza recited is specified by the *Zuo Tradition*. When it is not, it seems the first stanza of the Ode was intended. The first stanza of the Ode that Chonger chants, the "Heshui," reads:

> In flood those running waters
> Carry their tides to join the sea.
> Swift that flying kite
> Now flies, now lights.
> Alas that of my brothers,
> My countrymen and all my friends,
> Though each has father, has mother,
> None heeds the disorders of this land.[47]

There survives no explicit hermeneutic of the recitation of the Odes to aid us in the interpretation of the *Zuo Tradition* passage. However, the reactions and comments of participants at these occasions give an idea how these Odes were understood, and from this we can reconstruct an implicit hermeneutic. Sometimes the words of the Ode must have been taken as if they referred directly to the situation at hand. Several elements of the stanza recited by Chonger can be understood in this way. For example, in the last four lines, the reference to "disorders of this land" would have been understood to refer to the situation in Jin, and the mention of brothers and mother would have recalled to his auditors that Chonger's troubles stemmed from a feud within his family.

On the other hand, the first two lines could not have been taken to apply directly to the situation at hand; rather, they must have been understood much as later exegetes understood those portions of the Odes that they called *bi* ("analogy"): the sea is to the rivers that flow into it as a great king or hegemon—the Duke of Qin, in the view Chonger is proposing—is to lesser princes. Such associations of imagery and meaning were probably largely conventional. The image of the rivers and the sea, for instance, reappears in a number of early contexts as a conventional analogy for the relation between a true king and lesser vassals.[48] At the same time, such connections were not necessarily determined; there was a creative element in both the choice of an Ode to recite and in its interpretation, as we can see from the *Zuo Tradition* stories about uncouth or heedless individuals who fail to recognize the purport of an Ode recited to them.[49]

Chonger proposes through the chanting of this particular Ode a view of things: he has been unjustly denied his rightful position as ruler of Jin through the machinations of members of his family, and as a consequence his homeland is in disorder; the Duke of Qin is a great lord of men to whom others can come for help. But Chonger is proposing more than simply a picture of things as he envisions them to be; for while he is defining himself and his situation, he is also expressing his hopes for the future. He is in fact articulating something very like what later discussion of the Odes would call his *zhi* ("intention," "aim," "project").

The Duke of Qin expresses his willingness to help Chonger by quoting from Ode #177, the "Liuyue," whose first stanza reads:

> In the sixth month all is bustle,
> We put our war chariots in order,

Our four steeds are in good fettle,
We load our bowcases and quivers.
The Xianyun [nomads] are ablaze,
We have no time to lose.
We are going out to battle,
To set aright the king's lands.[50]

This recital serves as a reply to Chonger's request. The duke's choice of an Ode would also have been understood to articulate an aim (*yan zhi*), but an aim different not only in content but also in type from Chonger's. The duke does not make a statement about his own general situation or orientations, but simply expresses a determination to go to Chonger's aid, as a hermeneutically competent listener (or reader) would have understood from the references to preparations for a military campaign. It is significant that these lines would have been so understood even though the references to the Xianyun (a nomadic people displaced by the Zhou) and the place-names in the Ode clearly show that it originally referred to a completely different historical situation.[51] It is typical of the recitation of the Odes as portrayed in the *Zuo Tradition* that the lines quoted were not limited by their original context or historical reference, just as they were not in the *Analects* passages quoting the Odes.

That the meanings the Odes were used to convey in this practice were not thought to inhere in the Odes is confirmed by a passage preserved in the *Zuo Tradition*. In this speech, which appears associated with the 28th year of Duke Xiang of Lu, one Lupu Gui justifies his marriage to a woman of the same surname as he, then as now taboo in China, by saying: "The clan does not avoid me; why should I avoid it? In reciting the Odes [*fushi*], one breaks off a stanza [*duanzhang*]. I take what I want there; why should I worry about the clan?"[52]

The passage is significant because it implies that the people of the Spring and Autumn clearly understood that the stanzas from the Odes recited in the *fushi* practice were taken out of a larger context to which they "properly" belonged, just as Lupu Gui's betrothed was to be taken by her marriage out of the context, or clan, to which she belonged. In Lupu Gui's argument, the (tabooed) disregard of the social "meaning" of his wife was analogous to the disregard of the meaning of the Ode as a whole in the *fushi* practice. That Lupu Gui cites this principle in support of his argument—arguing, as people typically do, from the noncontroversial to the controversial—in a context quite unconcerned with the Odes recitation practice shows this was a commonly shared belief that did not require justification. Thus it was permissible according to well-understood although largely tacit rules to take lines from the Odes out of their original contexts and to ascribe to them new meanings, and such a practice implied no claims concerning the original meanings of the lines.

The practice of reciting the Odes depicted in the *Zuo Tradition* and that of quoting the Odes portrayed in the middle strata of the *Analects* have much in common. In both cases, it is not the musical qualities of the Odes that matter, but rather their language. The Odes serve as a rhetoric or source of good and usable phrases, which may be drawn upon in order to ornament or concisely express a point; in both cases, the original meaning of the Ode does not seem to have limited the uses that could be made of it. Although some modern students of these practices have been shocked by this way of using the Odes (one speaks of Confucius's "method of ruthless misinterpretation"),[53] their outrage is misplaced. Confucius and his contemporaries, who probably understood the original meanings of the Odes as well as or better than we do, were not, if my interpretation of the practice is correct, making claims concerning the original meaning of the Odes but simply availing themselves of their language for purposes of indirect or elegant expression. The Odes could help one to speak (*yan*), as the *Analects* tells us. If one was speaking about moral teachings, they could help with that too, but they were not thought to embody moral teachings. They were not yet the objects of study and exegesis.

The Latest Passages: The Odes as Strong Texts

The Odes as they were used in the middle strata of the *Analects* were not yet fully texts, but rather "pre-texts" used simply as the vehicles of elegant expression or doctrinal exposition. They were not thought to embody moral teachings or to repay careful and sustained study; nor was there, at least in surviving materials, a hermeneutic theory associated with them. In the latest stratum of *Analects* chapters, on the other hand, are three passages that deal with the role of the Odes in the Confucian curriculum and advocate their study. At least one of these passages (17.9) implies that the study of the Odes was to be pursued for its transformative effects, and another (16.3) seems to foreshadow the Mao school hermeneutic of the Odes; along with 17.10, all these energetically and explicitly advocate the study of the Odes. Indeed it is precisely these passages (along with 8.8) that are typically cited in support of the claim that Confucius advocated the study of the Odes. But the fact that these passages are found largely if not exclusively in the very latest stratum of chapters should make us wary of asserting any but the most tenuous connection between these doctrines and those of the historical Confucius; rather, these passages closely reflect and, I believe, derive from the concerns of the later schools that devoted themselves to the exposition of the Confucian teachings.

Perhaps the most important of these passages portraying Confucius as advocating the study of the Odes is *Analects* 17.9:

The Master said, "Little ones, how is it that you have not studied the Odes? The Odes can be used to stimulate [moral insight], to observe [character], to reaffirm one's commitment to the group, or to express resentment. Close at hand one can serve his father and farther away his lord; and you can increase your acquaintance with the names of birds, beasts, plants, and trees."

This passage both presupposes and promotes an institutionalized practice of the study of the Odes. First, Confucius enumerates four functions of the Odes, which have excited comment and speculation ever since. *Xing*, I suggested above, refers to the stimulation of the moral sense by the apt or pointed quotation of an Ode as an element of moral teaching or conversation. The other three functions deal with the mythology associated with the *Zuo Tradition* narratives concerning the recitation of the Odes. In this mythology, the recitation of the Odes could serve to affirm solidarity (*qun*; literally, to "group") or to express angry disappointment and resentment (*yuan*); or one might "observe" (*guan*) the intentions, concerns, and character that motivated these uses.[54] Thus *qun* and *yuan* have to do with the ways in which the Odes could help one to "speak" (*yan*); *xing* and *guan* with the lessons one might draw from someone else's use of the Odes.

The Odes were important not only as an element of the ritual or as a rhetoric of good phrases, but also as a text to be studied, from which the student could learn "the names of birds, beasts, plants, and trees." The identification of the numerous plant and animal names used in the Odes would be an important feature of later commentaries on the Odes; it was a natural outgrowth of the sort of textual exegesis that went on in a pedagogical setting. Finally, the student of the Odes could also learn how to serve his father and his lord. It is not clear whether this meant that the Odes were considered the agents of moral education, as they were in the Han; it may be that they simply helped the student by providing him with a repertoire of good phrases. In any case, this passage is clearly intended to lend prestige to and to justify the study of the Odes, and it probably reflects their increasing importance in the institutional milieu from which this passage derived. Even if the Odes had not yet been themselves invested with moral significance, the conditions were ripe for such a move.

The process of the institutionalization of the study of the Odes was clearly far advanced by the time the next passage became current.

> Chen Gang asked [Confucius's son] Boyu, "Have you heard anything [from your father] different [from what we, his disciples, have heard] [i.e., have you received any special teachings?]"
>
> [Boyu] replied, "I never have. Once, when he was standing alone and I was scurrying across the courtyard, he asked, 'Have you studied the Odes?' I replied, 'Not yet.' 'If you don't study the Odes, how will you speak?' I retired and studied the Odes.
>
> "Another day, he was again standing alone as I scurried across the courtyard. He said, 'Have you studied the rites?' I replied, 'Not yet.' 'If you don't study the rites, how will you establish yourself?' I retired and studied the rites. I have heard these two things."
>
> Chen Gang retired and said happily, "I asked one thing and got three [in reply]: I heard about the Odes, I heard about the rites, and moreover I heard that the superior man keeps distant from his son." (*Analects* 16.13)

This passage is interesting for a number of reasons. First, it clearly reflects a situation in which the study of the Odes had become a central and accepted element in the Confucian curriculum, on a par with the study of the rites. There is little in the first or second stratum of passages to suggest a similar status for the study of the Odes in the generations immediately after the death of Confucius. Second, the passage gives us a glimpse of what would become the characteristic approach to the study of the Odes, at least as it developed in the so-called orthodox "Mao school" tradition: the concern with the motivations that lay behind texts and utterances.

The original nucleus of this passage may have been an advertisement for the study of the Odes like 17.9 or the passage immediately following it in the present *Analects* (17.10): "The Master said to Boyu, 'Have you studied the Zhounan and Shaonan yet? Isn't a man who does not study the Zhounan and

Shaonan like someone who stands with his face to the wall?' "[55]

But the dialogue between Chen Gang and Boyu is more complex than either 17.9 or 17.10. Like certain other late passages from the *Analects* (especially 11.26; see below), its literary qualities are striking. One of Confucius's disciples asks the Master's son, Boyu, whether he has received any esoteric teachings from his father.[56] Boyu rejects this suggestion and reports rather two pieces of advice, which by the time this passage took its present form must have already seemed almost comically "Confucian": study the Odes, and study the rites.

Chen Gang, a good reader, knows that these clichés cannot exhaust Confucius's teaching. And so he seeks beneath the banality of this advice to discern its real motivation: Confucius's determination to maintain from his son a reserved distance, to check a parent's natural impulses to indulge and perhaps spoil a child. But the point of the passage was no more the homily "The superior man keeps distant from his son" than it was "Study the Odes." Rather it had to do with the hermeneutic acumen of Chen Gang, who, not satisfied with the manifest text of Confucius's utterance, searches out its motivations and its meaning in the particular situation in which it was uttered—that is, in the context of a dialogue between Confucius and his son.[57] We too should look beneath the manifest text of Chen Gang's gloss to the point of the narrative as a whole, which was to present and promote the kind of careful "reading" practiced by Chen Gang. This type of reading, which focused above all on the unsaid and on the hidden motivations behind an utterance, was to become a central concern of the Odes' hermeneutic tradition.

It was reading, then, the reflection upon a text, that was the subject of this passage. Indeed, such a passage was probably "written" in order to be read and reflected upon: the extended dialogue, the narrative detailing, and above all the hermeneutic concerns of the piece suggest that it was the product of a literary imagination nurtured on texts and their interpretation. Like 17.9 and 17.10, this anecdote reflects the increasing importance of the close study of texts—of hermeneutics—in the later Confucian schools.

In summary, we can distinguish in the *Analects* three types of passages concerned with the Odes. One group treats the Odes largely as the musical accompaniment to ritual; they are typical of those portions of the *Analects* with the best claim to represent early traditions concerning Confucius. A second group depicts Confucius or other figures quoting lines from the Odes in a way that recalls the recitation of the Odes portrayed in the *Zuo Tradition*, but with a moralizing twist largely absent in that text. These passages are typical of the middle strata of the *Analects*. Finally, the latest stratum of chapters of the *Analects* contains three passages in which Confucius is depicted as promoting the study of the Odes to his disciples.

There thus seems to be a clear chronological progression in the attitudes toward the Odes represented in the *Analects*, from the Odes as music to the Odes as rhetoric to the Odes as texts to study. This change must be understood in terms of two related developments. Perhaps already by the time of Confucius, certainly not long thereafter, the music of north China changed, perhaps under the impact of new types of music from the south. The advent of this "new music" inspired fear and contempt in the Confucian ritualists and teachers whose thought forms the background to works like the *Analects* and the *Mencius*, for it meant the displacement and eventual loss of the older, simpler music associated with the Odes.

The music of north China associated with the Odes was performed largely on bells and drums and was relatively simple and rhythmic. The new music from the south was performed on flutes and perhaps stringed instruments and was probably rhythmically and melodically more complex than the old music.[58] It was, as can be seen from the following passage, an altogether more seductive and attractive art than that of the music of the Odes.

Marquis Wen of Wei asked Zixia, "When I don my ritual regalia and listen to the ancient music, the only thing I fear is that I will keel over [from boredom]. But when I listen to the tones of Zheng and Wei, I never feel the least bit sated by it. May I be so bold as to ask why the ancient music is that way when the new is not?"[59]

Tonically, this new music from the south was characterized by its use of certain half or "changed" tones.[60] This was the feature most vehemently criticized by the defenders of the old music. Hence *Analects* 17.18: "The Master said, 'I hate the way that purple takes away from red, I hate the way that the sounds of Zheng confound the orthodox music [*yayue*], and I hate the way that skillful talkers overthrow states and houses.'"[61]

As Kenneth J. DeWoskin points out, purple and the "sounds of Zheng" were analogous in that both are mixtures, confusing and debasing a pure, primary color on the one hand and the purity of the "classical music" on the other.[62] The "Changed" (*bian*) Airs and Elegantiae of later Odes theory may have been associated with these "changed" tones.

Thus even as the teaching of the Odes was becoming institutionalized in the Confucian schools, the music that had been the raison d'être of the Odes was falling out of use, leaving behind the Odes as texts and texts only. Although traditions concerning the ritual uses and function of music continued to be taught, these teachings became increasingly speculative and abstract as they had fewer and fewer practical applications. The Odes, on the other hand, came to be seen largely as a repertoire of good phrases to be used in polite conversation or as the opportunities—the "pretexts"—for doctrinal exposition. In fact the tradition of quoting lines or stanzas from the Odes may have been quite old, perhaps deriving from the *fushi* practice depicted in the *Zuo Tradition*; now it became a central concern of the Confucian schools. But the quotation of the Odes as depicted in the middle strata of the

Analects differed from the use made of the Odes in the *fushi* practice (among other ways) in that the points made had to do with the illustration or opening up (*xing*) of points of Confucian teaching rather than with the more practical goals of the Spring and Autumn period warriors, wise men, and aristocrats portrayed in the *Zuo Tradition*.

This turn toward moral concerns was doubtless connected with the new role played by the Odes and texts generally in the curriculum of the Confucian schools of the Warring States. On the one hand, pressures of sectarian controversy led to the fixing—the "textualizing," if you will—of doctrine into stable and authoritative formulations. (The resulting texts may have included the earliest recensions of the teachings and traditions concerning Confucius, including the materials that survive in the *Analects*.) On the other hand, it was discovered that previously "weak" texts like the Odes could be glossed in such a way as to provide fruitful opportunities for doctrinal exposition. Both of these developments conspired to ensure that the reading and study of texts would come to occupy the central role in the Confucian curriculum we associate with them even today.

It was in connection with the study of such texts that questions of reading and hermeneutics first became thematic. In the *Zuo Tradition* narratives concerning the recitation of the Odes, that practice implied and presupposed a well-developed hermeneutic for interpreting the manifest content of the Ode and applying it to the situation at hand. So too with the *xing* practice, and so too with the Odes themselves. This earlier hermeneutic provided the structure of the later Mao school reading of the Odes. But it was only tacit; there was no "theory" of hermeneutics associated with the practices, and for good reason: the texts decoded in the earliest life of use of the Odes and in the *fushi* and *xing* practices were not the objects of *study*, of the careful and sustained reading that distinguishes the hermeneutic attitude proper. Such texts were used to make a point and then, as it were, discarded; it was not thought that they repaid a deep and searching engagement on the part of a student. In the latest stratum of the *Analects*, on the other hand, and in other texts from the mid and late Warring States period, texts like the Odes are treated not only as occasions for doctrinal exposition but as themselves embodying a kind of moral significance. It was in connection with the attempt to discover and reflect upon that inherent moral significance of the text that hermeneutics appeared.

At this moment in history, the decisive ascendancy of the Mao school and the hermeneutic associated with it were still centuries away. Rather, certainly at least two and perhaps many hermeneutics were associated with the Odes. One important type was represented by the dialogue between Confucius and Zixia (*Analects* 3.8). The discovery in the Odes of relatively abstract principles that seems to be represented in this passage had perhaps more in common with the traditional hermeneutics of the West than with the person-oriented hermeneutic associated with the Odes after the Han. Another kind of reading, the subject of this study, treated the Odes as deeds of words, as linguistic acts, whose significance was intimately related to the particular situation in which they were uttered: it was concerned more with their saying than with what they could be construed to have said. We can perhaps discern hints of this hermeneutic in certain passages discussed above (*Analects* 16.13 being the best example) that portray Confucius's disciples as ready and attentive to the nuances of their Master's teaching, especially as that teaching was to be understood in terms of Confucius's own motivations and concerns. Still, on the whole it is surprising how little of the later "Mao-style" reading of the Odes is to be found in the *Analects*. Its full development would depend upon the historicizing of the Odes visible in the thought of Mencius and perhaps Xunzi. But it would also draw upon certain other concerns to which we turn in the next chapter, concerns with what we might term the Confucian hermeneutic of character.

CHAPTER THREE

"The Odes Articulate Aims"

The Master said, "Look at what he uses, observe what he comes from, examine what he finds peace in. Can a man hide? Can a man hide?" —*Analects* 2.10

In the preceding chapter, we saw how the needs of Confucian teachers in the century or two after Confucius's death led to the canonization of the Odes, which from the musical accompaniment to ritual came to be treated as texts invested with moral significance. But such institutional pressures were in a sense vacuous: although they guaranteed that some such hermeneutic of the Odes would evolve, they did not determine its particular form. We could imagine, for instance, a dominant hermeneutic of the Odes in the form of the sort of exegesis engaged in by Confucius and Zixia at *Analects* 3.8, where the Ode is treated as a source for relatively abstract moral precepts. In the event, however, what emerged in the Mao tradition was a hermeneutic that saw the moral significance of the Odes to lie in their inscription and preservation of the paradigmatically normative aims, or *zhi*, of their authors. Although the origins of this view can arguably be sought in the Odes themselves or in the Odes recitation (*fushi*) practice described in Chapter 2, its fascination for later ages lay in its relevance to certain characteristic Confucian themes and concerns that seem to have been connected with what A. C. Graham has termed the metaphysical crisis of the fourth century B.C.E.[1]

During the fourth century, Confucianism was subjected to a searching critique on two fronts. On the one hand, the Mohists put the very raison d'être of the Confucians, their beloved music and ritual, to the test of utility and found them wasteful extravagances. On the other hand, the Confucian teachings concerning morality and ritual were attacked by "proto-Daoists" like Yang Zhu (fl. 350 B.C.E.?). Yang Zhu and those who thought like him claimed that the rituals and indeed the whole Confucian program ran counter to the demands of the "nature" (*xing*) endowed in humans by Heaven (*tian*); they thus placed upon the defenders of Confucianism the burden of showing how the demands of Confucian morality could be reconciled with those of an emotional nature admittedly disposed in other directions.

The proto-Daoists' attacks in particular brought to the forefront of Confucian discourse a new set of questions, all connected in some way with the problem of what we might term the opacity of the personality. Confucian thought became aware of and indeed preoccupied by the problem of the potential disjunction between, on the one hand, the nature and the emotions (*qing*) and, on the other hand, the normative standards of behavior as enunciated in Confucian teaching. This problem took two interrelated but analytically distinct forms: the mobilization of the emotions in the service of the Confucian norms; and a concern with distinguishing in others the authentic source of their actions—with the Confucian hermeneutic of character. The Odes were important to both concerns.

The Mobilization of the Emotions

A concern with what would come to be called "sincerity" (*cheng*) had perhaps always been part of Confucian thought.[2]

In the earliest stratum of the *Analects*, this concern was manifested in connection with emotional authenticity in ritual: "The Master said, 'If I do not participate in the sacrifice, it is as if I do not sacrifice'" (*Analects* 3.12). In Confucius's day, the ritual in which he believed so fervently seemed to have lost some of its efficacy; this phenomenon, which doubtless was connected to the social changes transforming China in his day, was ascribed here to a lack of commitment on the part of those who performed the rituals.

Perhaps as a result of the criticisms from Yang Zhu and other Daoists or proto-Daoist thinkers, this concern became central in later Confucianism. A new ideal emerged: the emotional nature, whatever its original dispositions, could be so nurtured or remade as to be in harmony with the demands of Confucian morality. Take, for example, Confucius's famous spiritual autobiography: "The Master said, 'At fifteen I had set my heart on learning. At thirty I had a foothold. At forty I was without any doubts. At fifty I knew Heaven's mandate. At sixty, my ears were suited [to hear the Way]. At seventy I could follow my heart's desires without trespassing the bounds [of what is right]'" (*Analects* 2.4).

This passage is unlikely to reflect an authentic tradition concerning Confucius, but it does indicate a relatively early interest in the notion of a self so completely remade that it does what is right spontaneously and naturally. Note that the apogee of moral accomplishment as portrayed here involves not the ability to make moral judgments but the ability to carry them out; or rather, to mobilize the emotional nature in their service in a spontaneous and unconflicted way. The central problematic was not the question of how to *determine* the good (for the norms were already known, or at least knowable through study) but how to *be* good. Much of the later history of Confucianism can be understood as a series of answers to this question. As we shall see below, the particular attraction of the Odes as a text was that they seemed to provide a privileged means for realizing these goals.

The Confucian Hermeneutic of Character

Closely linked with the problem of mobilizing the emotions was that of the Confucian hermeneutic of character. Confucianism had always had a strong interest in the evaluation of personality, as in the many passages in the *Analects* where Confucius and others discuss historical or contemporary figures or where Confucius evaluates his disciples. The problem of how to "know" men was a topic of interest in Confucius's circle because it was a useful skill in a society where patron-client relations predominated, both within government and without. Another reason was the interest in personalities as exemplary of different types or ways of "being a person" (*wei ren*): "A man's faults go together [with the rest of his personality] [*ge yu qi dang*]. Observe his faults, and you will know the man"[3] (*Analects* 4.7).

A person's faults were related here to character in what would be one of the most characteristic tropes of Chinese hermeneutics, synecdoche; the faults implied the whole character much as the microcosm does the macrocosm in later cosmology. As such, these faults resemble other "significant parts" thought in the later Confucianism of Mencius to reveal character: words (2.A.2) or the pupil of the eye (4.A.15).

The new awareness of the opacity of the personality precipitated by the metaphysical crisis of the fourth century seems to have complicated this concern as well. The Daoist and proto-Daoist critics of Confucianism energetically urged the possibility that the moral behavior of the Confucian gentleman reflected not his real desires and inclinations but only constraint, hypocrisy, and self-deception. Perhaps as a result, Confucian doctrine became aware of and concerned with the possibility that a person's character might not be exhausted in the manifest text of behavior. People and personalities came to be seen as complex and potentially opaque, and the question of understanding—of hermeneutics—came to the fore, especially as it was reflected in the figure of the moral-hermeneutical adept able to penetrate the evasions and deceptions of others.

The *Zhi*

The entity that exemplified the new complexity surrounding the possibility of knowing and understanding others was the *zhi*, or "aim." The term has a complex history. It was not exclusively associated with any single tradition, but appeared in a variety of contexts, with differing shades of meaning. In perhaps its earliest surviving appearance, in the "Pan Geng" chapter of the *Documents*, the term means "to aim": "I tell you about the difficulties [to be overcome], just as an archer aims [at the target; *yu gao ru yu nan ru shezhe you zhi*]."[4]

In the *Zuo Tradition*, *zhi* is a nominal expression meaning something like "ambitions." These "ambitions" were generally hopes for power or worldly success: "That we have not got our will [*zhi*] on the East of the Han is all owing to ourselves" and "Let him obtain his wish [*zhi*] [to become Prime Minister]" (Huan 6, 17).

In the *Analects*, *zhi* was adapted to Confucian concerns; it became the moral project or the ambition of a morally committed person. Thus we find the phrase *zhi yu* "to set oneself upon" completed in the *Analects* by *dao* "the Way" (7.6) and *ren* "humaneness" (4.4). Similarly, just as an unspecified *zhi* in the *Zuo Tradition* could be presumed to refer to an ambition for worldly success, in the *Analects* an undefined *zhi* was a moral commitment: a *zhi shi* (15.9) was someone committed to the Confucian project.

In late Warring States texts like the *Mencius* and the *Xunzi*, the *zhi* became an element of the common "philosophical anthropology" of the day.[5] In a famous passage at *Mencius* 2.A.2, for instance, Mencius debates the relation between language or doctrine (*yan*), the "heart-mind" (*xin*), the *zhi*, and that problematical entity known as the *qi*. In this view, the *zhi* was an integral element of the personality, connected to and "leading" the emotional nature.[6]

The *zhi* was thus an organizing and guiding preoccupation, either moral or frankly secular; I render it as "aim," but the term also covers some of the same ground as "intention," "ambition," "disposition," or even the Heideggerian "projection" (see Chapter 1). The *zhi* symbolized or rather exemplified the whole thrust of a person's being, for it was connected to and represented personality in a particularly direct and important way. If you knew an individual's *zhi*, you knew who that person was. But the *zhi* was different from, say, the pupil of the eye alluded to in *Mencius* or the faults Confucius observed in that it was not itself directly observable but had to be inferred from words or deeds. The revelation of the *zhi* could be, as it were, involuntary: that is, a casual word or deed might reveal to the hermeneutically astute observer everything about a person's orienting preoccupations and thus that individual's character and prospects. But the *zhi* could also be stated directly; in such a case the process was one of self-revelation. It was the self-revelation of *zhi* through speech—through direct statement or through the recital (or compositon) of an Ode—that was of particular concern for later hermeneutics.

Self-revelation is a complex and problematical activity, which takes away with one hand what it offers with the other. This particular complexity is illustrated by a pair of passages from the *Analects* that differ from one another only in respect to *zhi*. The first passage is from the earliest stratum of the *Analects*: "The Master said, 'If a man in three years [after his father's death] has not changed from his father's ways, he may be called filial'" (4.20). The concern of this passage is to specify the criteria for judging filiality. While a man's father was alive, he could only submit himself to his father's "ways," since he was not yet the head of his own household. Under such circumstances, his conformance to his father's ways was constrained, and so not significant. But when, after his father's death, he had become the head of his own household and could do as he pleased, he either followed his father's practices or he did not, and in that decision he showed whether he was truly devoted to his father—whether he was truly filial. We see in this passage both the early Confucian interest in determining and specifying character and the confidence, typical of the earliest sections of the *Analects*, that this character would be unproblematically revealed in observable behavior.

In another version of the story, which derives from the next stratum of chapters, a new perspective has been added: "The Master said, 'While his father is alive, observe his aim [*zhi*]; when his father is gone, observe his behavior. If in three years he has not changed from his father's ways, he may be called filial' " (*Analects* 1.11).[7] This fuller version differs from the last by the addition of the first sentence of Confucius's comment. This addition can be understood in one of two ways. In one view, the significance of the *zhi* is that it provides a means to judge a man's character before the text of his unconstrained behavior becomes available: the addition of the reference to *zhi* to the passage represents an addition to the hermeneutic repertoire. Considered in this light, the *zhi* resembles the other hermeneutic significata mentioned above (e.g., the pupil of the eye); it provides a window onto the character of the person observed, a criterion by which character could be judged and future actions predicted in the absence of an overt, or as we should say "behavioral," text. The inferring and interpreting of the *zhi* such a view presupposes would perhaps be a skill—they would perhaps require hermeneutic expertise—but there is no implication that the revelation of the *zhi* is necessarily self-revelation.

The other reading of this passage focuses on the contrast between the son's *zhi* as revealed before the death of his father and his behavior after that event. The motivating interest of the passage on this reading is in the question of whether the *zhi* will in fact be acted upon and borne out—whether the *zhi* is authentic. This is the interpretation implied by Arthur Waley's translation: "The Master said, While a man's father is alive, you can only see his intentions; it is when his father dies that you discover whether or not he is capable of carrying them out."[8] The central concern of the passage would thus be the problem of hypocrisy. Does the son truly intend to carry out the aims expressed while his father was alive? The son may well, while his father is alive and he has no other option, suggest that he does not chafe under that rule, but how will he behave when his father can no longer enforce his will? The possibility broached is the disjunction between a man's stated aims and his real aims. The *zhi* was, on this reading, generally available because self-revealed and yet requiring interpretation or certification. In this early context, *zhi* seems simultaneously to promise a privileged avenue for the understanding of character and to be hermeneutically problematical.

Such a reading presupposes that the expression or manifestation of the *zhi* was something public, something that could be observed, cited, and compared with the son's later behavior; indeed it is only in the context of some well-understood social practice by which the son might make his *zhi* known that a question like this could arise. A possible picture of such a practice is given in another linked pair of passages, these having to do with the "articulation of the *zhi*" (*yan zhi*).

Articulating the Aim

In the *Analects* a pair of closely related narratives concern the "direct" articulation of the aim. The first appears at *Analects* 5.26.

Yan Yuan [i.e., Yan Hui] and Zilu were in attendance. The Master said, "Why don't each of you tell your aim [*yan er zhi*]?"

Zilu said, "I would hope to share my chariot and my horses, my clothes and my furs, with my friends and not to resent it if they are so damaged."

Yan Yuan said, "I should like to make neither a show of my abilities nor a fuss over my labors."

Zilu said, "I would like to hear the Master's ambition."

The Master said, "To secure the elderly, keep faith with friends, and cherish the young."

In this brief narrative, Confucius asks two of his disciples to "tell his aim" (*yan zhi*). Zilu, Confucius's military-minded and least polished disciple, speaks first, and Confucius expresses his own ambition last. Almost certainly a "literary" (i.e., not a historical) text, this story is nevertheless quite unsophisticated. The function of the narrative is simply to articulate a hierarchy of moral accomplishment, with Zilu, as is so often the case in the *Analects*, serving as a foil, against whom the progressively more perfect aims of Yan Yuan and Confucius are contrasted. Although the passage seems to presuppose some well-understood convention of the presentation and evaluation of the *zhi*, Zilu and Yan Yuan nevertheless demonstrate a naiveté that renders their *zhi* hermeneutically transparent; Zilu in particular does not seem capable of imagining what Confucius would like to hear.

The situation is much more complex in another narrative of the same type, *Analects* 11.26 (numbered 11.24 and 11.25 in some editions).

Zilu, Zeng Xi, Ran You, and Gongxi Hua were sitting in attendance. The Master said, "You think of me as a day or two older than you. Do not think of me so. You are always saying, 'I am not recognized.' If someone were to recognize [your worth and give you a position], then what would you do?"

Zilu boldly and hastily replied, "Give me a state of [only] a thousand chariots, caught between two great states, with invading armies and drought and famine as well—I could handle it. Within three years, I could give the people courage and direction."

The Master smiled at him. "Qiu, what about you?"

[Ran You] replied, "A country sixty or seventy, or even fifty or sixty, *li* square—I would manage it. Within three years, I could see that the people had enough; but as for ritual and music, I would leave that to a [real] gentleman."

"Chi, what about you?"

[Gongxi Hua] replied, "I am not saying that I could do it, but I should like to learn. In the ceremonies at the ancestral temple or at a convocation of the feudal lords, dressed in a ceremonial cap and robes, I would like to be a minor assistant."

"Dian, what about you?"

He struck the zither, and its last notes faded away. Putting the zither aside, he stood and said, "It is different from what the other three have chosen."

The Master said, "What harm is in that. Each of us is simply telling his aim [*zhi*]."

[Zeng Xi] said, "In late spring, when the spring clothes have been made, with five or six newly capped youths and six or seven boys, to bathe in the River Yi, enjoy the breezes at the Rain Altar, and return home singing."

The Master sighed and said, "I am with Dian!"

When the other three had gone out, Zeng Xi remained behind. Zeng Xi said, "What about what the other three said?"

The Master said, "We were just telling our aims, that's all."

[Zeng Xi] said, "Then why did you smile at Zilu?"

"One governs a state with [adherence to] ritual. His words were forward, and so I smiled at him."

"But Qiu—he was not speaking of [being in charge of] a state?"

"Where have you ever seen [an area] sixty or seventy, or even fifty or sixty, *li* that was not a state?"

"But Chi—he was not speaking of a state?"

" 'Ancestral temples', 'convocations'—if these are not [the business of] a feudal lord, then what are they? If Chi would play a minor role, then who would play a major one?"

This passage, the longest in the *Analects*, is also one of the most narratively sophisticated and probably among the latest.[9] Clearly based upon *Analects* 5.26 (as well as upon 5.8), it reflects a deepened sense of the complexities involved in self-revelation and in understanding other people.

In this version, as in 5.26, several of Confucius's disciples are invited to state their *zhi*, or aims. As in 5.26, there is a progression from the relatively crude ambitions of Zilu to the culminating vision of Confucius, here articulated by Zeng Xi. But whereas the progression in 5.26 was from Zilu's unimaginative hope to attain some modest measure of self-control to Confucius's more complex and substantial ideal, in this passage the course is reversed, and moves from a relatively grandiose ambition on Zilu's part to a series of (seemingly) ever more modest visions, from Zilu's intention to accomplish the most difficult military, political, and moral tasks to Zeng Xi's modest and apolitical desire.

The narrative sophistication of the story is matched by its thematic complexity. In 5.26, the point of the narrative has to do with the content of the *zhi* articulated; the narrative simply provides a convenient structure to compare them. In 11.26, on the other hand, the focus is not simply on the content of the *zhi* of the first three disciples, but also on their hermeneutical status. As in the story about Chen Gang and Boyu at *Analects* 16.13, the concern of the anecdote is no longer the object of interpretation as such, but interpretation itself. Interpretation itself has become problematical and thematic.

Discussions of this passage have tended to focus on the significance of Zeng Xi's aim; the variety of interpretations given by traditional commentators is testimony to its difficulty and suggestiveness.[10] The absence in Zeng Xi's vision of any overtly political program or mechanically rigid morality has led some critics to characterize 11.26 as "Daoistic," and the aesthetic sensibility it seems to promote is reflected in the careful and skillful narrative detailing that characterizes the passage as a whole.

But the significance of Zeng Xi's aim cannot be understood apart from those of the other disciples. As the interpretive coda shows, although Ran You and Gongxi Hua purport to state their *zhi*, they do not in fact do so; whether from hypocrisy or from a lack of self-understanding, they do not say what they really want. Rather, they try to say what they think Confucius wants to hear. There is to each of their *zhi* a "sub-text," which is decoded by Confucius. The final *zhi* articulated, that of Zeng Xi, avoids this difficulty: it has no sub-text, and thus Confucius gives it not interpretation but only approval. Indeed, Zeng Xi's *zhi* may represent the culmination of the passage precisely because it eludes interpretation, even as it is placed in a frame that constantly solicits it.

Zeng Xi's aim is culminating not only because of the vision it implies, but because of its authenticity or sincerity: it is what Zeng Xi really wants. We are convinced by the narrative—by Zeng Xi's preoccupation with his lute and his initial reluctance to voice his aim and also by the qualities of the vision he articulates. The enjoyment of the wind, the return home singing, do not seem to be symbols of something else; rather, they are compelling features of a concrete and genuinely attractive scene.[11] It is in this connection that I think we must understand the curious feature of this passage that Confucius expresses himself by choosing Zeng Xi's *zhi* rather than by articulating one of his own, as he does in 5.26. The nod to Zeng Xi may reflect a move in the institutional and ideological politics of late Warring States or early Han Confucianism.[12] But surely the way in which this most literary of all *Analects* passages works has to do with Confucius's spontaneous and thus convincing choice of Zeng Xi's wish—Zeng Xi's wish appeals to Confucius in precisely the same way that the visit to the river appeals to Zeng Xi. Explicit, discursive self-revelation is always in danger of falling prey to the kinds of failure exemplified by Ran You and Gongxi Hua, if only because the very act of saying what it is that motivates one must necessarily stem from a motivation different from the one it states. Spontaneous movement toward a desired state, on the other hand, reveals the person completely.[13]

The Moral-hermeneutical Adept

Self-revelation, which promised to provide insight into character, has become intensely problematical in *Analects* 11.26. The passage, and the issues it raises, stands at the beginning of a long hermeneutical tradition. One line of development was pursued in the context of the *shi* "lyric," through which poets sought ways to demonstrate the sincerity and authenticity of the aims they voiced.[14] Another tradition of concern, more directly relevant to the history of hermeneutics and of the reading of the Odes, approached the problem from the opposite tack, asking how one could judge the authenticity and content of self-revelations like these. It is in connection with this deepened sense of the problematical character of interpretation and understanding—the opacity of the personality—that we begin to find in certain late Warring States and early Han materials the figure I call the *moral-hermeneutical adept*.

In *Analects* 11.26, it takes a good man—a sage, in fact—to understand the real meaning of the *zhi* articulated by the disciples. The idea that interpretation was difficult and problematical and that it could be accomplished only by the morally accomplished is common in late Warring States texts. The best and most famous example of the type is Confucius himself. One of the best examples in another context can be found in an Odes recitation narrative in the *Zuo Tradition* under Xiang 27. The story concerns the visit of the grandees Zhao Meng and Shu Xiang of Jin to the state of Zheng in the year 545 B.C.E. Jin was at this time still nominally the leader of the fragmented and contentious states of north China, but in reality it was increasingly undermined by the power of the semi-sinicized state of Chu to the south. Zhao Meng is one of the heroes of this story, an idealized bulwark who staves off the collapse of Jin. In the story below, Zhao Meng and Shu Xiang are just returning from a convocation of the states where they dealt with a series of troublesome encroachments by Chu.

The earl of Zheng feasted Zhao Meng at Chuilong. Zi Zhan, Bo You, Zi Xi, Zi Chan, Zi Dashu and the two Zishi were all in attendance. Zhao Meng said, "You seven sirs have done me the honor of accompanying your prince [to this banquet in my honor]. Please do you each now recite [an Ode], in order to complete your prince's kindnesses; and I, Wu, will thereby observe your seven aims [*yi guan qi zi zhi zhi*].

Each of the seven Zheng ministers then recites an Ode. With the exception of Bo You, each chooses an Ode that is politely welcoming and flattering in tone. For instance, Zi Chan, the famous minister, recites the "Xisang" Ode (Mao #228), the first stanza of which reads as follows, in Arthur Waley's translation:

> The mulberry on the lowland, how graceful!
> Its leaves, how tender!
> Now that I have seen my lord,
> Ah, what delight![15]

The third line of the stanza could as well be understood as "Now that I have seen you, sir"; that is, as referring to Zhao Meng. Zhao Meng replies to each of these polite gestures with suitably courteous replies.

Only Bo You, the second of the Zheng ministers to chant, does not take the opportunity to welcome Zhao Meng; rather he recites the "Chun zhi benben" Ode (Mao #49), which reads as follows, again in Waley's translation:

> How the quails bicker,
> How the magpies snatch!
> Evil are the men
> Whom I must call "brother."
>
> How the magpies snatch,
> How the quails bicker!
> Evil are the men
> Whom I must call "lord."[16]

The last couplet could just as easily be rendered "Evil is the man / Whom I must call 'lord.'" Bo You, as we are meant to discern, is malcontent and has plans to usurp the position of his lord, the Earl of Zheng. Zhao Meng urbanely deflects Bo You's suggestion, but later when he is alone with Shu Xiang, they discuss its implications.

Wenzi [i.e., Zhao Meng] said to Shu Xiang, "Bo You will be executed. We use the Odes in order to articulate our aims [*shi yi yan zhi*]. His aim [*zhi*] is to impose upon [*wu*] his superior, and he publicly complained about him when he should have been welcoming his guests. Can he last long? He will be lucky if he can delay his end."[17]

Shu Xiang said, "Right. He is already out of hand. What they say about not lasting another five harvests certainly applies to him."

They then review the characters and prospects of the other Zheng ministers, predicting that among them, "the family of Zi Chan will be the last to perish."

This narrative is significant in that it contains what is arguably the earliest appearance of a version of the *shi yan zhi* ("Odes articulate aims") formula. Moreover, it provides examples of three of the possible uses of the Odes according to *Analects* 17.9.[18] Although it is more likely in my opinion to reflect the concerns and interests of the fourth century B.C.E. (i.e., the period when the *Zuo Tradition* took its final form) than of the sixth century (the ostensible date of the events narrated), it is an important document in the history of the hermeneutics of the Odes.

One of the most striking features of this narrative is its structural similarity to the *Analects* 11.26 narrative concerning the aims of Confucius and his disciples. Both narratives begin with an invitation by someone to a group to articulate or reveal their aims (*zhi*). The implication is that this morally and hermeneutically accomplished individual will judge the others and that he is entitled and qualified to do so. Those who have been invited then articulate their aims—directly in *Analects* 11.26 and indirectly through the Odes they choose in the *Zuo Tradition* narrative. Finally, each passage closes with an interpretive coda, a dialogue in which the hero and an intimate decode and discuss the meaning of what they have just heard.

Common to these stories is the figure of the moral-hermeneutical adept about which they revolve. In both Confucius and Zhao Meng, we see the characteristic trait of this figure, his combination of moral accomplishment and hermeneutic acumen. In *Analects* 11.26, the Master is able to understand the motivations and concerns behind each gesture of self-revelation and to understand those gestures in turn as exemplary of the character or personality (the way of "being a person"; *wei ren*) of each of the disciples. Similarly, Zhao Meng demonstrates his hermeneutic acumen by interpreting in what would become a paradigmatic fashion. First, he discerns behind each recitation the aim that motivates it. From those aims, he is able to make inferences about the characters and dispositions of the various Zheng grandees and thus to (accurately) predict their fates. The link—Ode, *zhi*, character, social world—was to provide the basic structure of the Odes hermeneutic of the *Mao Preface* (except that there it would be the composition, rather than the recitation, of the Odes that was at stake).

This hermeneutic mastery was linked with moral accomplishment. In the case of Confucius, this need hardly be said: in the system we are now discussing, the figure "Confucius" has become a counter symbolizing the full realization of human potentialities. In the *Mencius* as well, claims concerning hermeneutic expertise are linked with claims about moral achievement. The unifying notion may be completeness: the faults Mencius is able to discern in his debating opponents seem to have to do with partiality or incompleteness.[19] Similarly the interpretive recalcitrance of Zeng Xi's *zhi* may have to do with the moral accomplishment it reveals: Zeng Xi (that is, Confucius) subsumes or contains the other disciples and so can understand them, but the relation is not mutual.

Zhao Meng is likewise a moral hero and exemplary figure, although not like Confucius "tautologically" good: his moral accomplishment must be demonstrated and certified by the narrative. Indeed, this is one of the functions of the Chuilong episode: Zhao Meng's hermeneutic acumen is one more ennobling, certifying attribute that contributes to the total picture of the man the *Zuo Tradition* wishes to paint. His invitation/command to the Zheng grandees, his "observation" (*guan*) of their characters, and the revelation of his mastery in the coda—all these are marks of moral authority, which we can conveniently sum up by saying that Zhao Meng has been assimilated to and identified with the figure of Confucius as portrayed in *Analects* 11.26 (whether that passage existed in its present form when this one took shape or not).

The point, then, is that in the doctrinal milieu in which this narrative took shape, hermeneutic expertise—the ability to read others—had become an assumed good, had become so highly valued that it could be, as it was here, borrowed for the purpose of building up someone who, it was claimed, possessed it.[20] The moral-hermeneutical adept had become a recognizable and admired *type*. The appearance of this type in these late materials reflects the increasing importance assigned to interpretation and hermeneutics at this moment in Chinese history, an importance stemming from the deepened sense that people could be complex, devious, and opaque—to others, and to themselves. The "articulation of the aim," which it was the particular promise of the Odes to realize, was an especially problematical case, for as *Analects* 11.26 shows, that activity was always both seductively attractive and yet hedged round with difficulties. Much of the subsequent history of the reading of the Odes, as well as of the "secular" lyric (*shi*), was concerned with overcoming, circumventing, or denying these difficulties. The hermeneutics of texts and hermeneutics of the personality deepened together.

Zhi as Historical: Mencius and the First Explicit Hermeneutic

It is a tricky and problematical business to date passages like *Analects* 11.26 and the *Zuo Tradition* narrative or their constituent elements. Nevertheless, both passages probably come from the later stages of their respective traditions; taking the redaction of the *Zuo Tradition* as an index, we might place them some time around the end of the fourth century B.C.E.

This would make these materials approximately contemporaneous with the teaching of Mencius (Meng Ke or Mengzi, 372–289), in whose teachings we find the first explicit hermeneutic of the Odes.

I argued above that it is in the latest strata of the *Analects* and the *Zuo Tradition* that we begin to see a deepened interest in the study and interpretation of texts, an interest manifested not only in teachings commending such study but also in stories and materials that seem to presuppose and anticipate it. This new importance of texts was related to the routinization of teaching in the schools and to the discovery that the explication of texts could provide a fruitful means of doctrinal exposition, as well as to the needs of the schools to specify—in the face of competing visions—what exactly they believed in, defined as what they believed Confucius and the Sages to have said. These pressures contributed to the institutionalization of the study of texts and the articulation of a hermeneutic in another way as well: it was probably in the context of contemporary doctrinal conflict that the Odes and Documents came to be quoted in arguments as authoritative sources for historical and normative truths. And it was from the desire to adjudicate among such readings that the first explicit hermeneutic of the Odes and of reading generally was born.

Both this atmosphere of doctrinal controversy and the hermeneutic it engendered are features of the famous conversation recorded at *Mencius* 5.A.4.

Xianqiu Meng said, "I now understand your teaching that Shun did not treat Yao as a subject. [But] the Ode [#205] says,

> Everywhere under Heaven
> Is no land that is not the king's.
> To the borders of all those lands
> None but is the king's subject.[21]

I venture to ask how it was that once Shun had become the Son of Heaven, the Blind Man [i.e., Shun's father] was not his subject?"

[Mencius] said, "That is not what the Ode says [*fei shi wei*]. [It is rather that the author] labored over the king's business and was not able to take care of his parents. [It is as if the author] said, 'This is all the king's business; why do I alone deserve to be so overworked?'

"Thus those who speak of the Odes should not let their literary qualities [*wen*] harm the [plain, literal meaning of the] words [*ci*], nor take the words in such a way as to harm the aim [*zhi*]; rather meet that aim with your own intentions [*yi*]. If one were to seize upon the words only, then when the 'Yunhan' [Ode #258] says,

> Of the masses of people who remained
> of the Zhou
> There is not one left.[22]

it would mean that none of the people of Zhou survived, if we are to believe these words."

Xianqiu Meng, Mencius's interlocutor, is identified by the late Han commentator Zhao Qi as a disciple of Mencius and may have been so, although the traditional commentators sometimes identify even hostile questioners as disciples.[23] His questions, however, reflect the intensive scrutiny to which the doctrines and mythology of Confucianism were being subjected in Mencius's day. The issue under discussion had to do with the status of the sovereign as it was defined vis-à-vis the man of "complete virtue" (*shengde*) on the one hand and the ruler's father on the other. Xianqiu Meng begins by suggesting that Mencius's hero and exemplar of complete virtue, Shun, was accorded the honors due to a king by his predecessor, the Sage Yao, a suggestion Mencius rejects. Then, in the passage quoted above, Xianqiu Meng cites lines from the "Beishan" Ode as evidence that everyone in the empire, including the sovereign's father, must be subordinated to him.

As Mencius points out, however, the lines Xianqiu Meng quotes have a very different meaning in the context of the Ode as a whole, and he supplies a paraphrase that takes account of the last two lines of the stanza, omitted by Xianqiu Meng:

> But the ministers are not just;
> Whatever is done, I bear the brunt alone.[24]

Arthur Waley suggests in a note to his translation of this Ode that the lines Xianqiu Meng quotes may have been a proverbial saying; if so, the saying might have had the sense Xianqiu Meng assigns the lines.[25] But whatever the original sense of the saying, within the context of the Ode the lines Xianqiu Meng quotes have just the sense Mencius assigns them. They must be understood not in terms of their literal meaning, but in terms of their use, as Mencius makes clear in his next example.

The passage is significant because Xianqiu Meng's quotation of the Ode in this context and fashion clearly assumed that the Odes have stable meanings that could be used to support historical or normative arguments. Such a view differed in important ways from that implicit in the ritual use of the Odes or in the *xing* and *fushi* practices. These neither made nor presupposed any claims concerning the historical meaning of the Odes, but sought only to quote lines in an apposite and witty fashion. Whatever controversies arose concerned the appropriate or inappropriate use of the Odes (as we saw in the cases of Confucius's comments on the misuse of the "Yong" Ode or of Bo You's poor choice of lines to recite). They rarely if ever touched upon questions of meaning as such, since the original, historical meaning of the Ode was irrelevant to the use made of its language in these practices. Even when, as in the *xing* practice, the Ode was used as the occasion for exegesis, it was simply "borrowed" as a starting point; no claims were made concerning its actual historical meaning.

Xianqiu Meng, however, takes it for granted that the lines quoted from the Ode have a kind of normative force, that they have the status of a teaching. In Mencius's day, such a view of the Odes was widespread, and it is easy to see how the use of a line or two from the Odes to provide an elegant and persuasive tag or cap to an argument would naturally evolve into a practice whereby that quotation served as a proof. Mencius himself was particularly fond of citing the first ten or so Greater Elegantiae as sources for the early history of the Zhou, and he also quoted the Airs as sources for moral teaching.[26] Such a view presupposed that the Odes quoted did in fact have stable, specifiable meanings and could thus be used in normative or historical arguments. This use of the Odes led eventually to the Mao school interpretations (discussed in Chapter 4) and to Mencius's formulation of the first explicit hermeneutic in Chinese history.

But although Xianqiu Meng's quotation of the Odes represents a break with (or rather an evolution from) the sort of hermeneutic implicit in the *xing* and *fushi* uses of the Odes, it does nevertheless share with those practices an important continuity. Meanings are inferred from individual lines or stanzas, not necessarily from the Ode as a whole: Xianqiu Meng is still "breaking off a stanza" from the Ode as a whole and ascribing to it a meaning. As we can see from the example above (or from any of the many examples of the *xing* and *fushi* practices discussed above), this quotation of lines out of context allowed for the assignment of meanings to the Ode that often were quite remote from any plausible reading of the Ode as a whole.

It is against this feature in Xianqiu Meng's use of the Odes that Mencius is arguing in this passage. In his reply, Mencius cautions against two types of reading: allowing the literary qualities of the Ode to interfere with ("harm") the plain, literal meaning of the words and allowing the plain, literal meaning of the words to harm the *zhi* of the passage. Although he does not give an example of the first, he was probably referring to the type of interpretation that seized upon some "literary" feature of the text (*wen*)—an inversion, a meaningless particle—to the detriment of the plain, literal meaning of the passage.[27]

The second kind of interpretation that Mencius warns

against is precisely what was done when stanzas were "broken off" and used in ways that suited the needs of the moment, as in the *Analects*, the *Zuo Tradition*, or here in the case of Xianqiu Meng. In the Song dynasty, this passage tended to be interpreted in terms of a scheme of parts and wholes, with *wen* standing for a single character or word, *ci* for a sentence or phrase, and *zhi* for the intention animating the piece as a whole (see Chapter 7). Although I think this interpretation incorrect, at least as regards the meaning of *wen*, there is a sense in which the last, organizing term of the series, *zhi* ("aim"), can be decided only by reference to the Ode as a whole. Thus Mencius supplies the context of the Ode as a whole to refute the reading of the lines that Xianqiu Meng gives them.

But although the *zhi* can be inferred only from the Ode as a whole, the understanding of *zhi* involves more than a simple reference to the whole Ode. Although there are passages in other texts from this era in which *zhi* seems to have become nothing more than a kind of generic "meaning,"[28] in the *Mencius* at least and in most of the texts that focus in this period on the relation between the Odes and *zhi*, the term is still closely linked with the idea of personality. Thus in the passage under discussion, Mencius says "meet that aim [*zhi*] with [i.e., in terms of] your own intentions [*yi*]." The term *yi*, which we encounter here for the first time, plays an important role in discussions of meaning and language in Warring States texts. It reappears in the third century C.E. in Wang Bi's famous comments about the meaning and interpretation of the *Changes* and then plays an important role in the eleventh-century Neoconfucian discussions about intention and significance (*yii*).* It is often used interchangeably or in combination with *zhi* in later texts, and indeed in this passage Mencius seems to use it as a synonym for *zhi*, suggesting that the reader must as it

---

* The term I am translating as "significance" would ordinarily be romanized in the *pinyin* system as *yi*. I use the form *yii* to distinguish it from *yi* "intention." On the importance of this distinction, see Chapters 6 and 7.

were mentally recreate the animating intention of the Ode. To translate Mencius's dictum into an anachronistic vocabulary, we might say that one must in reading presume that the text is the utterance or product of a person like oneself and try to understand it in terms of one's own existential situation. Texts are like people in this view and must be understood on the basis of one's own personality and experience.

Zhi as Normative: Xunzi

Probably no single figure exerted as great an influence over the institutionalization of the study of classics in Confucianism as Xunzi (Xun Qing; 310–ca. 211 B.C.E.)[29] The role of the only other figure of comparable influence in early Chinese history, Confucius, was, as I tried to show above, historically problematical.[30] The word *jing* in the sense of a canonical text never appears in the surviving teachings of Mencius, the other great figure of Warring States Confucianism. Although Mencius frequently quoted from and cited the Odes, he expressed skepticism concerning the value of the Documents, saying of them that "it would be better not to have the Documents than to believe everything in them."[31] In the work of Xunzi, on the other hand, we find not only frequent quotations from and references to what he himself called the classics, but also injunctions to their study. Moreover, it is clear that Xunzi's students took his advice: his influence can be traced in the subsequent history of the classics, especially the Odes, and their associated exegetical traditions well into the Han. After the Western Han the influence of his thought declined; and lacking influential partisans in subsequent ages, his contributions to classics studies have been overlooked.[32] They were, however, crucial to formation of the tradition of discourse we call classics studies.

For Xunzi, the canon consisted of the *Odes*, the *Documents*, certain ritual texts, a music text, and the *Spring and Autumn*

Annals (*Chunqiu*), traditionally ascribed to Confucius.[33] These works, and especially the first two, were of paramount importance for Xunzi. He frequently quoted from them, more frequently than did Mencius,[34] and unlike Mencius, he was more likely to use the Odes to back up a point of doctrine than as a source of historical precedents. Such uses presupposed an environment where the moral and doctrinal authority of the Odes and, to a lesser extent, the Documents was taken for granted. Xunzi, moreover, frequently mentions the importance of the classics in the Confucian curriculum: "Learning—where should it begin and where should it end! I say: Its proper method is to start with the recitation of the Classics and conclude with the reading of the *Rituals*."[35]

For Xunzi, the study of the classics was an integral element of the Confucian curriculum; it was one of the privileged means for remaking the character into the forms Xunzi advocated. This promotion of the classics in general and the thematicization of the ideal of the "classic" (*jing*) in particular represented the culmination of trends toward the institutionalization of classics study visible in the later stratum of the *Analects*, and these trends provided a paradigm for the reading and study of the classics that was to prove enormously influential on the scholarship of the Han.

The most important of the classics for Xunzi, if we are to judge by his own style of argumentation, was undoubtedly the *Odes*, which he referred to more frequently than any other text.[36] The Odes were important to Xunzi because, as in the earlier formulations of Mencius and the *Zuo Tradition*, they gave voice to or "articulated" (*yan*) the aims (*zhi*) of their authors. The crucial innovation of Xunzi was to make explicit a claim that, if indeed it existed at all, was only tacit in the teachings of Mencius: the authors of the Odes were in every case the morally accomplished individuals known in the mythology of Confucianism as the "Sages" (*sheng, shengren*), and the motivations behind the Odes—the aims they articulated—

were for that reason in every case paradigmatically normative: "The Sages were the channel of the Way [*shengren yezhe, dao zhi guan ye*]; they were the channel through which the Way [was realized] in the Empire. . . . What the Odes articulate are their aims [*shi yan shi qi zhi ye*]."[37] The notion that the *zhi* inscribed in the Odes were in every case correct and exemplary was central to Xunzi's view of the Odes and their role in moral education, and it was to become the central claim of the medieval view of the Odes adumbrated by the *Mao Preface* and developed by the Tang dynasty *Correct Significance of Mao's Odes*.

This claim should be understood as the natural development of the tendency to treat the Odes as strong texts—as the appropriate objects of study and the occasions for doctrinal exposition. Of course, lines from the Odes had been used as the starting points (the pretexts) for doctrinal exposition in the *xing* practice as well, but insofar as that way of using the Odes neither made nor presupposed any claims about the original, historical "meaning" of the texts, it was not necessary to speculate on the characters of their authors. But once, as with Mencius, it was felt necessary to specify and limit the sorts of uses that could be made of the Odes by referring them to their putative historical authors, then their authoritative character could be secured only by claiming that they were the products of morally correct impulses (*zhi*), stemming from morally correct authors (the Sages).[38]

But there was another dimension to this claim as well. In their earliest life of use, certain of the Odes were associated with the rituals of the Spring and Autumn period and for that reason were invested with an aura of solemnity and grandeur. Others, however, were probably, at least in the repertoire of the Zhou court musicians, simply entertainments. Although Confucius denies the possibility in the case of the "Guanju," references elsewhere seem to admit the possibility that some Odes embodied and fostered sentiments that were undesirable and even dangerous to Confucian morality. Indeed, Confucius acknowledges as much precisely by ruling this possibility out in the case of the "Guanju," and by criticizing the "sounds" of Zheng and Wei.[39] But early advocates of the Odes like Confucius did not feel it necessary to insist that the corpus as a whole was paradigmatically normative; nor did the *fushi* or *xing* practices require such a claim.

As the Odes became more and more central to the Confucian curriculum, however, and in particular as they became the objects of the kind of intensive and careful study I am calling "hermeneutical," their teachers were embarrassed and perplexed by those Odes that expressed or referred to sentiments seemingly out of keeping with Confucian morality, especially those concerned with love and romantic adventure. Insulated by their status as memorized texts from the smoothing and naturalizing effects of oral tradition, such Odes served, to use a familiar but apt comparison, like the foreign and irritating grain of sand that stimulates the oyster to the production of a pearl. The pearl in this case was an elaborate mythology of the Odes that insisted most strongly precisely upon the claim which seemed most manifestly contradicted by the Odes themselves: that they expressed not overwhelming passions or enervating grief but moderate and exemplary control.

The pressure of the denied possibility that the Odes reflected emotional excess shaped the language in which Xunzi defined the normative character of the Odes, especially the Airs. In the passage quoted above, for instance, he goes on to define the distinctive characters of the Airs, the Elegantiae, and the Lauds. Regarding the first, he says: "So the means whereby the Airs are not abandoned [*zhu*] is that they avail themselves of this [i.e., the *zhi* of the Sages] in order to modulate [themselves] [*jie zhi*]."[40] In other words, the particular virtue of the Airs is that they keep the potentially dangerous and anarchic sexual passions in check (*jie zhi*). Xunzi makes the same point in the "Dalue" (Great Digest) chapter: "Concerning erotic love [*hao se*] in the Airs, a tradition says that 'Desire is fulfilled but the stopping point is not exceeded.' "[41] Although the Odes, particularly the Airs, were concerned with potentially dangerous and disruptive emotions like sexual passion, they expressed these passions in a paradigmatically correct and normative way. It was for this reason, among others, that the Odes could play a role in the moral education of the Confucian devotee.

Of course, Xunzi's interest in the Odes and in the question of their normative character was not an abstract one; rather, it had to do with his vision of the function of the Odes in the Confucian curriculum. At times Xunzi seems to speak of the pedagogical function of the Odes in terms that recall the *Analects*, as when he refers to the "breadth" of the Odes and Documents.[42] The Tang commentator Yang Liang refers this passage, correctly I think, to the famous claim at *Analects* 17.9 that the study of the Odes could increase one's "acquaintance with the names of birds, beasts, plants, and trees."[43] More often, however, and more important, Xunzi maintained that the Odes could transform the emotions and inner lives of those who attended to them.

So men cannot but feel joy, and joy cannot but manifest itself [in music]. If, however, it is manifested and [is not in harmony] with the Way, then there must be disorder. The Former Kings abhorred this kind of disorder, and so they made the sounds of the Elegantiae and Lauds in order to lead and control it [*dao zhi*]. They made these sounds so that they were sufficient [to incite] joy, which did not, however, get out of hand, and they made their texts [*wen*] so that they made salient points without, however, giving cause for fear. They made the directness, the complexity, the intensity, and the rhythms of [these sounds] such that they were able to move the good in people's hearts [*gandong ren zhi shanxin*] and such that the filthy and depraved energies [*qi*] would be rejected. This was the way in which the Former Kings established the music.[44]

Music had the power to modulate and transform the emotional natures of those who listened to it. This language of emotional moderation and poise had been associated from an early date with the music of the Odes but not, I have argued, with their texts. It was, however, precisely as texts that Xunzi commended the Odes to his students and to later generations. If here the power of their music had not yet been claimed for the study of their texts, this step would soon be taken by those who, in the Han, were influenced by Xunzi's thought.

CHAPTER FOUR

The 'Preface to Mao's Odes'

To study the Odes without seeking the help of the *Preface* is like trying to enter a house without going through the door.
— Cheng Yi

The *Preface* . . . is the work of a rustic ignoramus.
— Zheng Qiao

The proscription in 213 B.C.E. by the First Emperor of the Qin of Confucian teachings and the burning of the Confucian classics, especially the *Odes*, the *Documents*, and the ritual texts, were events of mythic significance in Chinese history.[1] The rupture of the tradition implied by these events came to symbolize for later generations the increasing historical remoteness of the language, ideas, and assumed social background of the classics, and the overcoming of hermeneutical difficulty or distance was often conceived in terms of repairing this break in the textual and exegetical traditions. In the second century B.C.E., the sense that the great, canonical texts of the past had become historically remote gave rise to two interconnected phenomena. First, there was the rise of the textually and historically oriented scholarship associated with the so-called Old Text versions of the classics. This resulted in the fixing into authoritative form of much of the Old Text canon, both the texts of the classics themselves and the exegetical traditions associated with them. And second, closely related to this new interest in texts was a new awareness of the problematical character of the study of canonical texts and an interest in their hermeneutics.

One of the most important products of this new interest was that portion of the *Preface to Mao's Odes* (*Maoshi xu*) commonly known today as the "Great Preface" ("Daxu"). This text represented not only a culmination of many of the themes discussed in the preceding chapter but also the starting point for most later discussions of the hermeneutics of the Odes and of secular poetry, of the classics, and of reading generally. If, as Alfred North Whitehead is supposed to have maintained, the whole of Western philosophy can be considered a footnote to Plato, we might with equal justice say that most Chinese hermeneutical thought has been a commentary on the "Great Preface." The "Great Preface" was and is, however, a difficult and somewhat problematical document, composed in a fashion that has both stimulated and frustrated interpreters. Understanding the "Preface" (as I will call it) requires that we understand something of the institutional context in which it took shape, and it is to that institutional context that I turn first.

The Classics in the Western Han

The first half-century or so of Han rule was not hospitable to Confucian teaching. The antipathy of Gaozu (206–195 B.C.E.), the founder of the dynasty, toward Confucians was demonstrated when he urinated in the ceremonial cap of an importunate adviser.[2] Perhaps the most important and influential teaching at the court during this period was that of "the Yellow Emperor and Laozi" (Huang-Lao), a Legalistic Daoism that may have had roots in the famous Jixia Academy in Qi.[3] It was not until the reigns of the Emperors Wen (179–57 B.C.E.) and Jing (156–41 B.C.E.) that Confucians began to

enjoy the favor of the emperor and that the imperial institutions which were to be so important for the development of
Han Confucianism were established. The most important of
these imperial institutions were the offices of the erudites
(*boshi*), scholars who specialized in the exposition and teaching
of a text or discipline.[4] Among these erudites were specialists
on the Confucian classics, including three versions of the *Odes*
(see below). During the reign of Han Wudi (140–87 B.C.E.),
the erudites were limited to specialists on the five Confucian
classics (the *Changes*, the *Odes*, the *Documents*, the *Yi Ritual*
[*Yili*], and the *Spring and Autumn Annals* with the *Gongyang
Commentary*). In 125 B.C.E. an Imperial Academy was established, and by the end of the second century B.C.E. it had 3,000
students.[5]

Although it was not a unitary, self-conscious movement or
school, the court Confucianism that flourished in these imperial institutions can be characterized in general terms. Its
most famous representative and the engineer of its ascendancy
in the mid- and late second century was Dong Zhongshu (ca.
175–ca. 105 B.C.E.), "chief of the literati"[6] and specialist on the
Gongyang interpretation of the *Spring and Autumn Annals*. His
synthesizing, unifying, and optimistic teaching linked the human and cosmic realms together in a network of ramifying
correspondences. Ritual, music, and certain texts were
thought to have the power to unify and shape society. Moreover, Dong Zhongshu saw the universe as radically intelligi-
ble, a veritable sign of itself, which proclaimed everywhere in
relations of synecdoche the cosmic principles at work at any
given moment, particularly the success or failure of the emperor in his role as mediator between humanity and Heaven.

Hermeneutically speaking, this court Confucianism was
innovative for what might be called its idealism—its belief in
the radical intelligibility of the world and in the efficacy of
symbolic action. But in another sense it continued certain key
aspects of pre-Qin hermeneutics. Like Mencius, Xunzi, and
other Confucian teachers of the Warring States period, Dong

Zhongshu and his fellow New Text Confucians were confident of their grasp of the authentic Way, and they regarded their task as its restatement in terms that addressed the needs and concerns of their own day. Indeed it was precisely this confidence in their mastery of the meaning of the texts and received teachings of the tradition that allowed Dong Zhongshu and his fellows to create the elaborate and speculative systems that seem to us so remote from the original spirit of the classics.

Although dominant at the imperial court with which it was both institutionally and thematically linked, the thought of Dong Zhongshu was not the only Confucianism of the Western Han. Outside the radius of imperial favor, among private teachers and especially at certain regional courts, another kind of teaching attracted pupils and adherents. Historically, philologically, and above all textually oriented, this loosely defined movement, if we can use such a term, came to be known as the Old Text (*guwen*) school for its devotion to certain texts, both versions of existing classics taught at the Imperial Academy and other, noncanonical texts, which it claimed had survived the Qin bibliocaust.[7] (The common name for the court Confucianism of the Western Han, the "New Text" [*jinwen*] school, was originally a pejorative epithet devised by the Old Text partisans.) One of the most important centers of Old Text scholarship was the court of Liu De, Prince Xian of Hejian (r. 155–130 B.C.E.). This half-brother of the Emperor Wu is supposed to have sponsored the editing or compilation of the *Zuo Tradition*, the *Institutes of Zhou* (*Zhouli*), the "Record of Music" ("Yueji"), and various texts associated with the Mao school of the Odes.[8]

Like New Text Confucianism, the Old Text approach to the classics represented less a coherent and self-conscious school than a style of scholarship. Surviving exegetical works like the *Commentary on Mao's Odes* are characterized by a philological orientation and an interpretive reticence that tended to focus on the historical background of the text rather than on its speculative exposition. Indeed, Old Text scholarship as practiced in the Western Han and thereafter seems to represent an act of conscious self-denial, a deliberately austere and modest exegesis in which the interpreter subordinated his own vision to that of the text. Probing deeper, we might say that in contrast to the self-confident and optimistic court or New Text Confucianism, Old Text scholarship was founded upon a sense that the continuity between past and present had been lost. This sense of increasing remoteness from the world of the Sages manifested itself in the defining characteristic of the school and its raison d'être, its concern to obtain and specify the correct, exact wording of the texts of the classics. The Han abounded in stories of secret texts preserving the secrets of a wiser age (or another world);[9] what the Old Text school searched for, however, was not some prescription for military or alchemical accomplishment, but the authentic, historical versions of the classics. Its adherents thus concerned themselves with collecting, collating, and editing the best and oldest texts of the classics. This concern resulted not only in the collection of existing texts but also in the redaction and fixing of traditions that had hitherto existed largely as orally transmitted teachings or doctrines. The *Commentary* and the *Preface* associated with the "Mao school" of the *Odes* were such texts.

The Odes in the Western Han

In the study of the Odes, New Text Confucianism was exemplified by the three schools represented by chairs in the Imperial Academy of the mid-second century B.C.E.[10] Each of these Three Schools (*sanjia*), as they came later to be known, had its own text of the Odes and its own characteristic tradition of exegesis. These teachings were largely lost by the Tang dynasty, but subsequent attempts at their reconstruction, although not without problems, provide some sense of what they might have been.[11]

The first of the Three Schools to emerge was the Lu school, associated with the name of Shen Pei, who completed a work on the Odes probably before 178 B.C.E. and who was made an erudite during the reign of Emperor Wen.[12] Although perhaps the most influential school of Odes interpretation during the Western Han, no work of the Lu school survives, although there are several collections of fragments. Insofar as the teachings of the school can be reconstructed, the Lu interpretations of the Odes seem to have resembled those of the Mao school in their concern with the historical context of the Odes.

The Qi school was associated with the names of Yuan Gu, made an erudite during the reign of Emperor Jing, and of Yi Feng. The teachings of this school also survive only in fragments; it may have specialized in the numerological and cosmological speculation typically associated with New Text scholarship.[13]

Whereas the Lu and Qi schools were named after the geographical areas from which they originated, the Han school was so called after its founder, Han Ying. The *Exoteric Commentary on Han's Odes* (*Hanshi waizhuan*) is the only work of the Three Schools to survive intact;[14] it seems to be a rhetorical handbook illustrating the apt use of quotations from the Odes to "adorn an exposition or clinch an argument."[15]

The Old Text reading of the Odes was represented by the Mao school, the only one of Han traditions to have survived intact to the present day. Three texts are associated with this school. First, there is the Mao text of the Odes themselves, the so-called *Mao's Odes* (*Maoshi*); this formed the basis of the syncretic edition of Zheng Xuan (127–200), which in turn forms the basis of our received text of the *Odes*. Moreover, two works of exegesis are associated with the Mao text: the *Commentary on Mao's Odes* (*Maoshi zhuan*)[16] and the *Preface to Mao's Odes* (*Maoshi xu*). The *Preface*, especially that portion of it known as the "Great Preface," is famously plagued by problems of dating and attribution that admit no easy solution.

The *Commentary*, on the other hand, can be dated with some confidence to the mid-second century B.C.E.; it thus provides the best point to begin discussing the interpretive tradition that forms the background for the hermeneutical "theory" of the "Great Preface."

The *Commentary on Mao's Odes*

The *Commentary on Mao's Odes*, probably compiled at the court of Prince Xian sometime around the middle of the second century B.C.E., is the most important surviving document for the study of Western Han Old Text scholarship. The *Han History* (first century C.E.) attributes the work to "Master Mao" (Mao gong), an erudite at the court of Prince Xian of Hejian.[17] In the second-century C.E. account of Zheng Xuan, the *Commentary* was made by "the elder Mao" (Da Mao gong), and the erudite at Prince Xian's court was "the younger Mao" (Xiao Mao gong).[18] Lu Ji (third century C.E.) gives the names of the elder and younger Mao as Heng and Chang, respectively; he also says that the elder Mao was a student of Xunzi's.[19]

As with most of the texts associated with the Old Text school, the authenticity of the *Mao Commentary* has been questioned; but Karlgren argues convincingly for a date of about 150 B.C.E., which would agree well with the traditional account.[20] The authenticity of the *Mao Commentary* was recently given additional support by a pair of archaeological discoveries. One excavation in Fuyang, Anhui, in the mid-1970's produced a fragmentary text of the *Odes* including a few lines of exegesis. Buried no later than 165 B.C.E., its commentary resembles that of the *Mao Preface* in form, but differs in the interpretations it suggests from either the Mao school or any of the Three Schools as they have been reconstructed, suggesting that there may have been a number of regional traditions of the transmission of the Odes in the early Western

Han.[21] Another discovery, perhaps even more significant, was the famous store of texts found at Mawangdui in south-central China. Included in the "Wuxing" text appended to the so-called Text A of the *Laozi* found there are not only a number of glosses on the Odes, but also several brief remarks adumbrating a hermeneutic theory that differs in interesting and significant ways from that of the *Mao Preface*.[22] This important text awaits further study.

The *Commentary* gives the earliest surviving versions of the interpretations that were to become typical of the Mao tradition of the exegesis of the Odes. As we should expect, the *Commentary*'s interpretations are somewhat less schematic and also less historically specific than those contained in the *Preface*, which in all likelihood represents a somewhat later development of the tradition. An example of the *Commentary*'s style of exegesis is the following passage, which discusses the first of the Odes in the Mao text, the "Guanju."[23]

> Guan guan! cries the osprey
> On the island in the stream.

This is *xing*. "*Guan guan*" is a harmonious sound. The osprey is a kingly bird. It is a bird of prey, and keeps apart [from its mate]. An "island" is a place in the water where one can stand. The Consort was delighted by her lord's virtue; there was nothing in which they were inharmonious. Moreover, she did not debauch him with her beauty. She resolutely kept herself hidden away [in the women's quarters], just as the osprey keeps apart [from its mate]. This being the case, it was possible to transform the empire. [For] when husbands and wives keep a proper distance, then fathers and sons will be close. When fathers and sons are close, then lord and minister will be punctilious. When lord and minister are punctilious, then the court will be rectified. When the court is rectified, then the kingly transformations will be accomplished.

> Lithe and lovely that beautiful girl
> A good match for the prince.

"Lithe and lovely" means "retiring and quiet." "Beautiful" means "good." "Match" means "mate." This means that the Consort had the virtue of the osprey: she was a retiring and quiet, chaste and virtuous, good girl; it is right that she be thought a good match for the prince.

> Here and there the plantain
> Left and right we catch it.

"Plantain" is *jieyu* [another name for plantain]. "Catch" means "seek." The Consort has the virtue of the osprey; so she is able to present plantain and to supply all the goods for the services in the family temple.

> Lithe and lovely that beautiful girl
> Waking and slumbering he sought her.

"Waking" means "awake." "Slumbering" means "sleeping."

> Sought her, couldn't get her
> Waking and slumbering he thought of her.

"Thought" means "thought about her."

> Long O! Long O!
> Tossing and turning.

"Longing" means "thinking."

> Here and there the plantain
> Left and right we pluck it.
> Lithe and lovely that beautiful girl
> With lutes and zither we welcome her.

It is meet to use lutes and zither to welcome her.

> Here and there the plantain
> Left and right we choose it.

"Choose" means "pick."

> Lithe and lovely that beautiful girl
> With bells and drums we make music for her.

One whose virtue flourishes ought to have the music of bells and drums.

The Ode, originally an epithalamium, is referred here to "the Consort" (*houfei*), whose virtues it is supposed to praise. The *Commentary* uses two strategies to direct the reader toward this reading. The first is the dogmatic redefinition of certain terms. Thus in the second couplet "lithe and lovely" becomes "retiring and quiet," and "beautiful" becomes "good." These redefinitions are offered in the same form—and, it seems, in the same spirit—as the glosses of difficult and rare words like "plantain," "osprey," or "slumbering." The second means by which the song is naturalized is by reading the first few lines as *xing*. For the *Commentary*, this involves drawing an analogy between the ospreys and the royal couple.[24] Like the osprey that keeps apart from its mate, the Consort keeps apart from her prince (i.e., she does not interfere in court affairs or divert the prince from them). The island on which the osprey stands is likened to the secluded spot (the women's quarters?) where the Consort remains. Thus the relation of the ospreys is analogous to and emblematic of the harmonious yet correct relation of the Consort and the King.

The moral transformation of society is thus made possible, for that project begins, in the traditional Confucian view, with the right ordering of the prince's own family life. In later developments of the Mao tradition, the "Consort" was identified with Taisi, wife of the great King Wen of Zhou (ca. 12th century B.C.E.). This identification is not made explicit in the *Commentary*, but the gloss on the first couplet seems to refer to the "historical" event of King Wen's transformation of the empire, in the mythology of Confucianism a highwater mark of moral and political accomplishment. This transformation, which began in the king's personal and domestic life and spread outward to reform the whole life of the empire, was presented both as a historical event and as a present possibility; at the same time, it is worth noting, the claim typical of the "Preface" and its later developments that the Odes were the privileged instruments of this process is not made.

The view that the "Guanju" concerned the virtue of King Wen's consort was not the only opinion current in the Western Han. Comments in the *Records of the Historian* (*Shiji*) and other texts refer to the "Guanju" in connection with the decline of the Zhou house.[25] This would seem to indicate that at least one

of the Three Schools did not make the assumption that the
Odes near the beginning of the collection were chronologi-
cally early and thus the products of a virtuous age (or, what is
less likely, that their text of the Odes was arranged differently
from that of the Mao school).[26] The Mao school (especially the
Preface), on the other hand, tended to conflate three things:
priority in the ordering of the *Odes*, chronological priority,
and virtue. Thus those Odes that come earliest in the various
sections of the *Odes* were presumed to come from a relatively
early date and to reflect a golden age of virtue and political success, whereas those that come later within the various sections
were often associated with political and moral decline.

Neither do the alternative interpretations seem to take account of Confucius's famous comment at *Analects* 3.20 concerning the "Guanju," that it was "joyful, but not abandoned;
sorrowful, but not harmfully so." The *Commentary*, on the
other hand, clearly has this phrase in view when it says that
the Consort "delighted ["joyed"] in her lord's virtue" and that
"she did not debauch him ["make him abandoned"] with her
beauty." I argued in Chapter 3 that in their original context
Confucius's words referred primarily to the musical qualities
of the "Guanju." It is clear, however, that here doctrinal exposition of the text of the Odes (and of the *Analects* passage)
has led to the interpretation of the phrase as applying to the
words of the Ode. This concern to base interpretations upon
authoritative texts was typical of the Mao school and of Old
Text scholarship generally.

The *Preface to Mao's Odes*

The other document associated with the Mao text of the
Odes is the *Preface to Mao's Odes* (*Maoshi xu*), or as it is often
more simply called, the *Preface* (*Xu*). Whereas the *Commentary*
has generally been accepted as an authentic Western Han document, theories concerning the authorship of the *Preface* are,
in the words of the editors of the Qing *Complete Library in Four*

Treasuries (*Siku quanshu*), "confused and disorderly, a host of conflicting opinions."[27]

The most widely held view and the one that became orthodox in the Tang is given in the *Chronological Table of the Odes* (*Shipu*) of the great Eastern Han scholiast Zheng Xuan. Zheng said that the *Preface* was composed by Zixia, the disciple with whom Confucius discussed the Odes in *Analects* 3.8, and supplemented by "Master Mao."[28] According to Zheng Xuan, the *Preface* came down to Mao as a single document separate from the Odes. Mao broke the *Preface* up, placing before each Ode that portion of the *Preface* pertaining to it.[29] The Preface to the first of the Odes, the "Guanju," under this arrangement was, however, longer than almost all the other Prefaces, containing as it did a long, general discussion of the Odes, the conditions and circumstances of their composition, and their relation to history. From early on therefore, a distinction has been made between the Preface to the "Guanju," which was called the "Great Preface" ("Daxu"), and the Prefaces to the other Odes, which were called the Minor Prefaces ("Xiaoxu") (or Minor Preface—the Chinese term does not specify singular or plural).[30]

In such an arrangement, however, the "Guanju" alone of all the Odes was left without a Minor Preface. This anomaly was resolved by Zhu Xi, and it is his rearrangement of the *Preface* that has become familiar to most Western readers.[31] The Preface to the "Guanju" has traditionally been divided into 21 pericopes, or sections, for commentary.[32] In Zhu Xi's arrangement, Pericopes 4 through 18, which apply to the Odes generally (that is, the portion of the Preface to the "Guanju" that begins with "The Ode is where the aim goes" and ends with "These are the four beginnings. They represent the perfection of the Odes"), are separated out and called the "Great Preface." In many modern editions this "Great Preface" is printed at the head of the *Odes*. The remaining portions (Pericopes 1–3 and 19–21) are taken to constitute the Minor Preface to the "Guanju"; this "Minor Preface" thus parallels in length and content the Minor Prefaces preceding each of the other Odes.

There is, however, another division of the *Preface* text, one that cuts across and subsumes the distinction between the "Great" and "Minor" Prefaces. It has long been observed that the *Preface* is a heterogeneous document that can be divided into two strata.[33] One layer of the text, putatively the earlier and more authoritative, was typically ascribed to either Confucius or Zixia. It consists of the first sentence of each of the individual Prefaces: "The 'Huangyi' [Mao #241] praises the Zhou" or "The 'Xiongzhi' [Mao #33] satirizes Duke Xuan of Wei." This stratum was referred to as the "Anterior Preface" (*qianxu*) or the "Ancient Preface" (*guxu*); I will call it the "Upper Preface." It may have been compiled during the first great efflorescence of Old Text scholarship around the mid-second century B.C.E.

The second stratum was supposed to be relatively later; it was often ascribed to "Master Mao" or to Wei Hong (first century C.E.) It was called the "Later Preface" (*houxu*), the "Lower Preface" (*xiaxu*), or the "Greater Preface" (*daxu*);[34] I will refer to it as the "Lower Preface." This Lower Preface consists of the text that in each of the Prefaces follows the Upper Preface (i.e., after the first sentence). In a few cases, most notably the case of the six "Lost Odes," there is no Lower Preface.[35] In a few others, the Lower Preface is very long: that to Mao #177 ("Liuyue") is almost as long as the "Great Preface."[36] In most cases, however, the Lower Prefaces consist of two or three sentences expanding upon the sense of the Upper Preface. For example, the two Upper Prefaces quoted above were expanded as follows:

["Huangyi":] Heaven saw that for replacing Yin, there was no one like the Zhou, and that of the Zhou who had for generations cultivated their virtue, there was none like King Wen.

["Xiongzhi":] Debauched and disorderly, he did not concern himself with the affairs of the state. There were numerous military expeditions, and the officers of the state were sent on frequent missions. Men and women complained about their length, and so the people of the state [*guoren*] thought it a disaster and made this Ode.

As we shall see below, there is reason to suppose that these Lower Prefaces (including what we think of as the "Great Preface") were probably products of the second great phase of Old Text activity, which took place around the beginning of the Common Era.

What exactly is the relationship between the Upper and Lower Prefaces? We saw in Chapter 2 how the present text of the *Analects* represents the redaction of traditions that tended to grow—some more, and some less—in the course of their transmission. Such passages, we saw, can be examined for the marks of their transmission, some features (narrative complexity, for example) presumptively reflecting the degree to which a particular tradition was worked on and shaped by successive statement and restatement. At the same time, however, the relatively earlier elements in a given anecdote or saying are more difficult to separate out formally, for a pretextual tradition accommodates teaching to new circumstances or problems through a process of reformulation in which the original historical nucleus of a saying often disappears altogether.[37]

The *Preface* does not seem to have been created by this kind of reformulation. As noted above, the Prefaces are in most cases clearly distinguishable into two strata: a relatively concise and formulaic Upper Preface, and the Lower Preface, a discursive expansion upon the first. If, as I hypothesize, the first layer represents an authoritative teaching received and commented upon by the author of the second, it is not simply restated in an expanded form, but preserved and, as it were, commented upon.[38] At least as we have the text, however, the two layers are not formally distinguished as text and commentary.[39]

How might such an arrangement have come about? It may

of course have been a consequence of textual corruption; it is not uncommon in textual traditions for commentary to become assimilated by a careless copyist to the text on which it expands.[40] But it may also be the case that our hypothetical expositor felt no gulf between his discourse and the discourse he was commenting upon; or, conversely, he may have not felt it necessary to make a clear distinction precisely because the teachings represented by the Upper Prefaces were so well known and so authoritative as to need no identification.[41] In either case, he would not have felt the need, typical of later commentators, to clearly distinguish the two.

Whatever the particular historical process that gave rise to the Prefaces, we can see that they were structured by an exegetical rhetoric: that is, the Lower Prefaces expand and "comment" upon the Upper. Because the Minor Prefaces are relatively short and simple, this exegetical relation between their two strata is clear and easy to see. In the case of the "Great Preface," a similar exegetical rhetoric is at work, although it has not been so generally noted; moreover, its effects are more complex there, as we shall see.

The Minor Prefaces represent a relatively systematic, even schematic, working out of several trends in late Warring States discussions of the Odes. First, as with Mencius, the Odes are discussed not in terms of their possible rhetorical use in quotation or recital but rather in terms of their original meaning as that was determined by the motivations of their authors. Second, as with Xunzi, all the sentiments expressed in the Odes are paradigmatically correct and normative. Both of these developments can be understood as the results of the institutional context surrounding the teaching and exegesis of the Odes. The teachers and classicists who, as the Song historian Zheng Qiao was to put it, "took it as their responsibility to find significance [*yii*] in the Odes" found the Odes to be more richly meaningful when they were considered and expounded in these terms (see below). Relying in equal measure on their knowledge of the historical lore of the Spring and Autumn period (especially as it was contained in the *Zuo Tradition*) and on their imaginations, they constructed for the Odes a kind of mythology in which each Ode found a place in the sweep of early Chinese history. The theoretical assumptions that underlay and justified this way of talking about the Odes were made explicit at the beginning of the *Preface*, in the document we call the "Great Preface."

The Great Preface

Its influence notwithstanding, the "Great Preface" is a difficult and sometimes confusing text, as the volume of recuperative commentary that has grown up around it and Zhu Xi's famous reorganization of the text attest.* The text in its full version (that is, the complete "Preface to the 'Guanju'") reads as follows:

1. As for the "Guanju"—[it is to be understood in terms of] the virtue of the Consort.
2. It is the first of the Airs [*or* It is the beginning of the suasion], and it is that whereby the world is transformed and husband and wife put right. So it was performed at the village meetings and at the gatherings of the feudal lords.[42]
3. "Air" [*feng*] means "suasion" [*feng*]; it means "teaching." Suasion is exerted in order to move [one's prince?], and teaching aims to transform [the people].[43]
4. The Ode is where the aim [*zhi*] goes. While in the heart [*xin*], it is the aim; manifested in words, it is an Ode.
5. Emotion [*qing*] moves within and takes shape in words. Words are not enough, and so one sighs it. Sighing it is not enough, and so one draws it out in song. Drawing it out in song is not enough, and so all unawares one's hands dance it and one's feet tap it out.[44]
6. Emotion is manifested in the voice. When voice is patterned [*cheng wen*], we call it tone [*yin*].
7. The tones of a well-governed age are peaceful and happy; its

---

*Unless otherwise noted, by the "Great Preface" (or, as I sometimes call it for convenience' sake, the "Preface"), I mean the whole of the Preface to the "Guanju" and not just that portion of it called the "Great Preface" by Zhu Xi.

government is harmonious. The tones of a chaotic age are resentful and angry; its government is perverse. The tones of a lost state are sorrowful and longing; its people are suffering.

8. So for putting right the relations of gain and loss, moving Heaven and Earth, and affecting the manes and spirits, nothing comes close to the Odes.

9. The early kings therefore used them to regulate the relations between husbands and wives, to perfect filiality and respect, to enrich human relations, to beautify the tutelary transformation [of the people], and to change mores and customs.

10. So the Odes have Six Arts:[45] The first is called "Air" [*feng*]. The second is called "recitation" [*fu*]. The third is called "analogy" [*bi*]. The fourth is called "stimulus" [*xing*]. The fifth is called "Elegantia" [*ya*]. The sixth is called "Laud" [*song*].[46]

11. Superiors use the Airs to transform those below. Those below use the Airs to spur their superiors on. They strive for delicacy and thus remonstrate obliquely: the speaker does not offend, and still the hearer takes warning. Thus they are called "Airs."[47]

12. When the kingly way decayed and rites and righteousness were discarded, when the teaching of government was lost, so that states had different governments and families different customs, then the Changed Airs and Changed Elegantiae were made.

13. The state historians [*guoshi*] were knowledgeable about the records of success and failure.[48] They were pained at the desuetude of [correct] human relations and appalled by the cruelty of government by punishments. They sang of what they felt in order to sway their superiors.

14. They knew how things had changed and longed for the old customs. So the Changed Airs derive from feelings and yet stop within [the bounds of] ritual and righteousness. That they derive from feelings is because that's how people are. That they stop within ritual and rightness is all due to the beneficence [*ze*] of the early kings.

15. Thus it is that when the affairs of an entire state are tied to the person of a single individual, we deem it an "Air" [*feng*]. When [an Ode] articulates the affairs of the empire, giving form to the mores [*feng*] of the four quarters, we deem it an "Elegantia."

16. "Elegantia" means "correctness." They tell of the reasons for the rise and fall of kingly government. In government there are [matters] greater and lesser; and so there are the Greater Elegantiae and the Lesser Elegantiae.

17. The Lauds raise the forms and visage of flourishing virtue. They tell the ancestral manes of its successes.

18. These are the four beginnings. They represent the perfection of the Odes.

19. Thus the transformation of the "Guanju" and "Linzhi" [Mao #11][49] derive from the suasion of the kings; they are associated with the Duke of Zhou. That they are called "south" is because the transformation proceeded from north to south. The virtues of the "Quechao" [Mao #12] and the "Zouyu" [Mao #25] derive from the suasion of the feudal lords. They derive from what the early kings taught; they are associated with the Duke of Shao.[50]

20. The Zhounan [Zhou South] and the Shaonan [Shao South] represent the way of right beginning; they are the foundation of the kingly transformation.

21. Thus in the "Guanju" there is joy at getting a good girl to marry to the lord and concern at advancing the worthy, [but] no abandonment in her beauty. There is sorrow at her seclusion—that is concern for talent—but no harm to the [essential] goodness of the heart. This is the significance of the "Guanju."

Characterized by a choppy and allusive argument that moves abruptly from one subject to another and punctuated by connectives at precisely those points where connections seem weakest,[51] this is a text that may frustrate even a sympathetic reader. One source of this difficulty is that, like the Minor Prefaces discussed above, the "Great Preface" is a composite, layered text, structured according to a rhetoric of exegesis—that is, as a series of glosses or expansions of key terms or authoritative dicta. The nuclear material is developed in the familiar manner of textual exegesis but is not clearly marked off (e.g., by typographical arrangement) from its expansion. As with the Minor Prefaces, this "confusion" of exegetical material with a foundational text may be a consequence of textual corruption, or it may be the case that the "Preface" is the instantiation or redaction of an oral tradition of teaching concerning the Odes that developed over many generations, or it may have been created by someone writing in an exegetical rhetoric. At any rate, the transitions between the nuclear dicta and their exegesis or, again, between an exegetical passage and the next nuclear dictum—in short, the exegetical rhetoric of the text—foil and frustrate our expectation of a unitary exposition.

If we analyze the Preface to the "Guanju" according to the scheme outlined above (that is, into an Upper and a Lower Preface), then the first sentence, which is the first of the pericopes into which the text has traditionally been divided, constitutes the Upper Preface to the "Guanju." All of what follows constitutes the Lower Preface to the "Guanju." It would constitute an expansion, perhaps coming together in the present form around the beginning of the Common Era, of the nuclear teaching contained in Pericope 1. That the Lower Preface to the "Guanju" was so much longer than the majority of the other Lower Prefaces need not surprise us; it was typically and quite naturally the case that the first pericope of a text provided the occasion for an exposition of the nature and significance of the text as a whole. But if all the Lower Preface to the "Guanju" was in this sense simply an expansion upon the Upper Preface to that Ode, it is not the case that all of it was the same age or of equal weight. As I will show below, significant portions of the Lower Preface parallel other early texts, either deriving in some sense from those texts or from some ancestor thereof. Some of these elements were likely to have accrued to the Preface to the "Guanju" at a relatively early date, and they were very likely relatively authoritative. These authoritative elements originally adduced by way of expansion upon Pericope 1 have in their turn their own expansions attached to them. The Lower Preface is itself thus a structured, sedimented document, made up of authoritative teachings and their exposition. If it is impossible to specify in more than a few cases the sources or even the boundaries of those authoritative elements, this in no way diminishes our impression that the "Preface" is made up of a series of exegetical digressions unevenly yoked together.

Another source of difficulty has to do with a real complexity in the "Preface," a complexity that derives in part from its relation to its own past. In what follows, I discuss three themes integral to the "Preface." These themes concern the transformative power of the Odes, the perfect inscription of the aims in the Odes, and the relation between these two claims. Although I present these themes in a relatively systematic manner alien to the rhetoric of the "Preface" itself, I try to give some sense of the characteristic expository strategies of the "Preface."

The Transformative Power of the Odes

The exegetical rhetoric of the "Preface" lends itself to the articulation of complex, overlapping patterns of homologies and transformations. In the glosses given in the first three of its traditional pericopes, the "Preface" plays upon the rich semantic ambiguities of the character *feng* ("wind," "Air") developing a view in which the Odes inscribe and make available certain morally paradigmatic historical events.

The first sentence of the "Preface" both resembles and differs from the Upper Prefaces associated with the other Odes. Pericope I is like the Upper Prefaces to the other Odes in that it refers the Ode to a historical situation or phenomenon, here the "virtue [*de*] of the Consort."[52] It is unlike the typical Upper Preface in that it does not specify the intention of the poet in making the Ode (here, presumably, to "praise" [*mei*] the virtue of the Consort). Still, the relation between the two parts of the sentence is clear: it is a gloss of a type familiar to any reader of classical texts and their commentaries: "X, Y *ye*." As such, it says that the "Guanju" is to be referred to and understood in terms of the virtue of "the Consort."

The second pericope of the "Preface" is an expansion upon the first. The topic of the first sentence, although not explicitly stated, is still the "Guanju," and that topic is still being glossed. There are two possible readings of the first phrase, *feng zhi shi*; both are formed by reading "[It is] the first of the *feng*" as a second nominal complement to the subject of Pericope 1, the "Guanju." Thus the first three phrases of the "Preface" can be read either as "As for the 'Guanju'—the virtue of the Consort. It is the first of the Airs" *or* "As for the 'Guanju'—the virtue of the Consort. It is the beginning of the suasion."

The first of these two possible translations identifies the "Guanju" as the first of the "Airs" (i.e., the first of the four traditional divisions of the Odes) and thus the first of the Odes. It is perhaps the more "natural" reading and may represent the original sense of the phrase.

The reader is pulled away from this relatively simple and unproblematic reading of *feng zhi shi* by the rest of Pericope 2 and by Pericope 3. In this series of glosses and glosses upon glosses, the "Preface" develops a vision that is difficult, even counterintuitive, for modern readers: it asserts that the Odes can transform the moral and material life of society; they are, it is claimed, one of the privileged means by which the emperor can engage in the great Confucian project of the "suasive transformation" (*fenghua*) of the world.

At times, this claim is stated relatively directly in the "Preface," as in Pericope 8: "So for putting right the relations of gain and loss, moving Heaven and Earth, and affecting the manes and spirits, nothing comes close to the Odes." In the first three pericopes, however, this theme is developed in a way that is relatively oblique but more subtle and complex. This development depends upon the rich complex of meanings associated with the key term *feng*. Among the senses germane to the "Preface" are "wind," "suasive influence," "customs" or "mores," and "indirect, often satirical discourse."

Originally meaning "wind," *feng* early on acquired a variety of metaphorically connected meanings. An instructive text in this connection is *Analects* 12.19: "Confucius said, '. . . The charismatic virtue of the prince is like the wind, [the virtue] of the common people the grass. When the wind is on the grass, it must bend.'" The more idealistic versions of Confucianism current in Warring States and medieval China claimed that the prince could exert a powerful suasive influence over his subjects, transforming their conduct and character without resort to coercion or punishment; this suasive influence irresistibly swept over the people as a wind sweeps across and bends a field of grass. In this use, *feng* was often closely associated with *jiao* "teaching," as in the compound *fengjiao* "suasive teaching"; or with *hua* "transformation" in the compound *fenghua* "suasive transformation."[53] According to the view expressed in *Analects* 12.19, the policies and practices of the ruler were in effect constitutive of the customs and mores that obtained in his realm; the term *fengsu* "mores and customs" used in Pericope 9 reflects this identity. Finally, the (indirect) criticisms loyal subjects might use to sway their ruler to the exercise of virtue were also known as *feng* (sometimes written with the addition of the "word" or "speech" classifier or radical, number 149 in the modern order).

The "Preface" refers the "Airs" (*feng*) to this ideal of suasive transformation. First, the Airs were the responses of the authors of the Odes to the moral atmosphere fostered by their prince (Pericope 15). The notion that the Odes generally and the Airs especially were originally collected because they represented and expressed the prevailing mores and manners of the states and by extension the charismatic virtue of their princes was also expressed in several other Han texts, and it was caught up and expanded in Zhu Xi's influential account of the Odes.[54] In Zhu Xi's view, the Airs from badly ruled states reflect that failure in the values they embody and express; Confucius included them in the collection as negative examples. In the view of Pericopes 12–14 of the "Preface," on the other hand, Airs from states with degenerate morals were nevertheless expressive of paradigmatically correct moral responses to those negative circumstances.

The "Great Preface" (and the Minor Prefaces as well) thus

support and expand upon Xunzi's claim, discussed in the preceding chapter, that all the *zhi* or aims articulated in the Odes are paradigmatically normative and correct. The authors of the Odes were thus able to transcend their environments because of the charismatic virtue of earlier, greater princes like King Wen; the influence of these paragons shaped and constituted the characters of the authors of the Odes. This is a second sense in which the Airs derive from "suasive transformation."

The Odes are referred to another sense of "suasive transformation" in Pericope 3, where *feng* means "to subtly influence (someone, especially one's superior)": " 'Air' [*feng*] means 'suasion' [*feng*]; it means 'teaching.' Suasion is exerted in order to move [one's prince?], and teaching aims to transform [the people]." Pericopes 12 and 13 hold that the "Changed [*or* changing] Airs" (*bianfeng*) and perhaps all the Airs were composed in order to influence the rulers of the states from which they derived. Pericope 11 suggests that this kind of indirect discourse was adopted by the authors of the Odes for reasons of propriety and prudence, in order to avoid offending their prince. Pericope 3 suggests that the value of indirect, poetic discourse lies in its power to move its hearers at an emotional, preconscious level; thus it says that *feng* can be defined by *dong* "to move (emotionally)."[55]

Through the indirect criticisms of the Airs, their authors hoped to move the ruler; at the same time these criticisms were themselves the products of the transformative influence of the ruler or his predecessors. Presented by their authors and taken up and canonized, these paradigmatically correct Odes can be used by the perspicacious ruler in a program of moral and social transformation. For instance, the "Guanju," which in the view of the "Preface" is concerned with the harmonious and correct relations between King Wen and his consort, is particularly suited to set conjugal relations aright. This is another way in which the Airs are "suasive transformation."

In fact the "Preface" implies that the program of moral and social transformation it urges upon the prince had already been successfully undertaken during the heyday of the Zhou, a claim supported by what may be a reference to the *Yili* in the last two phrases of Preface 2: "So [the 'Guanju'] was performed at the village meetings and at the gatherings of the feudal lords."[56] Thus not only did the Ode preserve or institutionalize the original charismatic event of King Wen's influence, but the employment of that Ode, and thus the reenactment of the original event, was also itself a historical event that, as a kind of paradigmatic moral option, had been selected out from the flux of history and institutionalized or conventionalized as one of the *li* or "rites." This notion of the inscription in culture of a paradigmatic event, typical of the rites as well as of the Odes, is one of the central themes of the "Preface" and of the tradition that stems from it.

The idealistic and utopian vision of the role of texts that characterized the first three sections and the "Preface" generally was largely absent from the *Commentary*, but it was typical of court New Text classics studies, especially as they were developed by Dong Zhongshu, that school's leading representative. It may well be that the "Preface" was compiled to serve as a weapon in the great struggle between the advocates of the Old Texts and those of the New Texts at the end of the Western Han and beginning of the Eastern Han (end first century B.C.E. and early first century C.E.). The adoption by the Old Text Odes specialists (i.e., the school of Mao) of this idealistic and utopian rhetoric was perhaps an attempt to disarm and co-opt the strongest claims of their New Text opponents. To put the matter so, however, does not do justice to the sense that such a claim must have had for those making it and for those for whom it was intended. Some of that sense can be gleaned from the next turn the "Preface" takes.

The Production of the Odes

In Zhu Xi's rearrangement of the Preface to the "Guanju," the "Great Preface" proper begins with the account of the production of the Odes in Pericopes 4–7. The account is in two parts. The first part, Pericope 4, represents a transformation of the familiar *shi yan zhi*, "The Odes articulate aims," whose history we explored in the previous chapter. Its affiliations are with the tradition of the rhetorical use of the Odes—that is, with a tradition of discourse concerned largely with the Odes as "words" (*yan*) and as texts. The second part, consisting of Pericopes 5–7, closely parallels and may in some sense derive from the rather miscellaneous collection of music lore known as the "Record of Music" ("Yueji").[57] Deriving from Confucian apologetics concerning the music of the Odes, the "Record of Music" tends to associate the Odes with the language of emotions and emotional balance, which I argued in Chapter 2 is characteristic of the earliest stratum of the *Analects*.

The account of the production of the Odes contained in Pericopes 4–7 thus represents the fusion of two traditions that, if not incompatible, at least possessed different histories and orientations. This complexity in the relationship of the "Preface" to its antecedents existed because the "Preface" was pieced together from heterogeneous sources and traditions that often had little in common besides their reference to or association with the Odes. But it had also to do with a complexity in the relation of Han thinkers to the teachings and texts they had inherited.

The Claim of Perfect Inscription

Take, for instance, Pericope 4, perhaps the most famous passage in the "Preface," if not in all of Chinese literary theory and hermeneutics: "The Ode is where the *zhi* goes. While in the heart [*xin*], it is the *zhi*; manifested in words, it is an Ode."

This passage was based upon the earlier formula "The Odes articulate aims," which had already become a cliché by the third century B.C.E. if not before. The "Preface" both reaffirmed and subtly modified the force of the earlier claim.

Perhaps the original force of the claim that the Odes articulate aims was to assert that the *zhi* (rather than some other entity) generated and defined the Odes. There were at least two versions of the claim that the Odes derived from the *zhi*; each depended on a somewhat different sense of the key term *zhi*. One, relatively broader, derived from and recalled the "non-hermeneutical" use of the term in texts like the *Zuo Tradition* or the *Analects*. In the *Zuo Tradition*, the *zhi* was typically a frankly worldly ambition: to gain a piece of territory or to secure political power within a state. In the *Analects*, the *zhi* was the "moral ambition" that ruled and organized someone's behavior: to be "humane" (*ren*) or to live according to the Way (*zhi yu dao*). Of course, the moral and the "secular" dimensions of *zhi* were often only different aspects of the same orientation or disposition of the personality. A moral vision, if it was to be truly compelling, necessarily involved some idea of the place one might find in the world; the ambition to achieve a political goal also entailed a kind of moral vision or orientation. In the *Zuo Tradition* narratives concerning the chanting of the Odes and in the *Analects* passages dealing with the articulation and interpretation of the *zhi*, this entity was hermeneutically significant: at once both exemplifying and guiding the personality, the *zhi* revealed a person's deepest, organizing concerns. Reading Pericope 4 in the light of this tradition, we might give its first sentence a slightly different translation: "The Ode [tells, represents] where the *zhi* tends."

The other, narrower sense in which the Odes could be said to derive from and to be defined by the *zhi* of their authors may go back to the Odes themselves, but it found its most famous expression in the Upper Prefaces. In this view, the *zhi* is something like the "linguistic intention" behind a given utterance, as in this quotation from one of the latest strata of the *Zuo Tradition*:

Zhongni [i.e., Confucius] said, "In a book it is said: 'One speaks in order to do justice to [*zu*] one's *zhi*, and gives it literary form [*wen*] in order to do justice to one's words. If you don't speak, who will know your *zhi*? And if your words lack literary form, then they will not travel far.' "[58]

In the hermeneutic that informs the Upper Prefaces, the *zhi* is the motivation behind a given utterance that in the special case of the Odes could not, for reasons of propriety or prudence, be expressed directly. This sense of *zhi* is very close to that of the term which eventually replaced it in discussions of the Odes and hermeneutics generally, *yi* "intention."[59] The *zhi* here is not so much an enduring feature of the poet's personality as a specific linguistic intention—to "praise" or to "satirize" in the typical formulations of the *Preface*—that could be exhausted by its expression. The composition and recitation of the Odes in this view had to do with the saying of what could not be said and with the expression of disappointment, resentment, and frustrated ambition.

The two versions of the claim that the *zhi* is the important thing about an Ode tended to run together, or at least to evade analytic distinction. Even the relatively narrowly conceived version of *zhi* as linguistic intention was understood to exemplify a more general, orienting project of the personality. As we saw in the case of *Analects* 11.26 (see Chapter 3) and as was demonstrated by the subsequent history of the lyric, the articulation or specification of the project of the personality was best read in the impulses behind a particular instance of saying. In the case of a minister who was prevented from admonishing his prince by propriety or prudence, the two senses were virtually identical: the *zhi* articulated by the Ode he made or recited represented at once the substance of a vision of a remade world and the hidden or obliquely stated content of his Ode.

Pericope 4, I think it fair to say, presupposes all these meanings. Moreover, it introduces a new claim as well by emphasizing not *zhi* but *yan* "articulate": that is, it asserts not only that the *zhi* defined the essence of the Odes, but also that the Odes did indeed succeed in realizing and preserving in language the *zhi* of their authors. Such a reading is suggested by the emphasis of Pericope 4 on the underlying identity of *zhi* and *shi*: "In the heart, it is the *zhi*; manifested in words, it is an Ode [*shi*]."

In this, what I call the claim of perfect inscription, the Ode is said to inscribe and preserve the *zhi* in an enduring and integral fashion. As Stephen Owen says, there is implied here "a virtual transfer of substance."[60] Such a claim was many things: part of the rhetorical arsenal with which the Mao school exegetes pressed their claim for students and imperial patronage; the product and the promise of the discovery of a living voice in a canonical text; and the attempt to silence the disquieting claim that the Odes, like the other texts of concern to the Confucian school, were but empty husks, the "lees and scum of bygone men."[61]

Perhaps it was the last concern that mattered most. The earlier focus on "aims" was, in the *Mencius* at least, an attempt to limit and forestall certain sorts of speculative exegesis—to limit what the Odes could be said to mean. In Mencius's view, his debating opponents found in the Odes meanings that their authors could not have intended. The "Great Preface," on the other hand, addresses a different danger. The critics that the "Great Preface" had in view were skeptical about the validity of disputation (*bian*), about the adequacy of language as a representative medium, and about the value of texts and their study.

The Way the world values is the one found in books. Books are nothing but talk, but there is something valuable in talk. What is valuable in talk is intentions [*yi*]. Intentions have something with which they are concerned, but what the intentions are concerned with cannot be passed on in words. Yet because the world values words, it therefore hands on the books. Although the world values them, I do not, because what the world values in them is not what is valuable.[62]

Against skeptics who disbelieved that language and texts had stable, usable meanings, who claimed that "words do not exhaust intentions" (*yan bu jin yi*),[63] the "Preface" asserted that the original, animating impulse behind an Ode, indeed the very personality of the author, is there intact and persistent in the text, just as the character for *zhi* "aim" is contained within that for *shi* "Ode." In so arguing, the "Preface" provides a justification for a whole tradition of discursive, historical exposition of the Odes. Perhaps even more important, by asserting the hermeneutical integrity of the Odes, the "Preface" also asserts their transformative efficacy.

Poetry as Emotion

Of the many aporia of the "Preface," none has been more perplexing nor more fruitful than the problem of the relation between the account of the production of the Odes given at Pericope 4 and the parallel account immediately following in Pericope 5: "Emotion [*qing*] moves within and takes shape in words. Words are not enough, and so one sighs it. Sighing it is not enough, and so one draws it out in song. Drawing it out in song is not enough, and so all unawares one's hands dance it, and one's feet tap it out." As mentioned above, this passage and Pericopes 6 and 7 have close parallels in and probably derive from music lore, several versions of which survive today. Like most early Confucian speculation concerning music, this lore was concerned with the *yayue*—the "refined music" of the Odes and rites threatened by new forms and styles in the Warring States period. Although thus linked with the Odes and indeed with the Confucian use of the Odes, early Confucian music theory represented a tradition of discourse that had to a large extent developed independently of teaching concerning the reading and interpretation of the words of the Odes.

Like those *Analects* passages that touch on the Odes as the musical adjunct to ritual, the "Record of Music" and its congeners tend to speak in terms of a balance in the economy of the emotions (*qing*) that both generated and was fostered by the music of the Odes. [64] Music, it was believed, has the power to recreate in those who hear it the emotions that inspired it. [65] Because those emotions were the paradigmatically normative and accomplished ones of the Sages, music has the power, like the ritual with which it was closely connected in this system, to effect the moral transformation of those who hear it—to change not only the individual but society as a whole for the better. The language of Pericope 5 derives from and recalls these beliefs.

The tradition that discussed the Odes as texts and the tradition that discussed the Odes as music were not utterly foreign to one another, but they reflected different concerns and had different histories and vocabularies. So too with the "internal" terms of these two accounts—the *zhi* or "aim" manifested in the Odes in Pericope 4, and the *qing* ("feelings," "emotions") externalized in music according to Pericope 6. Although both of these terms belonged to the common vocabulary of the late Warring States philosophic anthropology, the nature of their relationship was rarely if ever specified. Nevertheless, their juxtaposition in this context requires that they be understood according to the rhetoric of exegesis discussed above: that Pericope 5, and to a lesser extent Pericopes 6 and 7, be understood as providing a gloss upon or expansion of Pericope 4. In this respect, the relationship between these two passages resembles that of the Upper and Lower Prefaces, or, better, that of the last section of Pericope 2 to the first part: that is, as the citation, by way of exposition, of an authoritative text or teaching.

But although the rhetoric of the "Preface" thus required

that the two passages be understood as connected, their relation could be construed in a number of different ways. In the next chapter, for instance, I will show how the disjunction between the Odes as texts and the Odes as music came to symbolize for the men of the Tang the gap they felt between their grasp of the classics and that of the Sages. In what follows here, however, I concentrate on the internal terms of these equations, on the relation between *zhi* and *qing*.

The simplest way to construe the relationship between *zhi* and *qing* is to suppose their identity. Recall that in the view implied by the readings in the "Preface," the Odes are the expressions of paradigmatically normative moral attitudes or reactions: joy at good government and distress at bad (see Pericope 7). We saw in Chapter 3, however, how already in a text like *Analects* 11.26 it had become apparent that the articulation of the *zhi* was not necessarily hermeneutically transparent: that the statement of what it is that motivates one might, perhaps must, respond to motivations different from those it names. Pericope 5, on this reading, addresses this concern: it claims that music (and thus the Odes, by the logic of the gloss) is the product of an overwhelming, spontaneous emotion that cannot be expressed or even contained by ordinary speech, an emotion that transforms and energizes the levels of a hierarchy of expressive means even as it overflows them. According to this account, the expression of the *zhi* in an Ode is spontaneous and unmediated by artistry or calculation. Just as Pericope 4 asserts the integrity of the relation between the *zhi* and the Ode, asserting that the former is perfectly inscribed in the latter, so this passage asserts the integrity of the relation between the *zhi* and the personality as a whole: the authors of the Odes could not help but say what they did. It was what they really felt.

The net effect of the claims made in Pericopes 4 and 5 is to assert the hermeneutic intelligibility (if not transparency) of the Odes: to assert that it is possible to discern in the Odes the aims of their authors—not only the particular, "linguistic" aims that inform the individual Odes, but also the more general, determining dispositions or "projects" of the authors themselves. Because these projects and intentions are, according to the "Preface," in every case normatively correct, it is possible to read back from the sentiments expressed there to the social context that provoked them: "The tones of a well-governed age are peaceful and happy; its government is harmonious. The tones of a chaotic age are resentful and angry; its government is perverse. The tones of a lost state are sorrowful and longing; its people are suffering."

The doctrinal exposition of the Odes could thus proceed from the manifest content of the Odes to the paradigmatically normative attitudes they inscribed and thence to their historical context as it was developed in ever more circumstantial detail. That such discursive exposition could improve those who read or heard it was implicit in the whole tradition. At the same time, it would be a mistake to think that the assertion of the integrity of the Ode—that is, that the Ode inscribed the authentic, unfeigned *zhi* of its author—responded only to concerns about the intelligibility of the Odes. The most important concerns of the hermeneutics of the Odes and indeed of Chinese hermeneutics considered as a whole lay elsewhere.

Transformation and Personality

In the preceding chapter, I suggested that traditional Confucian ethics tended to ask not "What is the good?" but rather "How can one *be* good?" Moral difficulty was thought of not as a problem concerning conflicts over or confusions about the content of the norms (not that there were no conflicts, simply that the tradition tended not to problematicize them), but rather as the problem of ensuring compliance with the norms, especially with the project of mobilizing the emotions so as to guarantee their reliable and enthusiastic enactment.

In a similar and related fashion, we might say, the central problematic of Chinese hermeneutics was not how to understand the text but how to be affected by it. Texts contained norms, to be sure, some of them explicitly and discursively developed. In other cases, notably the Odes, the normative content of the text had to do with the attitudes that inspired their composition and were inscribed there. In either case, the point of study was less intellectual apprehension of and reflection upon explicit, discursive norms than it was their internalization and realization. Intellectual understanding of the meaning of the text was not an end in itself; rather, it was one of the preconditions of being moved by it.

The particular promise articulated in the "Preface" is that the Odes have the power to move and affect their readers in a uniquely direct and profound way. This claim was facilitated by the assimilation of the rhetoric of music to the rhetoric of the Odes, in particular the assimilation of the *qing* to the *zhi*. By presenting the Odes as the products of an overwhelming emotion, the "Preface" also borrowed for its ends the other half of the music model: the claim that the products of overwhelming emotion are capable of inspiring powerful emotion in others. By virtue of their musical nature, the Odes can move their students in a way ordinary texts cannot. At the same time, unlike the music of the Odes, their texts persist to be studied and expounded.

This view of the function of the Odes is relevant to another, somewhat more complex version of the relation between *zhi* and the emotional nature. In this view, the *zhi* and the emotions are not identical, but still closely related, indeed "connected," in a very real, concrete sense. Perhaps the best source for this view is *Mencius* 2.A.2. In that passage, Mencius debated the nature of the relations among doctrine (*yan*), the heart-mind (*xin*), the *zhi*, and the *qi*, or "passion nature." The heart-mind (*xin*) and the *zhi* are closely related in Mencius's account; indeed the *zhi* might best be described as the heart-mind in its focused or directed state. The *qi* is a reservoir of psychic and physical energies, closely related to the emotions. Hence the *Zuo Tradition* says: "Liking and hating, delight and anger, grief and joy, are produced by the six *qi*."[66]

In the discussion at 2.A.2, Mencius says that the *zhi* is the "leader of the *qi*" (*qi zhi shuai*) and that where the *zhi* goes, the *qi* must follow. On the other hand, he cautions, just as the *zhi* can move the *qi*, so can the *qi* affect and move the *zhi*. The *zhi* can, but should not, force the *qi*. Nor can the *zhi* "take the *qi* by a surprise attack." In fact the power of the *zhi* to affect the *qi* is limited; in a famous simile, Mencius likened one who would force his *qi* to a farmer who tries to help the sprouts of grain grow by pulling on them.

If, as the *Zuo Tradition* passage cited above implies, the *qi* represents the emotional energies, then this passage from the *Mencius* says that the *zhi* has the power to shape or reshape the emotions—to "pull" them in a given direction—but that power is circumscribed and limited. Although Mencius is almost utopian at times about the power of the moral ambition, in this passage he seems to adopt a more modest view that acknowledges the finitude of any person's ability for self-change—that the self is not transparent to the moral will—while nevertheless claiming the *zhi* can exert a measure of influence over the emotions. And indeed there was always, as we saw in the *Analects* passages discussed in the preceding chapter, a tension in the notion of *zhi* as it was employed in early Confucianism. On the one hand, it is in a sense something to be "chosen"—thus one "sets himself upon humanity" or "on the Way" (*Analects* 4.4, 7.6). This implies a kind of conscious commitment to an ideal, and one sort of moral failing (exemplified by Zilu in *Analects*, 5.26, see Chapter 3) is the choice of an aim or goal that is insufficiently ambitious, that does not, in the language we are using, exist in a state of tension with the emotional nature, pulling and reshaping it. On the other hand, the *zhi* has to be "authentic"; it cannot get too far out in front of the emotional nature. That kind of naive voluntarism (which supposes that we can simply choose who we will be) is hermeneutically inauthentic as well. An authentic *zhi* exists in a state of tension with the emotional nature, at once leading it on to change and yet supported by it and representing it.

If this hypothesis about the relation of the aim and the emotional nature is correct, we can see something of the significance of the Odes for the Confucian project of moral self-transformation as it was conceived in the late Warring States and Han. The Odes inscribed—preserved and made available for the student—the aims or *zhi* of their authors, and these aims are in every case paradigmatically normative ones. By "studying" the Odes—that is, by attending to their discursive exposition, by memorizing, reciting, and internalizing them—the student is able to "take on" those aims, at least temporarily.[67] These aims, representative of their authors, exert over the emotional nature the kind of transformative influence alluded to by Mencius and the "Record of Music." The emotional nature is not transparent to the *zhi*, but it can be influenced or shaped by it; and so the Odes can help in the project of reshaping the emotional nature of the student in the image or pattern of the Confucian sages and worthies who had made the Odes. Moreover, they do this in a way that obviates the intractable problems about the mobilization of the emotions in the service of the Confucian norms as exemplified in the texts of the classics.

It is not clear that the Han Confucians whose exposition of the Odes resulted in the "Preface" would have fleshed out their account in this particular fashion. Certainly they would not have felt the need to give this kind of relatively analytic and detailed account. Nevertheless, this version of the "Preface," I believe, both makes sense of the passage and remains true to the conceptual vocabulary of the tradition of discourse in which that text occurred. And it is clear that the central

claims of the "Preface"—the insistence that the Odes fully inscribe the authentic aims or *zhi* of their authors, that these
aims are in every case paradigmatically normative, and that
the Odes are integral, privileged elements in a program for
personal and social transformation—are interlinked. At the
same time, the very assertion or implication of these linkages
implies a more problematical view in which these connections
are endangered. This more problematical view would come
to the fore in later discussions of the Odes.

CHAPTER FIVE

The Perfection of the Text

This method . . . presupposes the absolute authority of certain books, which are to be comprehended as containing an integrated and complete body of doctrine; but paradoxically, it also presupposes that there may be both gaps and contradictions within the text: and it sets as its main task the summation of the text, the closing of gaps within it, and the resolution of contradictions. . . . Both in law and theology, and later in philosophy, the scholastic mode of analysis and synthesis was promoted by the method of teaching in the university, particularly the method of glossing the text and posing questions for disputation. . . . In other words, science—scholarship—came from teaching, and not vice versa.   —Harold J. Berman, *Law and Revolution*

The preceding chapters of this study traced a steady growth in the authority and prestige of texts in Confucian culture. In Chapters 2 and 3 we saw how first the Odes and then certain other texts called "classics" (*jing*) came to occupy a central place in the Confucian curriculum as the appropriate objects of the most serious and devoted study. Chapter 4 attempted to show how in the Han the claims made for the canonical texts became ever more ambitious: they had the power, it was thought, to effect an almost magical transformation of the individual student and of society as a whole. At the same time the exegetical traditions associated with the classics were themselves fixed as texts, and certain of these authoritative commentaries soon acquired the same aura of unimpeachable authority as the classics themselves. In the "expositions of the classics" (*jiangjing*) made during the long Han–Tang interregnum (the so-called Northern and Southern Dynasties period, lasting from the final disintegration of the Han dynasty in the third century of our era to the rise of the Sui and then the Tang in the sixth and seventh centuries), not only the classics but also their authoritative commentaries came to be treated as magical objects invested with seemingly infinite "significance" (*yii*). The result was a body of enormous, exhaustive commentaries that represent the most extreme example of the tendency in Confucian hermeneutics to exalt texts in what might be called their "textuality"—in the specific, "contingent" particularity of their wording.

The expositions of the Northern and Southern Dynasties period were summed up and codified in the great early Tang compilation, the *Correct Significance of the Five Classics (Wujing zhengyii)*. This work decisively influenced later classics studies; at the same time it became the model of a type of scholarship against which scholars of the Song and later dynasties defined themselves.[1] That part of the *Correct Significance of the Five Classics* dealing with the *Odes*, *The Correct Significance of Mao's Odes (Maoshi zhengyii)*, was in the form of a subcommentary on the "Mao materials" discussed in Chapter 4 (i.e., the Mao text of the *Odes*, the *Commentary on Mao's Odes*, and the *Preface to Mao's Odes*), and on the "annotations" (*jian*) of the great Eastern Han scholiast Zheng Xuan (127–200).[2] It is a key document, perhaps the key document, in what might be called the medieval understanding of the *Odes*. In the first part of this chapter, I summarize the doctrinal and hermeneutical context out of which the *Correct Significance* developed; the second part consists of a discussion of the *Correct Significance*'s hermeneutic as revealed in its explication of the "Great Preface."

Classical Studies in the Medieval Period

The Northern and Southern Dynasties are typically portrayed in histories of classical scholarship as a period of decline and fragmentation for classics studies and Confucianism.[3] Many of the age's most vital intellects were attracted either by the new foreign religion Buddhism or by the speculations of the Learning of the Mysterious (*xuanxue*).[4] The political divisions of the day were matched by a fragmentation of orthodoxy in classical studies, and Confucians, or at least scholarly Confucians, seemed to have little or no role in the ferocious politics of the day.

There were, however, courts at which Confucian studies were patronized, even if political power was not delivered into the hands of the scholars. In the North, Emperor Xiaowen of the Wei (r. 471–99) and Emperor Wu of the Zhou (r. 560–78) were patrons of Confucianism, and in the South, Emperor Wu of the Liang (r. 502–49) not only sponsored court discussions of the classics but also attached his own name to an array of works of exegesis.[5] There were, moreover, centers of learning away from court, elaborate academies with sophisticated curricula and "private scholars," who in the manner of Confucius gathered a few students and developed their vision of the classics. It was the works of these centuries, now almost completely lost, that were the indispensable and now largely invisible foundation of the *Correct Significance of Mao's Odes*.[6]

Northern and Southern Learning

By the Northern and Southern Dynasties, the burning issue of Han classical scholarship—the Old Text–New Text controversy—had been largely forgotten, to be replaced by another dichotomy, which nevertheless preserved something of the structure of the earlier dispute. Like the Old Text–New

Text controversy, the split between the Northern and the Southern Learning (*beixue* and *nanxue*) contrasted a relatively austere, philologically and historically oriented style of exegesis with a scholarship that was visionary, speculative, and inclined to discern hidden meanings in the text. But whereas New Text scholarship was an indigenous development of the Confucian tradition (albeit one that borrowed from other schools like the "cosmologists" [*yinyangjia*]), Southern Learning was in many ways an apologetic movement intended to reconcile Confucianism with the two most vital intellectual movements of the period, the Learning of the Mysterious of the Wei and Jin dynasties, and Buddhism.

When later writers came to define the difference between Northern and Southern scholarship, they typically talked in terms of the commentaries on the classics favored by each tradition, as, for example, the famous formulation in the "Biographies of Scholars" chapter of the *History of the Northern Dynasties.*

On the River's left [i.e., south of the Yangtze], it's Wang Fusi [i.e., Wang Bi (226–49)] for the *Changes*, Kong Anguo [fl. 2nd century B.C.E.]) for the *Documents*, and Du Yuankai [i.e., Du Yu (222–84)] for the *Zuo Tradition*; whereas in the region of the Ho and Lo [rivers] [i.e., in North China], it's Fu Zishen [i.e., Fu Qian (d. ca. 220 C.E.)] for the *Zuo Tradition* and Zheng Kangcheng [i.e., Zheng Xuan (127–200)] for the *Documents* and the *Changes*. For the *Odes*, both favor Master Mao [i.e., Mao Chang (2nd century B.C.E.)], and for the *Rites* both follow Zheng [Xuan].[7]

The text continues:

The Southerners are simple and concise; they take only the flower. Northern Learning is deep and profuse; the Northerners go all the way to the ends of things [lit., "the leaves and branches"].

The regional labels "Northern" and "Southern" had, however, only a very general application. Not only were there Northern scholars who were taken with Wang Bi and the speculative style in exegesis that he represented and Southerners who took Zheng Xuan as their master, but as time went on and contacts between the Northern and Southern intellectual worlds increased, more and more scholars made use of both Northern and Southern approaches. This synthetic tendency culminated in the work of the "Two Liu"—the Sui scholars Liu Zhuo (540–610) and Liu Xuan (sixth century)—whose commentaries in the explication (*yiishu*) form were extensively utilized in the composition of the *Correct Significance*.

Nevertheless, the Northern-Southern dichotomy was a central category in the Tang understanding of recent scholarship, and the terms do indicate identifiable styles in classical studies, if not hard and fast regional filiations. Northern Learning, it has been well said, was Zheng Xuan learning; it took the scholarship of the great Eastern Han scholiast not only as the authoritative, foundational interpretation of the classics but also as a model exegetical style.[8] The Northern scholars followed Zheng Xuan on the *Changes*, the *Documents*, the *Rites*,[9] and probably the *Odes*; and Fu Qian's commentary on the *Zuo Tradition* was, according to a *New Tales of the World* anecdote, very much in the spirit of and perhaps partially based on that of Zheng Xuan.[10] As far as can be judged (only one, inferior work of Northern scholarship survives intact), the exegesis of the Northern scholars was in the historically oriented manner of Zheng Xuan. In a style familiar to any student of the Chinese classics, it provided readings for difficult characters or usages; institutional, geographical, or historical background; and a bit of interpretive guidance. A particular, "practical" concern was to provide the specifics of various rituals and ritual objects mentioned in the text. Yan Zhitui (531–91), a Southerner resident in the north, expressed his impatience with this sort of exegesis in his *Family Instructions for the Yan Clan*: "Why is it necessary to have two pages of commentary on Confucius's dwelling, his dining hall, bedroom, and classrooms? And now where do such things exist? In adhering to such formalities, what actual benefit can one obtain?"[11]

As with the Northern Learning, most of the many works of Southern scholarship have been lost; we know them only from quotations in the great Tang commentaries, which overshadowed them and caused their disappearance. One source for the Southern style does survive, however: the *Explication of the Analects* (*Lunyu yiishu*) by Huang Kan (488–544).[12] This work was lost in China in the Song dynasty (perhaps because of the success of the *Correct Significance of the Analects* [*Lunyu zhengyii*] of Xing Bing [932–1010]) but rediscovered in Japan, and returned to China during the Qianlong period (1736–96).[13] In form, Huang's work is a subcommentary on the *Collected Explanations of the Analects* (*Lunyu jijie*) of He Yan (d. 249 C.E.); but Huang also cites a wide variety of other commentators, including the Learning of the Mysterious luminaries Wang Bi (226–49) and Guo Xiang (d. 312 C.E.) and Buddhist figures like Sun Chuo (fl. 330–65) and the monk Huilin (fl. 424–53). It is an invaluable source for the Southern Learning as represented by the earlier exegetes whom Huang quotes and by Huang's own commentary.

Both Learning of the Mysterious and Buddhist interpretations are prominent in the *Explication of the Analects*. It was central to the Learning of the Mysterious to deny that words or doctrines could fully express intentions or ideas (*yi*); in particular, it was claimed, they could never express the nature of non-being (*wu*), which was embodied (*ti*) by the sage Confucius and which subsumed all distinctions among things or qualities. Knowledge that derived from language was discounted, and a premium was placed on pre-sensory or supersensory gnosis.[14] Thus when in his famous spiritual autobiography at *Analects* 2.4, Confucius says of himself that "at sixty, my ears were suited [to hear the Way]," Huang Kan appends the following two comments:

Wang Bi says: "My ears were suited" means that his heart knew before he heard it. Sun Chuo says: "My ears were suited" [means] that hearing was not used. Brilliantly he mysteriously understood; he didn't have to make an effort and then understand. It's what was referred to [in the *Odes*] when it was said:

> Without [need of] knowledge or wisdom
> In accordance with the pattern of God.[15]

In this reading, Confucius is made into a Daoist adept possessed of gnostic pre-knowledge.

Since words (and texts) were for the Southern school only imperfect realizations of a prior translinguistic truth, any verbal teachings, even Confucius's, had only a provisional and conditional validity; they were what Buddhist commentators called *upaya*, "expediency." Thus when Confucius asks "When you do not yet know about life, how can you know about death?"[16] Huang Kan comments: "That the outer teaching lacks the idea of the Three Ages can be seen from this passage. The teaching of Kong of Zhou [i.e., Confucius] only discusses the present; it casts no light on the past or the future." The Confucianism of the *Analects*—the "outer teaching"— was just an exoteric, provisional doctrine; the true teaching that Confucius embodied was more adequately expressed later in Buddhism.

This discussion does not do justice to the complexities of the hermeneutics of the Southern Learning; the sophisticated and intriguing theories of Wang Bi in particular deserve a more detailed treatment.[17] I hope, however, that the examples given serve to illustrate one important way in which the Southern hermeneutic differed from that of the *Correct Significance*. Like the *Correct Significance*, the Southern Learning looked beyond the apparent meaning of the text for a "deeper," more authentic meaning. It typically did this, however, in a way that discounted the authority of the wording of the text. The *Correct Significance*, as we shall see, preserved and even exalted the particular language and phrasing of the text.

The impatience of the Southern Learning with particular "texts" was also illustrated in its attitude toward ritual. Concerning the *di* ritual mentioned in *Analects* 3.10, Huang Kan says: "Earlier scholars disagreed over this; we won't go into all their theories here." Elsewhere he says of an inconsistency between the Eastern Han exegete Ma Rong (79–166) and the *Institutes of Zhou* (*Zhouli*) in the explanation of a ritual that "they are slightly different, but can be made to agree; it's not necessary to get all worked up over the details."[18] As with texts, so with rituals: the intentions that lay behind them were capable of realization in any number of ways; the forms (textual or ritual) of another age appropriate to that age are not necessarily appropriate to another. Nothing could contrast more vividly to this attitude than the literalism of the *Correct Significance*, where, as we shall see, rituals and texts were the decisive and authoritative realization of their (sagely) author's intentions, unadventitious and significant even in their most seemingly trivial formal features.

The paucity of surviving Northern and Southern Dynasties works, particularly works on the *Odes*, makes it difficult to assess the relative influence of the Northern and Southern Learning on the *Correct Significance*. In a famous complaint, Pi Xirui (1850–1908) noted that "after the unification of classical studies [in the Sui], there was Southern Learning but no Northern Learning."[19] It is true that the *Correct Significance* accepted the Southern and not the Northern canon of commentaries as authoritative. Moreover, we are told in the *Correct Significance*'s prefaces that it drew heavily on the work of such eclectic scholars as Liu Zhuo and Liu Xuan. In its attention to historical and ritual detail, however, the *Correct Significance* seems in many ways to stand more in the Northern than in the Southern style as we understand them.

The Northern and Southern Dynasties works of exegesis were the crucible in which many of the opinions in the *Correct Significance* were forged. Another innovation of that period was, however, crucial for the form of the *Correct Significance* and subtly shaped and influenced the opinions expressed there. This was the rise and development of the explication (*yiishu*) genre of commentary.

The Rise of the Explication Genre

Commentaries upon the classics were composed in a bewildering variety of forms in Han China. Many of these forms do not survive and are known only from the bibliographic record, and many of those for which we do have surviving examples are so fragmentary that it is difficult to tell just how they differed from one another.[20] A general distinction can be made, however, between "annotation style" commentaries, which were relatively terse and philologically oriented, and "chapter and sentence" (*zhangju*)–style works, which expounded the text's significance and which were famously prolix. In the late fourth century or early fifth century, a new genre of commentary appeared, the explication (*yiishu*). It resembled the chapter and sentence expositions in its lengthy and comprehensive treatment of the classic, but nevertheless it differed in important ways from any exegetical genre in use up to that time. By the next century, the explication had become the single most important literary medium for Confucian doctrinal exposition, and hundreds of explications were composed on various canonical and semi-canonical works.

This new form was distinguished by its detailed and systematic analysis of the text. Here, for instance, is Huang Kan's gloss on the first character in the title of the *Analects* (*Lunyu*):

Speaking generally, there are three ways to gloss the character *lun*. One way involves putting aside the written form and following the sound; this means reading it as *lun* "to relate." Another way puts aside the sound and follows the written form, making it *lun* "to discuss." Still another way says that there is no difference in meaning between *lun* "to relate" and *lun* "to discuss."

In the first school, which says to discard the written form and follow the sound, reading *lun* "to relate," there are many versions. Basically, however, there are no more than four kinds. One says *lun* means "to order"; it means that in this work, events and their significances generate one another; its beginning and its end are in order. The second says *lun* means "principle"; it says that within this work are contained the ten thousand principles. The third says *lun* means *lun* "to arrange"; it means that this book arrays the present and antiquity. The fourth says *lun* means *lun* "wheel"; it means that this book's significance is complete and comprehensive, endlessly circulating like the wheel of a cart.

This kind of systematic analysis was largely unprecedented in the history of Chinese exegesis, and it is not surprising that scholars, beginning with Liang Qichao (1873–1929), have looked outside the mainstream Confucian tradition for a model. Recently several writers, notably Mou Runsun and Dai Junren, have discussed and refined Liang's thesis that the Confucian explications were decisively influenced by Buddhist doctrinal exposition.[21]

The explication genre developed out of the practice of *jiangjing* ("exposition of the scriptures/classics") current in both Buddhist and Confucian circles in the Northern and Southern Dynasties period. In both the Confucian and the Buddhist versions, "scriptures/classics exposition" involved public dialogues before an audience of students or scholars, sometimes at court, between a master who would expound the text and a *dujiang* "interlocutor" who would either ask questions concerning problematic passages or simply read off passages to be commented upon by the master. Exposition of the Buddhist scriptures is supposed to have grown either out of debates over contested points of doctrine or in the context of missionary activity; the Confucian practice seems to have had its roots in the teacher-student dialogue. The problem of the relative priority of Buddhism as regards the discussion practice and the composition of explications is a difficult and contested question, but it is generally agreed that a native

Chinese tradition of dialogic exposition (like that reflected in the *Gongyang* and *Guliang Commentary* exegeses of the *Spring and Autumn Annals*) was transformed under the influence of Buddhist practice, the most important result being the tendency toward systematic analysis described above.

In the Confucian version the master and his interlocutor, typically a favorite disciple, engaged in a stylized dialogue of question and explication before an audience of other students and scholars. The topics of the "debate" would have been standard; here we can recall the practice of "pure conversation" (*qingtan*) described in the *New Tales of the World* (*Shishuo xinyu*), where "adversaries" discussed set topics like "Music has neither joy nor sadness." In a similar way, the scriptural expositors probably specialized in set topics—the meaning of the arrangement of the sections of the text, or some particularly difficult and fruitful aporia—about which their interlocutor would not omit to ask. The total body of interpretations and views held by some expositor would have been a complexly sedimented structure of the interpretations of earlier scholars, modifications of those views, and original interpretations.

Such an approach tended to result in the expansion of the interpretive-doctrinal tradition. There is no reason why old questions should drop out of the repertoire even when "solved"—when alternative interpretations had been decisively refuted—for they would still provide opportunities for the illustration and discussion of the Confucian moral principles that their expositors thought immanent in the material. In addition, new points could always be raised, new questions asked, the answers to which would themselves generate new opportunities for discussion. The process thus lent itself to the creation of a body of tradition that was at once refined and yet steadily expanded over the generations. This process continued even when explications were composed in written rather than in oral form, and in fact written and oral explications of scripture doubtless influenced one another for generations.[22]

Of the many explications listed in the bibliographic record of the Northern and Southern Dynasties period and of the many more not listed there, only the *Explication of the Analects* survives intact. The huge amount of discussion contained in the lost works, however, and the even larger body of oral discussion that lay behind the explications constitute the invisible but crucial background to the *Correct Significance* and to early Tang Confucianism.

The Composition of the *Correct Significance of the Five Classics*

No single orthodoxy prevailed among students of the Confucian classics during the long Northern and Southern Dynasties period. As Wei Zheng put it in the "Biographies of the Literati" in the *Sui History*: "Since the date of New Year's ceased being the same [i.e., since the onset of political division], nearly three hundred years have passed; the teachings of the ancient masters have become disordered, and there is no way to choose what is right."[23]

When the Tang assumed power in the early part of the seventh century, one of its first priorities was to right this situation.[24] The connections between doctrinal and political unity were deeply interwoven in traditional thought. Beginning with its role as promulgator of the agricultural and ritual calendar (note Wei Zheng's use of calendrical disunity as a synecdoche for political fragmentation in the above quote) and continuing through the idealistic Confucian notion of the emperor as teacher-sage, the state had been seen as the source of doctrinal orthodoxy; heterodoxy was often seen either as the sign of a moral failure on the part of the emperor or as sedition or as both. As with the concern to reconstitute the ritual armature of the state, moreover, there was a sense that the achievement of doctrinal orthodoxy was constitutive of good social and political order. Both the famously exhaustive Han commentaries and the *Correct Significance* arose from expository practices in the academies, and both alike aimed at enunciating a comprehensive interpretation of the classics that would parallel, presage, and contribute to the renovation of the political and ritual-cosmological spheres.

Finally, on a more practical note, the Tang required standard interpretations of the classics for the newly reinstated examination system. The composition of *shi* lyrics was made part of the examinations at least in part so that the examiners could utilize objective standards to judge candidates (i.e., compliance with the rules of tonal prosody and poetic decorum). Bureaucratic rationality demanded clearly defined standards for the judgment of the performance of candidates.

The *Correct Significance of the Five Classics* was the second great project of classical scholarship sponsored by the Tang emperors in the first decades of their rule.[25] In 630, Taizong, concerned that "the texts of the classics are remote from the Sage, their texts confused and mistaken," ordered Yan Shigu (581–645) to establish definitive texts (*dingben*) of the Five Classics (the *Changes*, the *Documents*, the *Odes*, the *Rites*, and the *Spring and Autumn Annals* with the *Zuo Tradition*).[26] After completing his work, Yan defended it in a court debate, defeating his opponents through his quotation of old editions and through the clarity and detail of his citation of authorities. In the eleventh month of Zhenguan 7 (633), the text was promulgated.

In 638 Taizong further ordered a committee of scholars under the direction of Kong Yingda (574–648) to prepare an authoritative commentary on the Five Classics. The committee for the preparation of the commentary on the *Odes* included, in addition to Kong Yingda, Wang Deshao and Qi Wei. The work was completed between 640 and 642, probably in 641. It was vehemently criticized by one Ma Jiayun for its prolixity, and in 642 the emperor decreed that the work be revised; Kong, Wang, and Qi were joined in this work by Zhao Qianxie, Jia Puyao, and Zhao Hongzhi.

Kong Yingda died in 648, before this revision was completed. In 651, Gaozong commissioned Zhangsun Wuji (d. 659) and a group of erudites to undertake further revisions. This they submitted along with a memorial on the 24th day of the second month of Yonghui 4 (28 March 653); the work was promulgated on the first day of the third month (3 April) of the same year and thereafter formed the standard commentary on the classics for the Tang examinations.

Some writers have claimed that Kong Yingda was listed as the chief compiler of the *Correct Significance* project simply because he was the eldest of the compilers, or the one with the highest rank. Whether this is true, or whether Kong really had overall responsibility for its composition, it is certainly the case that the *Correct Significance* was the product of more than one intelligence. Kong's early collaborators and the two revisions of the work, one undertaken after Kong's death, must surely have left a mark on the work we have today.

There is, however, another, more significant sense in which the *Correct Significance* was a collaborative project. The *Correct Significance* is borne upon the support of earlier interpretations. Yu Zhengxie, among others, has shown from textual evidence that the *Correct Significance* quoted extensively from earlier commentaries.[27] In its preface, the *Correct Significance* acknowledges its debt to the Sui scholars Liu Zhuo and Liu Xuan, and it must have drawn on other explications as well. These works would have drawn in turn on earlier explications, which grew out of generations of classics exposition in the academies and at court debates. Like an oral epic, the *Correct Significance* was the product of many retellings and many minds, not the work of one person or time.

The opinions expressed in the *Correct Significance* thus imply a whole universe of discourse. We must, through an act of the imagination, place them synchronically in a field of possible interpretations that the *Correct Significance* attempted to rule out or to affirm. We must also site the *Correct Significance*'s opinions diachronically, understanding them as the products of a centuries-long process of evolution wherein individual interpretations were proposed, attacked, and refined time and time again, at first in oral debates and then in written commentaries.

Viewed in this way, the *Correct Significance* was one more attempt to come to grips with the problematical legacy of the past as it was represented both by the classical text itself and by the weight of tradition: it was itself one more instance of the process that created it. There was, however, one crucial difference between the *Correct Significance* and the expositions it drew upon: the *Correct Significance* was intended to halt the long proliferation of interpretations, to establish an orthodoxy that would have as its support the power and prestige of the state. Or perhaps it would be more accurate to say that the significance of the *Correct Significance* was that for some time at least and in some measure it achieved this ambition, an ambition shared by other, earlier such compilations. The *Correct Significance* did, with the help of the Tang state, succeed in establishing itself as the orthodox interpretation of the classics, and this hegemony of the text of the *Correct Significance* resulted in the gradual disuse and eventual disappearance of the whole, vast expository literature on which it was based.[28]

The Perfection of the Text

There is a characteristic order to the *Correct Significance* commentary. Comments typically (although not invariably) begin with a short explanation of the order of the text's exposition;[29] these passages, which I call the "Sequences," can be understood as a practical response to the task of managing the

Correct Significance's exposition.* Given the length and complexity of an explication-style commentary, especially when heard rather than read, the student could easily lose the thread of the argument; all the more so when, as with the "Preface," the connecting links in the original text are loose to begin with. By summarizing the point of the last passage and anticipating the one about to be commented on, the Sequence shows how the order of the text's exposition proceeds in a perspicuous and significant way, thus orienting the reader in the vast landscape of the *Correct Significance*.

The Sequence is usually followed by a Paraphrase, restating in an expanded and perhaps somewhat more colloquial form the text of the pericope at hand.[30] Like most paraphrases, these both expand and define the original text, ostensibly in order to render it transparent to the understanding; at the same time, however, they revise its meaning, often quite radically. A favorite strategy of the *Correct Significance* is to restate the monosyllables of Classical Chinese into the bisyllabic expressions typical of the modern language. Thus *zhi* "aim" becomes *zhiyi* (literally, "aim and intention"), *xin* "heart/mind" becomes *xinfu* (literally, "heart and belly"), and *le* "happiness" becomes *huanle* (literally, "joy and happiness").[31]

The third element in the *Correct Significance* commentary, and by far the largest, is the "Topics," discussions, sometimes quite lengthy, of questions that probably formed the subject matter of earlier expositions of the scriptures (*jiangjing*) and explications (*yiishu*). It is in these Topics that the traces of the

---

* The *Correct Significance* commentary on the first sentence of the Preface to the "Guanju" says that it has divided the text into fifteen sections. As we have it now, however, the *Correct Significance* text of the Preface to the "Guanju" (hereafter the *CSPG*) is divided into 21 pericopes. I therefore follow the same convention that I observed in the discussion of the Preface to the "Guanju" in Chapter 4, numbering the *CSPG* pericopes 1 to 21, and I also number the lines of the *Correct Significance*'s commentary as it appears in the *Guoxue jiben congshu* edition. Thus a reference to "Pericope 7" is to the seventh of the *CSPG* pericopes, and "*CSPG* 7.12" or simply "7.12" refers to the twelfth line of the *Correct Significance* commentary on that pericope. When not otherwise specified, "the Preface" means the Preface to the "Guanju."

oral-dialogic background of the *Correct Significance* commentaries are most clearly seen.

The Topics section of a *Correct Significance* commentary on a given pericope tends to treat a series of discrete questions about the classical text. Some questions are narrowly philological. For example, difficult words may be glossed, or the interpretation of an ambiguous or potentially deceptive phrase fixed. Others are concerned with parallel texts, explaining differences in language or dealing with the problem of seemingly contradictory doctrines.[32] Questions concerning the internal organization of the text, particularly the problem of order, are treated, and counterintuitive or ambitious claims are naturalized and justified. Or the Topics may refer explicitly or implicitly to other interpretations of the passage at hand and rebut them; this was certainly a feature of scriptural and classics exposition. The Topics contain a wealth of material about those elements in the text of the "Preface" that the compilers of the *Correct Significance* saw as problematical, and these concerns, as well as the arguments used to address them, reveal a good deal about the views of the *Correct Significance* concerning texts, interpretation, and authority.

The Sequences, Paraphrases, and Topics may be understood as practical responses to the problems of commenting upon the classics and their authoritative exegeses. They address both the problems inherent in understanding a text that has become historically remote and the problems created by the *Correct Significance*'s enormous length and complexity. But they serve another function as well. Like the discussions of moot or refuted interpretations that I hypothesized were a common feature of the expositions, the discussion of the "problems" of the organization and content of the classical text was an end in itself, for it allowed one more opportunity to enunciate the Confucian message that was the purpose and function of exegetical activity.

Overcoming Difficulty

As we saw in the preceding chapter, the "Preface" was a bricolage, a compilation patched together from earlier texts and logia that was anything but systematic. It aimed to be comprehensive only in the sense that it attempted to bring together what its compilers thought the most important, authoritative traditions concerning the Odes. The *Correct Significance*, on the other hand, undertook to present a unified and comprehensive, even systematic, account of the Odes.[33] It was therefore constantly forced to explain that the relatively narrow and particular claims made in the "Preface" in fact presupposed or implied a more general, unified vision.[34] These discussions served an apologetic function, remedying seeming deficiencies in the presentation of the "Preface," but they also represented opportunities for the discursive exposition of Confucian teaching.

Take, for example, Pericope 15: "Thus it is that when the affairs of an entire state are expressed through [*xi*; lit., "bound up with," "tied to"] the person of a single individual, we deem it an 'Air' [*feng*]. When [an Ode] articulates the affairs of the empire, giving form to the mores of the four quarters, we deem it an 'Elegantia.'" The "Preface" here reflects the tradition that associated each of the Airs with one of fifteen small feudatory "states" (*guo*). The Airs were understood as the responses of their authors to the social and political lives of these states, whereas the Elegantiae were supposed to be addressed to the affairs of the Zhou kings, whose authority nominally extended over all the empire (*tianxia*), including the states.

For the *Correct Significance*, the problem with Pericope 15 was that it did not state clearly that the Elegantiae were, like the Airs, the products of representative individuals, who reflected and articulated the community's concerns by saying what they felt. Rather, it seemed to allow for the possibility that the Elegantiae were composed in some other way. This would have violated the unitary conception of poetry the *Correct Significance* was concerned to maintain. The *Correct Significance* argued that the Three Forms (*san ti*)—the Airs, Elegantiae, and Lauds—were realized through the same stock of rhetorical devices (direct presentation or *fu*, analogy or *bi*, and stimulus or *xing*) and were the products of the same psychological and social processes. Only the variation in the nature and quality of the government of the day produced variation in the form and content of the Odes.[35] Hence among the Topics discussed in connection with Pericope 15 is the following:

[a] Each of the Airs and Elegantiae was made by a single person. [b] It is said of the Airs that in them the affairs of the whole state are expressed through the person of a single individual. [c] In the case of the Elegantiae, the affairs of the empire are likewise expressed through the person of a single individual. [d] [To say that] the Elegantiae articulate the affairs of the empire means that a single individual articulates the affairs of the empire. [e] As for the Airs, there too a single individual articulates the affairs of the entire state. [f] Backward and forward, the author of the "Preface" built [the meanings of] his text; [g] they are reciprocally articulated [*huyan*].[36]

The first sentence of this comment (labeled *a* in the translation) claims that the Airs and Elegantiae were individually authored; the rest of the passage justifies this claim. Behind this justification, structuring and validating it, is a pair of interconnected assumptions concerning categorical analogies (*lei*). According to the logic presupposed here, analogous concepts or entities (that is, concepts or entities belonging to the same "category" or *lei*) have analogous structures and characteristics.[37] What is more, for the *Correct Significance*, these analogous relations are depicted in and can be inferred from the parallelism that characterizes the text of the "Preface." The nature of this parallelism is clear if we diagram Pericope 15:

		一	國	事	繫	一	人	風
(	)	one	country's	affairs	tied to	one	person:	Airs
言		天	下	事				雅
articulate		the empire's	affairs	(			) :	Elegantiae

Both the Airs and the Elegantiae are concerned with "affairs" (*shi*). This is an analogical relation of the simplest kind, of identity. A more complex relation obtains between "an entire state" (*yiguo*) and "the empire" (*tianxia*); these terms are analogous because they belong to the same "category" (*lei*) of political entities. This sort of analogical relation is typical of the parallel couplets of Chinese regulated-style poetry.[38]

The difficulty for the *Correct Significance* arises from the imperfect parallelism between these two expressions. In connection with the Airs it is mentioned that the affairs of the state are "expressed through the person of a single individual," but not in the case of the Elegantiae. Of the latter but not of the former, it is said that they "articulate" (*yan*) the affairs. It is possible, however, to regard this asymmetry as another kind of parallelism: each of the two expressions has an element the other lacks and lacks something the other has. These missing elements are thus supplied—"mutually" or "reciprocally" articulated (*huyan*), as the *Correct Significance* puts it—in the parallel expression.[39] What is true of the one (the Airs)—that it is the product of a single individual—is thus true of the other (the Elegantiae).

The point the *Correct Significance* wants to make is expressed in sentences *b* and *c*, but the economy of supplement and deficiency the *Correct Significance* posits here requires that there be an exchange of elements between the two expressions. For symmetry's sake, then, it must assert what was never in question, that in the Airs a single person *articulates* the affairs of the state (sentence *e*).

The symmetry that obtains between the Airs and the Elegantiae can be discerned because it is modeled in the text of the "Preface." The form of that discussion—that is, the text of the "Preface" *qua* text (what the *Correct Significance* would call its "way of being a text," or *wei wen*)—is itself categorically analogous to the entities and concepts it discusses. This claim is in keeping with one of the most characteristic features of the *Correct Significance*—its presumption of what might be called "the perfection of the text." Although the presumption that the formal, seemingly adventitious features of the text are in fact significant and liable to discursive exposition was in a sense required by the apologetic ends of the Confucian expositors in whose charge these texts were, it must also have appealed to them precisely because it was so fruitful and allowed the creation of so much "significance" (*yii*). From its beginnings in the need to smooth over the difficulties of the canonical text in the course of its academic exposition, the presumption of the perfection of the text acquired a life of its own as a way to generate meaning.

The Production of Significance

An instance of the generation of meaning is the Sequence passage at the head of the *Correct Significance* comment on Pericope 2 of the "Preface." The two pericopes this Sequence discusses are:

1. As for the "Guanju"—the virtue of the Consort.
2. It is the first of the Airs [*or* It is the beginning of the suasion], and it is that whereby the world is transformed and husband and wife put right. So it was performed at the village meetings and at the gatherings of the feudal lords.

For the *Correct Significance*, the "difficulty" of Pericope 1 is its expectation that—all other things being equal—a reference to that which is most important will come at the most important position in the text, at its head (*shou* or *guan*), and what is less important will be mentioned in less prominent places below (*zai xia, tui zai xia*). To put it another way, the *Correct Significance* presumes that the hierarchical order of the world is reproduced in the sequential order of the text. There are any number of these hierarchical orders. The text's arrangement may, for instance, reflect the practical order of moral-political tasks in the world,[40] a hierarchy of clarity in the means of expression,[41] the temporal order of events in the world,[42] or the order of the socio-political hierarchy.[43] This is one more aspect of the homology between text and world the *Correct Significance* assumes is a feature of the canon.

In the passage at hand, the *Correct Significance* expects the editor of the classic to have placed at this, the "head of the Odes" *shi shou*, a reference to someone or something important.[44] Instead there is an Ode dealing with relations within King Wen's household—"trivial domestic matters" (*jiaren xishi*), in the *Correct Significance*'s phrase. In the *Correct Significance*'s view, the "Preface" also sees this arrangement as violating the presumption of the perfection of the text and so goes on in Pericope 2 to dispel the apparent anomaly.

The "Preface" considers just trivial domestic matters that the Consort was delighted to get a virtuous girl or that she did not debauch [King Wen] with her beauty. Yet [this Ode] was placed at the head of the Odes and used as a song. So beneath "the virtue of the Consort" this [i.e., the following] idea [*yi* "intention"] is developed.[45]

The *Correct Significance* dispels the aporia by resorting to the rich ambiguity of the key term *feng*. As discussed in the preceding chapter, Pericope 2 admits of two different interpretations. The first reading (followed, for instance, in the Lu Deming comment included with the *Correct Significance* commentary on this passage) takes *feng* as "Airs," the first of the canonical divisions of the Odes. The other reading, advocated by the *Correct Significance*, takes it as "suasion" or "suasive transformation." The *Correct Significance* thus reads Pericope 2 to say that the "Guanju" speaks of or celebrates the beginning of King Wen's project: the Consort's virtue was the first accomplishment in King Wen's suasive transformation, which was to lead to the foundation of the Zhou dynasty: "That the Consort had this perfect virtue was because this was the beginning of King Wen's suasive transformation."[46]

In the mythology of Confucianism, the early years of the

Zhou, specifically the reigns of Kings Wen, Wu, Cheng, and Kang (eleventh and twelfth centuries B.C.E.), represented a historic highwater mark of moral and political accomplishment. The seemingly "trivial" domestic life of King Wen was redeemed by being a part, albeit a small part, in a larger, historically significant project of political and moral endeavor. Indeed, King Wen's relation with his wife not only foreshadowed his moral transformation of the empire, it represented the indispensable first step in that project. The term *shi* "beginning" is related to *tai* "embryo, fetus";[47] like an embryo, the *shi* is both *xi*—"small, trivial"—and *zhong*—"weighty, important"—by virtue of its potential. Just as an organism cannot grow except from a seed or embryo, the transformation of the empire, it was thought, could not begin except from what seemed relatively unimportant: the personal, domestic relations of the king. This was the old Confucian idea, famously expressed in the "Great Learning" (*Daxue*), of the moral and political project moving outward in a staged progression from one's most intimate relations to a larger political realm (but, it is interesting to note, without the preliminary emphasis on "inner" personal cultivation that so interested the Song Confucians).[48]

The view that the Consort's virtue represented the indispensable first accomplishment in the historical event of King Wen's larger moral-political project was closely related to a second claim. Just as King Wen's moral-political project began with his marriage, so too did the Duke of Zhou's historical program. So too had the Tang dynasty's program for the moral renovation of society to begin by setting aright the personal relationships upon which any more ambitious project must be founded. The "Guanju" made this possible by inscribing and keeping available for reenactment the paradigmatic instance of that process: "When the Duke of Zhou made the rites and fashioned the music, he used [the 'Guanju'] among the villagers, causing the village grandees to use it to teach their people; and he used it among the feudatories, causing the Empire's feudal lords to use it to instruct and transform their vassals."[49]

The "Guanju" was appropriately placed first in the *Odes* because it was the first Ode that had to be used by the prince bent on the moral renovation of the empire. The placement of the "Guanju" was not an anomaly; rather, it was one more aspect of the perfection of the text of the Odes. It not only symbolized but also facilitated the staged progression through which the sentimental education of the individual student and society as a whole were to be accomplished.[50]

The *Correct Significance* aimed not only to explicate but also to create meaning. The *Correct Significance*'s presumption that the canonical text was perfect gave rise here to a "problem" that had to be solved, an aporia to be glossed, but the point of the passage was less the difficulty than the exposition that arose from it. The project of explaining the text was in the service less of historical understanding than of doctrinal exposition.

Word-meanings and Music-meanings

The *Correct Significance of the Five Classics* represents the apotheosis of the text in Confucian doctrinal culture. It was the culmination of a tendency that had been growing for almost a thousand years to focus upon texts in their "textuality"—in their fixity and in the details and form of their language. Not only the texts of the classics but also those of their authoritative commentaries were treated as richly meaningful and explicated in their every nuance of phrase. This elevation of the authority of the classical and exegetical canon was linked with the *Correct Significance*'s own ambition to specify an orthodoxy in matters doctrinal. Backed by the power of the Tang state, the *Correct Significance* attempted to define the limits of orthodoxy for those who would enter officialdom via the official examinations, and its wide circulation and use led to the disappearance of the vast *yiishu* "exposition" literature it summed up and defined.

At the same time, however, no single work, no matter how privileged, could utterly stop the processes by which readers attempted to accommodate to their understandings the sometimes puzzling and problematical teachings of the classics. Less than one hundred years after the promulgation of the *Correct Significance*, skeptical and iconoclastic intelligences were proposing subversive new interpretations of texts like the *Spring and Autumn*; by the eleventh century, the *Correct Significance* interpretations had become a byword for a dry and crabbed literalism. The particular failing of the *Correct Significance* in the view of many of its critics was its *wordiness*: its verbosity and its focus on the language (*yan*, "words") of the text that led to this extravagance. In the Song, Chinese hermeneutics would swing back again from the confidence that inspired the *Correct Significance* to a skepticism concerning language and texts. But perhaps we will not be surprised to find in the extremity of literalism the germ of attitudes that were to lead to its criticism and rejection.

In the preceding chapter we discussed the problem of the relation between Pericope 4 and Pericope 5, perhaps hermeneutically the most influential passage in the "Great Preface," if not indeed in all of Chinese hermeneutical thought:

> 4. The Ode is where the *zhi* goes. While in the heart [*xin*], it is *zhi*; manifested in words, it is an Ode.
> 5. Emotion moves within and takes shape in words. Words are not enough, and so one sighs it. Sighing it is not enough, and so one draws it out in song. Drawing it out in song is not enough, and so all unawares one's hands dance it, and one's feet tap it out.

I argued above that the relationship between *zhi* ("aim" or "project") and *qing* ("feeling" or "emotion") suggested by the juxtaposition of these two traditions was a crucial concern of the compilers of the "Preface." In the *Correct Significance* commentary on this passage is an aporia, a mismatch in the identification of the terms of Pericope 4 with those of "music materials" found in Pericopes 5–7. The *Correct Significance* commentary focuses, however, not on the terms *zhi* and *qing* but on their external complements. In Pericope 4, the external term associated with *zhi* is *yan* "words, language." In the case of Pericopes 5–7, the term associated with *qing* is *yin* "tone."

6. Emotion is manifested in the voice. When voice is patterned, we call it tone [*yin*].

7. The tones of a well-governed age are peaceful and happy; its government is harmonious. The tones of a chaotic age are resentful and angry; its government is perverse. The tones of a lost state are sorrowful and longing; its people are suffering.

These two terms do not coexist peacefully: for the *Correct Significance*, tones rather than words permit real understanding. The words of the Odes can be interpreted, to be sure; after all, most of the *Correct Significance* commentary is devoted to the elaboration and development of interpretations of what the words of the Odes mean. But words alone are treacherous and undependable. As we saw in *Analects* 11.26, it had already been discovered that they could conceal as well as reveal, and the Confucius of the *Analects* was only the first of a long series of influential figures to cast doubt on the adequacy of language.[51] The *Correct Significance* was similarly skeptical: "If you take only his words and are not knowledgeable about tone and voice, then although someone is in behavior like the notorious tyrants Jie or Zhou but in his words like the sage-kings Yao or Shun, you will not know it."[52]

The Odes were liable to this sort of misunderstanding.

Thus the "Chuci" [Mao #209], "Datian" [Mao #212], and their ilk all set forth the excellence of King Cheng; and the "Xinglu" [Mao #17] and "Rufen" [Mao #10] both narrate the evils of the time of the tyrant Zhou. That the "Rufen" is understood to be one of the Kingly Airs, and the "Chuci" a reproachful Elegantia—this is because the Music Master knew the impetus for their creation [*zuoyi*], knew their originative emotion [*benqing*].[53]

The words of the Odes alone could not enable an interpreter to decide between competing readings—to decide whether an apparent paean of praise was just that or rather a withering satire. The reading had to be validated by another kind of knowledge, a knowledge that did not have as its object the plain words of the Ode. Interpretation had to be informed by a knowledge of *yin*, musically patterned sound or tone.

The emotions [*renqing*] of joy and sorrow are manifested in the sounds of speech. At such a time, although joyous or sorrowful affairs may be spoken of, there is still not yet a *gong* or *shang* mode-key [i.e., there is not yet music], but only voice. When one comes to make a poem, however, one orders the clear and the turgid and rhythmically arranges the high and the low, thereby making the five sounds into a tune just as the five colors are made into a pattern.[54]

It was through the contemplation of musically patterned sounds or tones of this kind that the adept was able to know the real, authentic purport of the Ode, to know not only the sentiments that originally animated it but also the political circumstances to which it responded. And this knowledge was of a finer, more authentic type than the knowledge that could be gleaned from mere words.

Voice can represent [*xie*] emotion, and emotion can be completely discerned there. Listening to tones, you can know about order and chaos; observing [*guan*] music, you can be aware of ascendancy and decay. Thus an inspired [*shen*] blind musician has what it takes to know the drift [of an Ode or a state]. Suppose there are words that do not represent someone's aim [*zhi*]; we call that hypocrisy [*jiaoqing*; literally, "falsifying the emotions"]. The emotions will be manifest in the voice, and the hypocrisy can be discerned. Take some plain silk and weave it into fine silk garments. With some the colors are beautiful, but the material is thin; with some the pattern is ugly, but the stuff is good. Only a good merchant can distinguish them.

Take a folk song and put it to music. In some cases the words will be correct, and the intentions [*yi*] wrong; in some the words will be depraved, but the aim correct. Only one accomplished in music will know.[55]

Two kinds of knowledge of the meaning of the Odes were thus possible. One, conditional and perhaps defective, was produced by reading back from the words of an Ode to the aim of its maker; this was associated with the well-known account of production at Pericope 4. The other, veridical, authentic, and infallible (for the adept), was based on a parallel mode of production, that described in Pericopes 5–7. In this view, words had only a conditional validity. Although the meanings generated by skillfully and intelligently reading words were not discarded in the light of the more accurate knowledge provided by the music of the Odes, these "word-readings" had to be subsumed or put into the proper hermeneutic context by the "music-readings." To put it another way, one that perhaps reflects the *Correct Significance*'s own perspective more accurately, the music-readings defined the general purport of an Ode; the word-meanings then worked this general meaning out in more detailed terms. But the word-meaning reading was only conditional, potentially fallible, if not informed and validated by the music-reading. In the *Correct Significance*, for perhaps the first but certainly not the last time in the history of the reading of those texts, full understanding of the Odes was represented by music, and hermeneutic remoteness by its absence.

For the authors of the *Correct Significance*, the music of the Odes was absent. Even had they fancied themselves "music adepts" (*dayuezhe*), there was no way for them to avail themselves directly of the insights that only music could communicate; by the Tang, the music of the Odes had long been lost.[56] Thus the music-meanings of the Odes had to be sought in the exegetical tradition. The received tradition provided the crucial information concerning the purport of the Odes, information that no reader, no matter how astute, could hope to glean on his own from the words of the Odes.

There was, however, a difficulty. Mistrustful of words, which can lie and which do not come stamped with the guarantee of their authenticity, the *Correct Significance* aspired to the knowledge of tones, which certify themselves and which could validate the understandings derived from language. But the *Correct Significance* was separated from this sort of knowledge; it could receive it only secondhand, through testimony embodied in the words of the exegetical tradition, through the very fallible medium the testimony of the exegetical tradition was supposed to circumvent. Both a historical and an epistemological gulf yawned between the adept—the *dayuezhe* with the incommunicable knack of understanding—and the authors of the *Correct Significance*—the epigones, the sifters of traditions, of texts, of words.

Considered in this light, the *Correct Significance*'s presumption of the perfection of the text takes on a new aspect. On the one hand, the elevation of the authoritative exegetical tradition guaranteed the authenticity of the understandings embodied there. On the other hand, however, the punctilious, even ostentatious attention of the *Correct Significance* to the nuances of the text of the *Preface* suggests a deep and disquieting—although unacknowledged—anxiety about the transparency of the message of tradition.

In its concern to work out in painstaking detail what the "Preface" said, in its concern to cite, compare, and dispose of parallel texts, and in its concern to demonstrate the infallibility of the *Preface*, the *Correct Significance* contrasts with both confident interpretations like those of the *Mao Preface* or Zhu Xi and with the readings of later scholars who cited texts for their philological rather than doctrinal interest. Thomas Metzger speaks in his *Escape from Predicament* of the Neoconfucians' belief in their "godlike power" or in the "transnatural power of the mind" they thought available to them.[57] Although Metzger was talking about the Neoconfucian hopes of transforming the world, it is not hard to see this vaunting ambition at work in the Neoconfucian attitude toward the texts of the classics. Zhu Xi felt quite confident that he could understand the classics directly; he believed that he had no need of a "Preface" to establish for him the range of possible correct readings of the Ode.[58] The Han and the Song interpreters were very different, but they were alike in their confidence that they could grasp the meaning of the classics. The *Correct Significance* was painfully aware of the gaps—between word and intent, and between Han and Tang—that threatened its understanding, and of its dependence upon the received traditions it glossed so carefully.

Epilogue: The Disintegration of the *Correct Significance* Orthodoxy

The *Correct Significance*'s elevation of the received exegetical tradition to the status of canon and its ambition to specify a hermeneutic orthodoxy regarding the classics were two sides of the same coin; the *Correct Significance* hoped to claim for itself the same authority it accorded to the Han commentaries. But the position staked out by the *Correct Significance* did not hold; its attempt to put a limit on discussion of the classics and to establish their definitive interpretations was not successful. By the eighth century a new, more skeptical spirit was at work in classics studies.

There had always been individuals skeptical of the claims of the "orthodox" traditions in classics studies. Not only outside critics like the Mohists or Daoists but also those within the Confucian tradition had expressed doubts about elements of the canon. Mencius, that fierce defender of the received tradition, remarked that "it would be better to be without the Documents than to give entire credit to them."[59] The great first-century skeptical thinker Wang Chong made many critical comments on the classical tradition of his day; and in the seventh century Liu Zhiji expressed various iconoclastic opinions, including critical comments concerning the *Spring and Autumn Annals* traditionally ascribed to Confucius. But as E. G. Pulleyblank points out, Liu Zhiji did not contemplate a thorough or methodically informed revision of the tradition; most of his criticisms were, like Wang Chong's, ad hoc objections to "particular, often minor, details."[60]

In the eighth century, however, in the work of Dan Zhu (725–70), Zhao Kuang (fl. 770), and Lu Chun (fl. 773–804) on the *Spring and Autumn Annals*, there appeared a new approach to the classics, not only skeptical but also historiographically astute.[61] Traditionally, sectarian piety (*shifa, jiafa*) had demanded that students of that classic devote themselves to one of the three great exegetical traditions associated with it, the *Zuo Tradition*, the *Gongyang Commentary*, or the *Guliang Commentary*. Attached to each of these, but most especially to the *Zuo Tradition* (which had become orthodox), were various subcommentaries, such as that of Du Yu (222–84) on the *Zuo Tradition*. These subcommentaries had assumed a semicanonical status analogous to that of Zheng Xuan in the case of the *Odes*. Dan Zhu, in what would become one of the characteristic moves of Song hermeneutics, dispensed with the authoritative exegetical tradition, electing to try to understand the *Spring and Autumn Annals* directly, while retaining, however, the traditional assumption that the style of the *Spring and Autumn Annals* encoded Confucius's moral judgments upon the events narrated there. Dan Zhu moreover recognized that the *Zuo Tradition* represented the relatively late redaction of an oral tradition, leavened with a large admixture of "family biographies of leading figures, books of divination, collections of anecdotes, and proposals of the School of Politicians, etc."[62] His disciple, Zhao Kuang, rejected the traditional attribution of the *Zuo Tradition* to Zuo Qiuming.[63]

Thus certain of the key themes of the Song skeptical tradition were already broached during the mid-Tang revival of the Zhenyuan (785–805) and Yuanhe (806–20) periods: the impulse, which I will call "foundational," to evaluate and strip away layers of the exegetical tradition in search of some primitive orthodoxy; and closely allied with that, the attempt to understand the processes by which that exegetical tradition had grown up. These developments were also reflected in studies of the Odes, although they cannot be dated with such precision there as they can in the case of the *Spring and Autumn Annals*.

New Readings of the Odes in the Middle and Late Tang

Two names, one famous and one obscure, stand out in Tang studies of the *Odes* after the *Correct Significance*. One, that of the great poet, essayist, and thinker Han Yu (768–824), is attached to a strange and somewhat anomalous work entitled "A Discussion of the *Preface to the Odes*" ("*Shi zhi xu* yi"); associated with the otherwise largely unknown Cheng Boyu is a text that foreshadowed much of what was new in Northern Song studies of the Odes.

The "Discussion of the *Preface to the Odes*" attributed to Han Yu is a strange and difficult document. The text is almost certainly corrupt, and critics since Zhu Xi have doubted its attribution to Han Yu.[64] The piece is in the form of a catechism or interview, in which "Han Yu" answers a series of questions concerning the *Preface*. He claims that the *Preface* is "inconsistent with the aims of the classics" because its interpretations of the Odes "do not taboo their prince above"—literally, "fail to observe the taboos on the prince's name," but more generally are "insufficiently respectful of the prince." In contrast to Confucius's practice in the *Spring and Autumn Annals*, the *Preface* holds up to view "the hideous face of disorder" and "private intimacies of canopy and mat [i.e., the boudoir]."[65] Also, Zixia was born too late and thus "could not have known" about the affairs the *Preface* discusses.⁶⁶ As for the real author of the *Preface*, "It was that some Han scholar wanted to establish what he had been taught and so attributed it to Zixia. Thus the *Preface* is detailed when it comes to big states, and patchy when it comes to the small ones."⁶⁷

Certainly this is critical; it does not attempt to salvage any part of the authority of the *Preface*. At the same time, however, it is not subversive of the medieval notion that all the Odes inscribe paradigmatically normative impulses. It is not clear what sort of exegesis of the Odes the author of this piece would have preferred to that of the *Preface*, but the strong concern with ritual propriety suggests that an interpretation which took some of the Odes to represent abandoned or depraved attitudes was not intended. The "Discussion" is, so far as I can tell, a fragment from a tradition of exegesis, perhaps even more committed than the *Correct Significance* to the notion of the normative character of the Odes, that has not otherwise survived.

The "Discussion" did not exert much influence on the Song thinkers who wrestled with the problem of the *Preface*. When they began in the eleventh century to try to discover what, if any, value the *Preface* had for the understanding of the Odes, they neither cited not emulated it.⁶⁸ Rather, they were taken with the strategy of another Tang work of unconventional scholarship on the Odes.

No evidence to my knowledge allows us to date the *Explanation of the Points of the Odes* (*Maoshi zhishuo*) any more precisely than to the Tang dynasty. I can find no mention of its author, Cheng Boyu, in any Tang source; nor does the *Explanation of the Points of the Odes* carry any internal evidence that would allow us to date it. It seems to resemble in content and approach other skeptical works of the mid to late Tang, such as the writings of Dan Zhu and Chao Kuang on the *Spring and Autumn Annals* or the "Discussion of the *Preface to the Odes*." Its placement in the listing of Zhu Yizun suggests that it is a late Tang work,[69] but there is nothing that I know of in the work to rule out an earlier (or a later) date.

The *Explanation of the Points of the Odes* as it survives today consists of four *juan*, or chapters.[70] The first, "Origins" ("Xing shu"), deals with the origins of the Odes, relying heavily upon the accounts in the *Han History*, the "Kingly Institutions" ("Wangzhi") of the *Record of Ritual*, and the *Records of the Historian*. In this account the Odes were collected by a special official charged with this task and presented to the Zhou king so that he could judge the success or failure of his policies among the people. Later they were edited by Confucius. In Zhu Xi's influential reformulation, this account was modified to allow for the possibility that some of the Odes did not derive from correct impulses, but Cheng Boyu did not take this step. Stemming from ordinary people, the Odes must originally have been "not good in every case," but Confucius's editorship certified that each Ode preserved in the collection was in fact paradigmatically normative.[71]

The titles of the third and fourth chapters are "Transmission" ("Chuanshou") and "Forms" ("Wenti"), respectively. "Transmission" gives the history of the transmission of the interpretation of the Odes by listing the genealogies of the various schools. "Forms" gives examples of long and short lines, long and short Odes, strange rhymes, and particles used in the Odes.

The second chapter, "Explanations" ("Jieshuo"), consists of fourteen short essays on various traditional questions or topics connected with Odes—the order of the "Airs of the States," "the four beginnings" (*si shi*), and the like. The ninth of these short essays is concerned with the *Preface*;[72] in it, Cheng argues that all the *Preface* cannot be from the hand of Zixia. Rather, he claims, Zixia authored the "Great Preface" (i.e., the complete Preface to the "Guanju") and the first sentences of each of the Minor Prefaces. The Elder Mao added what follows in the Minor Prefaces (i.e., what I call the

"Lower Preface") on the basis of the Odes themselves, but since the Han had no texts of the six "lost Odes," Mao was not able to supplement Zixia's comments there, and their Minor Prefaces for the most part consist only of a single sentence. Moreover, the "Master Gao" mentioned in the Lower Preface to the "Siyi" Ode (Mao #292) was a Warring States figure who lived after Zixia; this is further proof that the Lower Prefaces were not by Zixia but by Mao.[73]

As with the "Discussion of the *Preface to the Odes*," the interpretative consequences of Cheng Boyu's skepticism about the *Preface* are not clear. Had there been an integral commentary originally attached to these four chapters of general observations, we should expect to have at least a few quotations from it, but none survive. The brief discussion of the "Guanju" that forms the eleventh of the fourteen essays in the second chapter is essentially a rehearsal of the *Correct Significance*'s reading of that Ode. But although the suggestion that the *Preface* was divisible into two strata possessing unequal measures of authority did not substantially affect Cheng Boyu's readings of the Odes, it would play a decisive role in the Northern Song critique of the received exegetical tradition.

CHAPTER SIX

The Claims of Tradition

Our age lacks teachers. Let the classics be your teachers.
—Ouyang Xiu, "Reply to Zuze's Letter"

The Song marked a major turning point in the history of classics studies, analogous in many ways to the revolution in the reading and authority of scripture in the Christian Reformation. In the Song case, this revision of the tradition involved on the one hand the criticizing and loosening of traditional and institutional authority over interpretation and on the other hand a renewed and deepened engagement with the classics. Both dimensions of the Song renaissance in classics studies were connected with new ways of reading the classics, ways of reading that culminated in a new, general hermeneutic which drew upon and summed up the key themes of the older Odes hermeneutic and which was to exert a lasting influence over the reading of texts in China down to the present day. The next three chapters trace both the course of the Song critique of the received exegetical tradition and the rise and development of the new general hermeneutic with which it was so closely linked.

One of the key figures in the formulation of this new Song hermeneutic was the great poet, historian, statesman, and scholar Ouyang Xiu

(1007–72). This protean figure exerted an influence over both the political and the intellectual worlds of the Northern Song.[1] Although his advocacy of political parties (*dang* "factions") would earn him the opprobrium of later absolutists, Ouyang's patronage of younger scholars and his association with the reforming program of Fan Zhongyan (989–1052) made him one of the heroes of eleventh-century Confucianism, and his innovations in the composition of the lyric, song (*ci*), and prose make him one of the most important figures in the literary history of the Northern Song.[2] Author or architect of the revision of two of the dynastic histories,[3] he also engaged in pioneering studies of epigraphy, genealogy, and the classics.[4]

Ouyang Xiu studied and wrote on several canonical texts, including the *Changes* and the *Spring and Autumn Annals*.[5] But it was his work on the *Odes* that made Ouyang famous in the history of Song classics studies, where he is often given credit (or blamed, by conservative scholars like Pi Xirui) for initiating the great realignment of the understanding of the Odes during the eleventh and twelfth centuries. It is true that Ouyang was one of the first to skeptically reconsider the Han exegetical tradition and to advocate a direct, unmediated engagement with the classics. Moreover, his readings of a number of the Odes, especially the love songs that would be called "debauched Odes" by Zhu Xi, were refreshingly simple and direct, cutting through and eliminating the worst apologetic excesses of the medieval tradition.

Most accounts, however, whether conservative ones blaming Ouyang for the destruction of some primitive orthodoxy or modern ones making him the hero of an empiricist fable about the transcendence of tradition, tend to exaggerate the skeptical strain in Ouyang's thinking and to discount his conservatism. Ouyang Xiu was no iconoclast: he hoped not to destroy but to refine and to preserve the authority and value of the exegetical tradition that he criticized. Indeed, part of the interest of his thought for the history of hermeneutics lies precisely in the care and seriousness with which he grappled with the problems of the tradition, neither dogmatically asserting its authority like the *Correct Significance* before him nor flatly denying its claims like many writers after him. Like his counterpart in the European Reformation, Erasmus, Ouyang Xiu was at once the last medieval and the first modern, engaged with issues whose importance would be overlooked by many of those who came after him.

Classics Studies in the Early Song

Like the great "Neoconfucian" revival with which it was so closely connected, the Song reformation of classics studies was a complex phenomenon, with no single feature linking all its elements.[6] I have already mentioned the analytic distinction between the critique of the tradition on the one hand and the new involvement with the classics on the other. But the new, deepened engagement with the classics was by no means of a single type. Perhaps we can distinguish three main tendencies.[7] The earliest to appear was the "institutional" approach. As adumbrated by such influential early figures of the Song revival as Sun Fu (992–1057) and Hu Yuan (993–1059), it sought to discover in the classics the blueprints for institutional reform of the state and society.[8] Its most famous practitioner was Wang Anshi (1021–86), whose reading of the *Institutes of Zhou* served to justify his ambitious and controversial reforms.[9] This development, which first appeared in the early eleventh century, was followed a generation or so later by the first works in what might be termed a "metaphysical" approach to the classics; exemplified by such seminal figures as Shao Yong (1011–77) and Zhou Dunyi (1017–73), this approach sought to discover in the classics the outlines of a moral cosmology.[10]

The readings generated by the institutional and metaphysical approaches, although suggestive and ingenious (some thought too ingenious), were not for the most part accompanied by any well worked out hermeneutical teaching.[11] In the case of the third dimension of the classics revival, the situation was very different. Indeed it was in connection with the "personal-devotional" approach to the classics advocated by such Neoconfucian luminaries as the brothers Cheng Yi (1033–1107) and Cheng Hao (1032–85), Zhang Zai (1020–77), and Zhu Xi (1130–1200) that there was developed for the first time in the history of China a kind of general hermeneutic, concerned not just with the particular set of problems associated with one classic but rather with formulating an approach valid for all the canon, indeed all texts. We might say that it was at this point that hermeneutics really became a subject of conscious, thematic reflection in China.

As with the Reformation in the West, the rise of a body of hermeneutical teaching in China was connected with the desire to overthrow and transcend a tradition that was seen as superfluous or even misleading. But the relation between the two dimensions of Song classics studies, the critique of the received exegetical tradition and the deepened engagement with the classics with its associated new general hermeneutic, was a complex one, for the two impulses stood in a dialectical relation, each serving to deepen and promote the other. The new general hermeneutic of the classics generated readings that could not be accounted for in the terms of the orthodox exegetical tradition, and in so doing, it served to promote the critique of that tradition. At the same time, the critique of tradition had a logic of its own and helped to create a space in which not only the new hermeneutic associated with the personal-devotional approach but also institutional and metaphysical readings of the classics could flourish.

These two orientations were not found in equal measures in every student of the classics. As we shall see in the next chapter, Cheng Yi, for instance, was largely uninterested in the evaluation and criticism of the tradition, even though the new general hermeneutic that he enunciated depended upon and presupposed such a critique. In a similar way, there were figures who, while employing new ways of reading, were nevertheless concerned less with the specification of a hermeneutical method than with the tradition and its problems; Ouyang Xiu was such a figure. And if we were to assign a priority, historical and perhaps structural, to one or the other of these two elements, it would necessarily be to the critique of tradition.

Critical Scholarship in the Early Song

As we saw in the last chapter, already by the late eighth and early ninth centuries writings dissenting from the officially sanctioned *Correct Significance* orthodoxy had appeared. In the tenth and eleventh centuries, this trickle of heterodox scholarship grew to a flood. As the conservative scholar and poet Lu You (1125–1210) was to complain, not only the received exegetical tradition, but also the classics themselves were subjected to a skeptical critique.

In the Tang and the early years of the Song, scholars did not dare to critically discuss Kong Anguo or Zheng Xuan; how much less the Sages! Since the Qingli [1041–48] era, scholars have explicated the classics in a way unmatched by earlier generations. But they exclude the [*Commentary on the*] *Appended Words* (*Xici* [*zhuan*]), destroy the *Institutes of Zhou*, doubt the *Mencius*, ridicule the "Punitive Expedition of Yin" ["Yin zheng"] and "Testamentary Charge" ["Gu ming"] chapters of the *Documents*, and reject the *Preface* to the *Odes*. They do not balk at criticizing the classics themselves; how much less the [authoritative] commentaries![12]

Although the critical scholarship of the Song may have lacked the methodological rigor and philological sophistication of Qing dynasty *kaozheng* ("empirical studies") scholarship, its accomplishments were by no means negligible. In addition to criticizing the traditional attribution of such Han documents as the *Preface* and the *Commentary on the Appended Words* to Confucius or his disciples, the Song classicists provided an insightful account of the process by which the exegetical tradition was generated, explored new materials like the Three Schools of Han Odes scholarship, and produced a variety of works of historical, geographical, and phonological scholarship.[13]

The sources of this newly independent spirit in Song classics studies were various. Some were internal to the tradition. The new ways of reading the classics that appeared in the Song generated new readings that made the interpretations of the received tradition seem inadequate. And, as we shall see below, the critique of the exegetical tradition tended to feed upon itself; the discrediting of each layer of the received tradition served to diminish the authority of the tradition as a whole and rendered the remaining layers that much more vulnerable to criticism. If we look outside the tradition of classics studies for influences, we can note an empirical spirit that seems to have informed not only classics studies, but also poetry, painting, and the arts in the Song. Certainly the changing status of the Confucian bureaucrats and gentry also exerted an influence, however subtle and indirect.[14]

Another significant development outside the sphere of classics studies proper was the spread of block printing in China in the ninth and tenth centuries. Most of the materials printed in the ninth century were Buddhist, as were the earliest surviving items, dating from the eighth century, but in the middle decades of the tenth century, the Confucian canon was printed and promulgated on several occasions.[15] Detailed research on the consequences of the proliferation of cheap, readily available editions of the canon upon classics studies and the examination culture still remains to be done, but it seems likely that, as with the printing of the Bible in the West, this development had the effect of subverting the authority of both the exegetical tradition and the hierarchies in whose care that tradition was, and of making possible the kind of individual, "devotional," engagement with the classics that became one of the ideals and the hallmarks of Song classics studies.[16]

These developments notwithstanding, the iconoclastic spirit that had begun to manifest itself in the middle and later Tang was not conspicuous in the early decades of the Song. Like their Tang predecessors, the new Song dynasts sought to define and promote an authoritative orthodoxy in matters doctrinal,[17] and the world of early Song classical scholarship was dominated in its official aspect by the *Correct Significance* commentaries and by a sterile and authoritarian traditionalism.[18] The spirit of the institutional guardians of the state orthodoxy is exemplified by a comment of the early Song scholar and statesman Wang Dan (957–1017): "It would be inadvisable to allow scholars either to put aside the [authoritative] annotations and commentaries or to set forth different ideas, for this might lead students astray and deprive them of standards [on which to base themselves]."[19]

Wang's stricture suggests that he was concerned not only with hypothetical heterodoxies but also with clear and present dangers to the authority of the received tradition. In fact by the mid-eleventh century, famous teachers such as Sun Fu and Hu Yuan were expressing unorthodox and critical opinions.[20] During the short-lived reform government of 1043–44, Fan Zhongyan brought these two scholars to the capital as lecturers in the Imperial Academy,[21] and the Qingli reign period (1041–48) in which these reforms took place has traditionally been held to mark the beginning of a distinctively Song classical scholarship.[22] Also frequently cited as one of the inaugural works of Song iconoclastic scholarship is the *Qijing xiaozhuan* (Short commentaries on the Seven Classics) of Liu Chang (1019–68), a man of the generation of 1020 discussed in the next chapter. It is significant that Liu's work was not in the form of a subcommentary, either upon the *Correct Signif-icance* exposition of the classics or upon the Han glossarists; rather, it was a direct commentary upon the text of the classic itself. This form concretely exemplified the characteristic Song faith in the ability of the student to confront and to understand the classics directly.[23]

In the field of Odes scholarship, the early Song does not seem to have capitalized upon the insights of Cheng Boyu discussed in the preceding chapter. Ouyang Xiu's friend, the poet Mei Yaochen (1002–60), is supposed to have authored an integral commentary upon the Odes, and given Mei's lively intellect and willingness to innovate, we might suppose that he initiated new readings of the Odes. The work does not survive, however, and the absence of quotations from it in later works suggests that it was not widely influential.[24] During the Five Dynasties period (907–60) or the early Song, Qiu Guangting discussed, as later Song iconoclasts would, the inconsistencies between the *Mao Commentary* on the Odes and the *Preface*, but Qiu's point was a conservative one, intended to prove that the *Preface* predated the *Commentary*.[25]

Perhaps the best indication of the relative conservatism of most Odes scholarship in the early eleventh century is the collection of materials pertaining to the imperial consort presented to the court in 1019 and entitled *Tongguan yifan* (Models of female virtue as recorded by the crimson brush). The "crimson brush" of the title referred to the *tong guan* mentioned in the "Jingnü" Ode (Mao #42). In the medieval reading of the Ode as developed in the *Preface* and the *Correct Significance*, this *tong guan* was the writing brush with which the virtues and demerits of the imperial harem were noted, but in the interpretation Ouyang Xiu was to propose some forty years later, it was a love token (see below). As Cheng Yuanmin has argued, this allusion would never have been made in the title of a collection intended for the consort had even a suggestion of the latter reading been current.[26] Thus the readings of the Odes proposed by Ouyang Xiu constituted a revolution in the understanding of the Odes.

The Fundamental Significance of the Odes

The structure of a work of exegesis is shaped by and revealing of the hermeneutical attitudes of its author or authors, especially as regards the problem of the authority of the received tradition. The subcommentary form, for instance, of which the Tang dynasty *Correct Significance of Mao's Odes* discussed in the preceding chapter is good example, as a commentary upon a commentary (or a commentary upon a commentary upon a commentary, depending upon how one conceives the relations between Zheng Xuan's work, the *Preface*, and *Mao's Commentary*) reflected the authoritative, semicanonical status it accorded to the received exegetical tradition. In the same way, a "direct" commentary like Zhu Xi's *Collected Commentaries on the Odes* (*Shi jizhuan*) implied a hermeneutic that deemed the exegetical tradition unessential, or even an impediment to the understanding of the classics.

There was yet a third type of commentary, one that emerged relatively late but was to be important in the great Song realignment of classics studies. This was what we might term the "foundationalist" commentary. For the foundationalist scholar, the history of the transmission and exegesis of the classics was a story of bibliographic catastrophes, misunderstandings, and entropic decay in which an original, primitive understanding of the classic—usually attributed to Confucius—had been progressively garbled and lost. Unable like the authors of the *Correct Significance* to believe that the received tradition reflected an authentic understanding of the classics, nor yet willing like the iconoclast to abandon this flawed tradition and to attempt to understand the classics directly, the foundationalist scholar instead strove to discover within the accumulated layers of tradition an authentic, uncorrupted stratum upon which to found understanding.

Thus the Song scholars moved back layer by layer through the received exegetical tradition in a search for a secure basis for their readings of the classics. In the studies of the Odes, their critique of the exegetical tradition began with the foundation of the early Song orthodoxy, the Tang *Correct Significance* commentary on the Odes, and then proceeded to a critical examination of the Han "Mao-Zheng" materials (that is, the *Mao Commentary* and the *Annotations* of Zheng Xuan). In the following generations, the foundation of the Mao tradition, the *Preface* itself, was subjected to intense scrutiny and eventually rejected by many scholars. The foundationalist impulse reached its logical conclusion in the work of Wang Bo (1197–1274), where the Odes themselves were criticized and expurgated.[27]

The Song review of the orthodox exegetical tradition thus led eventually to the criticism of even its most primitive layers and to a series of direct interpretations of the classics by (among others) Zhu Xi. These interpretations came in time to constitute the basis of a new orthodoxy, expounded and commented upon in their turn.[28] In the Qing, a reaction against this new orthodoxy arose, and the foundationalist critique was repeated, beginning this time with Ming and Qing Neoconfucian scholarship and proceeding thence to the Song Neoconfucians themselves, there picking up the thread of earlier Song scholarship and criticizing the *Correct Significance*, Zheng Xuan, and various of the Han scholars in their turn.[29]

The Song progression back through the exegetical tradition is one of the topics of the next two chapters, and I will not say more about it here, but it is worth spending a moment upon the foundationalist scholarship of the Qing, if only because it provides an instructive contrast with the hermeneutic Ouyang Xiu embraced. Qing foundationalism differed in at least one

important way from the Song version as exemplified by Ouyang Xiu, and this difference points up what is perhaps most
distinctive and important about Ouyang's thought. Qing
foundationalist scholars may have differed in their estimate of
which was the last uncorrupted layer of the tradition, but having made their choice, they were for the most part tenacious
in their commitment to its authority. Chen Huan (1786–
1863), and Chen Qiaocong (1809–69) differed in choosing to
focus upon the Mao *Preface* and *Commentary* and upon the
Three Schools, respectively, in their studies of the Odes, but
they were alike in tending not to question the integrity of the
foundation on which they constructed their scholarly edifices.
Indeed the aggressive assertion of sectarian piety (*jiafa*, *shifa*)
became one of the most salient features of Qing classics studies.[30]

Ouyang Xiu, on the other hand, was engaged in a more
complex relationship with the Han interpreters who were the
proximate locus of his exegetical concern, and this complexity
was reflected in the structure of the *Fundamental Significance*
(*Shi benyii*).[31] In his integral commentary upon the *Odes*, Ouyang discussed only 144 of the Odes; for the remaining 167
Odes, Ouyang accepted the received Han interpretations as
they were reflected in the orthodoxy of his own day: the *Preface to Mao's Odes*; the *Commentary on Mao's Odes*; and the *Annotations to Mao's Odes* of Zheng Xuan (the last two texts are
often referred to together in Ouyang's discussions as "Mao-
Zheng"). As for the 144 Odes he did discuss, Ouyang neither
rejected out of hand nor yet dogmatically asserted the authority of the *Preface* or the "Mao-Zheng" interpretations;
rather, he discussed their merits, sometimes affirming the traditional interpretations and sometimes criticizing and reject-
ing them. When critical, Ouyang sometimes rejected the *Preface* and the interpretations that flowed from it, but at other
times he criticized the "Mao-Zheng" interpretations for failing to do justice to the *Preface*. His engagement with the Han

commentators was not in the debunking spirit of a Zheng Qiao;[32] nor did he take the Han commentators as the irrefutable basis of a foundationalist reinterpretation. Rather, his was an attempt to glean insight into the meanings of the Odes from a source (or rather a set of sources) that was, in his view, at once deeply flawed and at the same time authoritative and indispensable.

The Contrast Between "Intention" and "Significance"

In the work of certain eleventh- and twelfth-century classicists appears a systematic contrast between a pair of homophonous or nearly homophonous terms, *yi* ("intention") and *yii* ("significance") that was to play a key role in later Chinese hermeneutics.[33] This contrast, which was perhaps first exploited to a significant extent in the work of Ouyang Xiu, was taken up and developed by other eleventh-century thinkers like Cheng Yi, Cheng Hao, and Zhang Zai, where it formed one of the centerpieces of the new general hermeneutic they formulated. The terms *yi* and *yii* had long histories, and the contrast between them was not limited to discussions of the Odes. Still, the career of this contrast was closely connected to the controversies surrounding the *Odes*, the *Preface*, and the traditional medieval claim that all the Odes inscribed their authors' paradigmatically normative attitudes. When in the twelfth century this claim was subverted and discredited in the work of Zheng Qiao and Zhu Xi, the contrast between *yi* and *yii* lost its fascination, even though the two terms continued to form part of the basic vocabulary of hermeneutical discussion.

Yi "intention." In the early Song, the key term of the old medieval hermeneutic of the Odes, *zhi* ("aim," "project") was displaced by a new term with which it had much in common but from which it also differed in significant ways. In many contexts, *yi* "intention" seems to cover much the same ground as *zhi* "aim." In the *Mozi*, for instance, *tianyi* "Heaven's intention" seems to vary freely with *tianzhi* "Heaven's will" (*or* "aim"), and *yi* and *zhi* were often used to gloss one another in traditional texts.[34] In such early contexts, *yi* referred like *zhi* to the motivating impulse behind some deed or action. As in the case of *zhi*, that deed or action could be a deed of words—an Ode, for instance. In such contexts, *yi* served (like *zhi*) some of same functions that "meaning" does in modern Western discussions of language: it was what was "behind" a given speech act. At the same time, *yi* was a more limited concept than *zhi*: the *zhi*, it will be recalled, referred to a whole orientation or disposition of a person, an "ambition" or "project" that was an ongoing feature of the personality; whereas the *yi* was specific to the particular act or statement in which it (potentially) exhausted itself.

There were other differences as well. In the late Warring States period, *yi* became part of the Mohist dialectical vocabulary; in these contexts it meant not "intention" or "aim" but something like "mental image."[35] It was part of the technical apparatus by which the Mohists attempted to assign words stable, definable standards of use.[36] In the third century, this sense of *yi* as "mental images" or "ideas" enjoyed a revival in the influential hermeneutic of the *Changes* developed by Wang Bi; perhaps not coincidentally, Wang also asserted that language was adequate to represent *yi*.[37]

But in most late Zhou and early Han discussions of language and *yi*, the sense of "intention" remained paramount. The tendency in these discussions was to assert (perhaps in opposition to the Mohist logicians) that language was inadequate to express its animating intentions.

Words do not exhaust intentions.[38]

The fish trap exists because of the fish; once you've gotten the fish, you can forget the trap. The rabbit snare exists because of the rabbit; once you've gotten the rabbit, you can forget the snare. Words exist because of intentions [*yi*]; once you've gotten the intentions, you can forget the words. Where can I find a man who has forgotten words so I can have a word with him?[39]

Perhaps as a result of discussions like these, *yi* served during most of the medieval period as the preferred term for "meaning" in a general sense. But the problem of language was usually treated only obliquely in the medieval period, and apart from certain sporadic uses in the discussions of, say, the Odes, *yi* functioned largely as part of the specialized vocabulary associated with the hermeneutic of the *Changes*. In the early Song, on the other hand, *yi* became the central term not only of the new general hermeneutic, but also in the hermeneutics of the Odes, where it displaced the older key term *zhi*. In this tradition of use, the late Mohist / Wang Bi sense of the term as "mental image" played little or no role; rather, the term was largely restricted to the sense of "intention,"

To make this Ode telling of this affair, praising what is good and censuring evil, is what is called "the intention [*yi*] of the poet." It is fundamental.

His intention in saying this [*suoyi yun zhi yi*] was to remind [literally, to "stimulate," *xing*] the bride that in her position as a new wife she ought to reflect upon the effort and difficulty with which the Zhou had amassed its legacy of accomplishment.

The "Guanju" and the "Linzhi" [Mao #11] were not made by the same person. The person who made the "Linzhi" had no intention [*yi*] of referring to the "Guanju."[40]

The *yi* was thus the intention of an author or a speaker, defined either relatively narrowly as the aim behind a given speech act or utterance or more broadly as the intentions that led, say, to the composition of one of the classics. Like the *zhi*, the *yi* was the core of the Ode, a prelinguistic state or act that resulted in an instance of saying. The hermeneutical clarity of the intention was threatened by its realization in language, especially by the *yii* or "significance."

Yii "significance." *Yii* was engaged in the *Fundamental Sig-*

nificance in a complex motion of identity and differentiation with *yi* "intention." The two terms may have been homophonous in the eleventh century; in the compound *wenyi/wenyii* "literal significance," the two characters tend to vary freely: either may appear with no evident difference in meaning.[41] When used apart from *wen*, however, especially in contexts where they were contrasted directly, *yi* "intention" and *yii* "significance" had different centers of meaning.

Yii was a complex term. In the texts of Ouyang Xiu and the other teachers with whom we are concerned, *yii* most typically referred to one of the classical Confucian virtues, usually rendered into English as "morality" or "oughtness." This sense of the term was linked to another mentioned above in connection with the Tang *Correct Significance* commentaries and the "exposition" (*yiishu*) genre of exegesis, that of "discussion" or "explication."[42] In hermeneutical contexts *yii* meant something like "meaning"; as a property of texts, *yii* was the "lesson" (or its "moral," if that did not imply some notion of a story) of a text. It was the morality to be found in or advocated there, especially as that morality was developed or explicated in the course of doctrinal exposition. "Significance" may be as close as we can come—that element or understanding of texts most consequential for character and moral behavior.

Moreover, in certain special contexts, *yii* was used to refer to the meanings that words had in and of themselves, apart from considerations of context or authorial intention. Although this sense of *yii* and the concept of *yii* as the expounded significance of a text are analytically distinct, they were, I believe, two facets of the same concept, and so I translate *yii* as "significance" in both contexts, even when this results in some awkwardness.

The "significance" of a text could, for the eleventh century at least, contrast with its intended meaning. For although the intended meaning of a text was determined by the intention of its author and was thus unitary and unambiguous, a passage or text or even an image could have more than one significance. For instance, Ouyang Xiu distinguished between the significance originally intended by its author for an Ode and the significance "established" for it by its placement within the collection as a whole by the Music Master (*taishi*).[43] For Ouyang Xiu, the hermeneutic problem consisted of discovering which of the possible significances of a text or image had been intended in a given context. The contrast was between a unitary, originating intention and a potentially complex and deceptive significance. This contrast was in turn involved with one between an austere and committed orientation toward the classics that aimed to recapture and relive the intentions of their authors and a prolix, discursive scholarship that focused on the detailed exposition of the significance of the text.

Ouyang's Reading of the Odes

The contrast between *yi* "intention" and *yii* "significance" played a crucial role in Ouyang Xiu's interpretations of the Odes. On the one hand, the *yi* served to specify and limit the meaning of the Odes, restoring to them their functions as deeds of words rather than as complex "maps" of the world in which a word or image might have a wealth of significance (*yii*). On the other hand, they served to unify the collection as a whole: their manifest content ("significance") notwithstanding, all the Odes, it could be maintained, were animated by a single intention, or at least a single type of intention. In this respect, *yi* "intention" served to negate certain disturbing possibilities raised by Ouyang's own interpretations.

"Intention" as a means to specify meaning: the "Quechao" Ode. Ouyang Xiu's readings of the Odes present a striking contrast with those of the *Correct Significance*. Above all, they are simpler, less forced, and less ambitious than those of Kong

Yingda and the tradition he summed up. Take, for instance, Ouyang's comments on the "Quechao" Ode (Mao #12):

> Now the magpie [*que*] had a nest,
> But the cuckoo [*jiu*] lived in it.
> Here comes a girl to be married;
> With a hundred coaches we'll meet her.
>
> Now the magpie had a nest,
> But the cuckoo made a home in it.
> Here comes a girl to be married;
> With a hundred coaches we'll escort her.
>
> Now the magpie had a nest,
> But the cuckoo filled it.
> Here comes a girl to be married;
> With a hundred coaches we'll gird her.[44]

The original Ode as we have it was an epithalamium. The significance of the *xing* image of the "magpie" (*que*) and the "cuckoo" (*jiu*) is not certain, but Mao's comment that the *jiu* does not build its own nest but occupies those of other birds is certainly relevant. Waley suggests that the *jiu* is the cuckoo, alluding to that bird's well-known habit of leaving its young to be raised in the nests of other birds.[45] Whatever the identification, it is clear that the *jiu* is analogous to a new bride who goes to live in the house of her husband's family.

In the interpretations of the *Preface* and of Zheng Xuan, this bride was associated with the wife (*furen*) of some prince, perhaps Taisi, the wife of the great King Wen of Zhou.[46] These expositors developed or expanded upon the *Commentary*'s interpretation of the Ode by ascribing to the *jiu* moral qualities appropriate to the wife of a great lord: it was "virtuous" (the *Preface*); it had the "virtue of uniting [two houses]" (Zheng Xuan).[47] In this style of exegesis, the Ode came to map the world in an ever more detailed way, and the study of the Odes consisted of pointing out and observing those correspondences and the moral lessons they implied.

Ouyang Xiu offered a reading of this Ode that was simpler and "less interpreted" than that of the medieval exegetes. Ouyang agreed with the *Correct Significance* that the *jiu* represented the young Taisi on her way to her new husband's home, but for Ouyang Xiu the *jiu* represented only that single feature of Taisi's situation. It did not necessarily symbolize anything else about her (i.e., her moral qualities). Ouyang made this point in terms of the contrast of *yi* "intention" and *yii* "significance." In the medieval reading, the image of the cuckoo had what Ouyang would have called two "significances": it represented both the bride going to a new home *and* feminine virtue. For Ouyang, it represented only the bride.

When the poet selected an object for the purposes of *bi* or *xing*, he would choose only one of its significances to express his intention. As for the significance of the "Quechao," the poet only referred to [literally *qu* "selected"] the magpie's merit in building a nest in order to make an analogy [*bi*] with the way in which the house of Zhou had established its kingly legacy through piling up accomplishment and merit, and he referred to the *jiu*'s occupation of the magpie's nest in order to make an analogy with the bride's leaving home to reside in that already established Zhou house. The poet's intention in saying this was to stimulate [*xing*] the bride to reflect on how difficult it had been for the Zhou house to build up its legacy and on how she ought to assist the prince to preserve and not lose it.[48]

Ouyang's reading did not make the imagery of the poem do so much work as the traditional interpretation; we might say that the Ode or at least the image of the *jiu* had less *yii* "significance" for Ouyang than it did for the *Correct Significance* or Zheng Xuan. But Ouyang's reading was not simply "less interpreted." Ouyang also insisted that the moral significance of the Ode was located not in the *jiu* as an emblem of the virtue of the consort Taisi but in the intention of the poet that lay behind the Ode as a whole. In the former reading, the "Quechao" had to do with the character of Taisi as it was symbolized by the *jiu*; in Ouyang's view, the poem's moral interest lay in the act performed by the Ode and in the intentions of its author, who enjoined Taisi to be a worthy steward of her husband's house. The source of the moral interest of the Ode was the intention that animated and spoke through it, and reading the Ode was an engagement with that force or intention rather than a pedantic point-for-point mapping of the Ode onto history.

   "Intention" as a means to limit meaning: The "debauched" Odes. Ouyang is perhaps best known in the history of the hermeneutics of the Odes for his reinterpretations of those songs the twelfth century would call *yin* "debauched."[49] Recall that in the medieval view all the Odes were composed by morally accomplished individuals and expressed and inscribed morally paradigmatic attitudes or reactions to the political and moral history of the Zhou dynasty. In the eleventh century, discussions of the Odes began to mention an idea that had been energetically and effectively denied for a thousand years: the possibility that certain of the Odes expressed sentiments and attitudes which were not only not canonically correct and normative but actually inimical to the foundations of the Confucian vision of society and morality.[50] These Odes, which came to be called the "debauched Odes" (*yinshi*), dealt with love and romance, not necessarily confined within what Confucians insisted were the indispensable bounds of marriage. To modern readers these poems evoke an innocent, pastoral world of infatuations, assignations, and festivals, but for Confucians who believed that the natural harmony of society was founded above all on the regulation and maintenance of the family, they seemed both to bespeak and to promote the disintegration of the social order.

   Ouyang Xiu was the first writer on the Odes after the Tang, perhaps the first since the Han, to suggest readings of these Odes that acknowledged them to be love songs. Take, as an example, the "Jingnü" Ode (Mao #42):

Of fair girls the loveliest
Was to meet me at the corner of the Wall.
But she hides and will not show herself;
I scratch my head, pace up and down.

Of fair girls the prettiest
Gave me a red flute.
The flush of that red flute
Is pleasure at the girl's beauty.

She has been in the pastures and brought
     for me rush wool,
Very beautiful and rare.
It is not you that are beautiful;
But you were given by a lovely girl.[51]

The medieval interpretation as developed by Zheng Xuan and the *Correct Significance* grew out of that of the *Mao Commentary* and the *Preface*. The *Preface* states that the Ode was directed against Duke Xuan of Wei (r. 717–699 B.C.E.), who, with his wife, was "guilty of licentious conduct."[52] On this reading the Ode described a beautiful and virtuous young woman, an appropriate mate and implicit reproach for the duke. The "corner of the Wall" in the first stanza was emblematic of the young woman's unassailable virtue (because the wall was high), and the red tube of the second was a writing brush with which the "female historians" (*nüshi*) of the Zhou court recorded the rules and activities of the harem. By so rebuking the duke and his consort, the poet demonstrated an appropriate emotional response to their conduct, and the Ode that inscribed that response could serve as an instrument of moral education.

Ouyang dispensed with most of what he termed the "far-fetched" (*yu*) features of the medieval interpretation. For Ouyang the Ode concerned a meeting between two lovers; the "red tube" of the second stanza was a love token, and the corner of the wall a trysting spot. Although he was able, by a deft interpretive move to be described below, to avoid challenging

the central assumption of the tradition that the Odes represented morally paradigmatic attitudes, Ouyang nevertheless
radically transformed the way that the Ode was read, produc-
ing a reading that was refreshingly simple and direct. It is for
such reinterpretations that he is justly famous in the history of
the reading of the Odes.

But although Ouyang's interpretations often departed from
the received readings, it would be a mistake to exaggerate their
iconoclastic character. It is often claimed that Ouyang was the
first of the Song scholars to depart from the medieval view
that all the Odes inscribed paradigmatically normative attitudes and to designate certain Odes as *yin* "debauched."[53] In
fact, a little more than a century later, the "Jingnü" Ode would
be widely thought "the Ode of a debauched eloper."[54] This
revolution in the understanding of the Odes, which was to be
made famous and influential by Zhu Xi, is of interest because
it involves a turn toward the reading of the Odes favored by
most modern interpreters. But although Ouyang's readings
provided a crucial bridge between the classical, Han-style
readings and the Song-style readings of Zhu Xi, Ouyang
never to my knowledge used the term *yinshi* "debauched
Ode" in the *Fundamental Significance*. Rather, he held to the
classical view that explicitly ruled out the possibility that any
of the Odes could have been composed by debauched, abandoned people and were valuable only as negative examples.

Like Zhu Xi, Ouyang took the "Jingnü" to concern a love
affair, and he moreover agreed in understanding the speaker
of the Ode to rejoice in the illicit connection he had formed
with the "beautiful girl" of the Ode. But whereas Zhu Xi
thought the Ode to thus inscribe the (morally distasteful) attitudes of its author, Ouyang drew a distinction between the
reprehensible attitudes expressed by the Ode's speaker on the
one hand and the good intentions of its author on the other.
The author, he claimed, sought to satirize Duke Xuan by illustrating the degree to which his behavior had corrupted his

people. Thus although the author of the Ode adopted, as we should say, the persona of one who was morally abandoned, he did it with the classically correct intention of satirizing (*ci*) and correcting his prince.[55] In Ouyang's interpretation, then, the classical assumption that all the Odes represented good, morally enjoined attitudes was preserved, even as the Ode itself was given a new and, to modern tastes, more natural and plausible reading. It was but a short step from this kind of reading to that of Zhu Xi, which dispenses with the presumption of the normative character of the Ode's source, but it is a short step Ouyang did not take in his classical scholarship.[56]

There is a temptation to conceive of Ouyang Xiu's scholarship in teleological terms—that Ouyang was the forerunner, but only the forerunner, of the modern reading of the Odes. It is true that Ouyang Xiu seemed to draw back before an explicit statement that some of the Odes were "debauched." Ouyang's readings were, however, less puritanical than, say, Zhu Xi's, for whom the "Jingnü" exemplified not the dewy innocence that we tend to see there but the moral collapse of the state of Wei. Confucius had included it in the collection as a negative example or warning, and this warning was to be taken to heart, but not to be enjoyed.[57] A generation later, Zhu Xi's "disciple" Wang Bo would carry these ideas to their logical conclusion by expurgating the "debauched Odes" from his edition of the *Odes*.[58] Ouyang's reading, on the other hand, allowed, even in a sense required, the pleasure of the Ode—the pleasure of becoming that hopeful lover—even as it claimed to caution against it.[59]

Ouyang Xiu's Mythology of the Tradition

A particular hermeneutical vision, with specifiable assumptions, orientations, and even rules, is implicit in the interpretations discussed above. Some of these assumptions, orientations, and rules are stated explicitly in the various essays and obiter dicta of Ouyang Xiu's to be discussed below. But interpretations can be justified in other, less direct ways as well. One of the most important of these, which we have already seen at work in both the *Preface* and the *Correct Significance*, is through the "mythologies" of the Odes presented by these sources: their stories about the origins, composition, collection, and transmission of the Odes. In the work of Ouyang Xiu, perhaps the most interesting and significant of these accounts is found in a short essay included in Chapter 14 of the *Fundamental Significance*, the "Discussion on Fundamentals and Peripherals" ("Benmo lun").[60]

In this piece Ouyang advises a questioner perplexed by certain notoriously difficult questions concerning the arrangement of the Odes to devote himself to a study of the fundamental (*ben*) elements of the tradition and to disregard or at least defer the study of its peripheral (*mo*) features. The *ben/mo* dichotomy was a favorite organizing trope of Confucian discourse and provided a means whereby to master and to hierarchically order complex phenomena like the exegetical tradition. *Ben* was literally the root or trunk, *mo* the branch tips of a tree. The root and trunk were conceived to be fundamental and essential; the branch tips were peripheral, marginal, or trivial. The root was also original, that out of which the branch tips grew; it controlled and in a sense implied or contained the branch tips. But the relation was not symmetrical: although the peripheral was not in itself bad, if the student were to devote himself to it at the expense of the fundamentals, he would be lost in a bewildering and insubstantial proliferation. Grasp well the trunk and you will be secure; put your faith in the branch tips and you will fall!

The first fundamental element of the tradition in Ouyang's scheme was authorial *yi*, or "intention." In traditional poetic and linguistic theory, *yi* "intention" and aim (*zhi*) were closely connected with the notion of centrality (they were themselves central to that tradition): the Ode, or indeed any speech act, was founded in and emerged from the intention or the aim. The intention was the foundation and origin (*ben*) of the Ode, which in this formulation was itself peripheral (*mo*); it provided the structural "core" of the Ode, limiting and defining the plurality of significance that arose from the ambiguities of language and history. The Ode was in its turn fundamental when considered in relation to the tradition as a whole; and this tradition could itself be conceptualized in terms of a fundamental/peripheral dichotomy in which a multitude of competing interpretations and schools branched out from a single, authoritative source.

Finally, the *yi* "intention" was fundamental because it was only when understood in terms of its motivations that the Ode became a gesture in the world, vital and consequential; the *yi* was fundamental to the use of the Odes as agents of moral transformation. Ouyang's insistence that the Ode be reflected upon as a deed of words, rather than pedantically expounded as a map of the world, was thus in effect a call for a return to the sources of the hermeneutics of the Odes as it had developed in the late Zhou and Han periods. In the thought of the Chengs and others in the next generation, this kind of "existential" understanding of the text would become the centerpiece of a new, general hermeneutic.

The moral involvement stemming from an engagement with the fundamental, originating intentions of the Odes was threatened by the next element of the tradition discussed by Ouyang, the "office" of the Music Master. The Music Master was supposed to have been a Zhou dynasty official entrusted, among other responsibilities, with the collection and preservation of the Odes. Ouyang defines his responsibilities as "rectifying the names [of the Odes] and distinguishing their categories, placing some here and some there."[61] Great amounts of energy had been spent on questions concerned with the details of the notoriously unsystematic and quirky classifications and subclassifications of the Odes into Airs, Elegantiae, and Lauds; these are the questions with which Ouyang begins the "Essay on Fundamentals and Peripherals." The danger, Ouyang believed, was that the student would become preoccupied with the significance of the Music Master's arrangement of the Odes and so overlook the fundamental significance of the Ode itself, which derived from the intention of its author. Questions concerning organization were not necessarily misguided or meaningless, but they were not central or fundamental; they did not allow one to become engaged with the Odes in a morally significant way, but only in a pedantic, antiquarian way. They were, in a word, "peripheral."

Ouyang spoke of the Music Master's labors in terms of the second term of the contrast drawn above, *yii* "significance." For instance, in his discussion of the "Lin zhi zhi" Ode (Mao #11), Ouyang says: "What the *Preface* gives is not the original intention of the poet; it is a significance established by the Music Master when he edited the Odes."[62]

We thus see here another version of the contrast between intentions and significance that Ouyang used to discuss problems of language and meaning. The choice of a word or an image, or the composition of an Ode or a text, was inspired in Ouyang's view by a single intention, and this intention determined the "real meaning" of the word, image, or text in question. But words, images, and texts could have more than one significance, either because of the inherent ambiguity of language (as in the case of the "Quechao" Ode discussed above) or because additional significance had been "established" for an Ode by the Music Master's placement of it in the collection as a whole. The significance of such an arrangement was one of the significances of the Ode, to be sure, but it was not the significance originally intended by its author; it was not the "fundamental significance" that Ouyang's title suggests he hoped to supply in his work.

In general, Ouyang Xiu saw the history of the classical tradition as one of decline and dispersal in which the original, unitary significances of the Odes were lost and confused. The third element of the "Discussion of Fundamentals and Peripherals," however, represented a reversal of this tendency. The "aim of the Sage" (*shengren zhi zhi*) was to "make right the Elegantiae and Lauds, eliminate duplications and repetitions, and place the Odes among the Six Classics, making manifest the good and bad that they might serve as encouragements or warnings."[63]

The reference is, of course, to Confucius's supposed labors on the Odes, labors that constituted the second fundamental element of the tradition in Ouyang's scheme. In Ouyang's account, Confucius's accomplishment was to canonize the Odes: to select out and include in the anthology those Odes that were paradigmatically normative and elevate that text to the status of a classic, and to unfold and make manifest the intentions of the Odes and thereby provide later readers with the hermeneutic key to understanding. Although one might, simply by reading the Odes over, be able to understand the "genre" to which they belonged—to tell whether they praised or censured—the student could not, in most cases, discover the specific historical circumstances to which they responded.[64] In Ouyang's account, Confucius was able to do just that. After he "examined the praising and censuring" in the Odes, he was able to "make manifest the good and evil"—that is, he was able to identify the good and bad actors and actions that formed the historical context of the Odes.[65] Confucius stated the intentions of the poets in ordinary, unambiguous, unpoetic language, so that it was possible to discern the correct, fundamental significance of the Odes.

The interpretations of Confucius—the highlighting of the historical circumstances of the Odes in morally charged language—was an exegetical gesture, founded on a reading of the original text and finally reducible and corrigible according to that original text. Confucius simply "made manifest" (*zhuo*) what was already there in the Ode. As Ouyang says at the close of the essay, "if you already know the intention of the poet, then you will have [i.e., understand] the aim of the Sage."[66] Confucius's labors were in this sense derivative, but because they were accomplished by Confucius—who was both supremely insightful and historically well situated to learn the intentions of the authors of the Odes—they were located unambiguously among the fundamental, foundational elements of the tradition, an indispensable focus of study. Although Confucius was located historically later than the Odes themselves or the Music Masters, nevertheless his interpretations could lead the reader though the obstacles to understanding. In this respect, Ouyang's account—his myth, if you will—resembled that of the *Correct Significance*; that is, it seemed to argue for the indispensability of the exegetical tradition.

There was, however, a complication.

For the *Correct Significance*, the exegetical tradition was both indispensable and reliable, even if, as I suggested, it was prey in the final analysis to the same difficulties concerning language it purported to obviate. In Ouyang's formulation, on the other hand, the exegetical tradition was itself badly flawed. Confucius's teachings were exemplary in this respect. Confucius was the first and best exegete of the Odes; it was his normative understanding of the Odes that all later commentators would try to recapture. But where were Confucius's interpretations to be found? No document on the Odes survived from Confucius's hand. Although the *Analects* ascribes some twenty-odd comments concerning the Odes to

Confucius, only a few of them actually present interpretations of particular Odes. Even when the "Confucian" interpretations gleaned from such sources and the *Record of Rites* or the *Mencius* were added, there were hardly enough statements in the classics ascribed to Confucius on which to found a school of interpretation.

The teachings of Confucius thus had to be sought in the fourth and final element of the tradition discussed by Ouyang, the "legacy of the classicists" (*jingshi zhi ye*). By "the classicists," Ouyang seems to have meant first the author(s) of the *Preface*, and second those of the *Mao Commentary on the Odes* and Zheng Xuan. According to our present understanding, of the three the *Mao Commentary* was the earliest (probably Western Han, see Chapter 4), followed by the *Mao Preface* (probably written down early in the Eastern Han, but based on traditional materials), and later by the *Annotations* of Zheng Xuan. In Ouyang's view, however, the *Preface* represented the earliest layer of the tradition, followed first by the *Mao Commentary* and then by Zheng Xuan, both of whom he understood as commenting upon the *Preface*. That Ouyang could construe the relation between the *Preface* and the *Commentary* in this way was due to the *Commentary*'s extreme terseness. Its interpretive comments are so brief that, given the notorious ambiguity of literary Chinese and the fact that those interpretations do stand within the same general hermeneutic tradition as the *Preface*, it was quite possible to see them as developing upon the *Preface*.

For Ouyang Xiu, then, the earliest and thus the best and most authoritative of the Han sources was the *Preface to Mao's Odes*. In the traditional account, the *Preface* was supposed to have been authored by Zixia, the disciple with whom Confucius could discuss the Odes. This attribution had long been doubted, and Ouyang himself said in his "Questions on the *Preface*" that the *Preface* was not the work of Zixia.[67] But Ouyang did not doubt that Confucius had in fact personally taught Zixia the meanings of the Odes.[68] We should understand his comment that Zixia did not author the *Preface* to mean that Zixia did not personally author it; rather, the *Preface* was the crystallization of a tradition that derived—not without corruption—from Zixia and thence Confucius. Thus Ouyang could say that the Mao teachings displaced those of the other Three Schools "because of the source from which they derived" and because they "got more of the Sage's points."[69]

The *Preface* was thus for Ouyang the most authoritative element of the "legacy of the classicists." He says at one point, "I often use the *Preface* as an authority in my writings on the Odes,"[70] and in fact he often employed the *Preface*'s interpretations in the *Fundamental Significance* as a yardstick to measure those of "Mao and Zheng" (i.e., the *Commentary* and the *Annotations*). The following passages are typical of the argumentation found in his "Discussions" of the Odes.

Mao and Zheng fail to use the *Preface*'s intention to seek the significance of the Ode. Since they are mistaken about the fundamentals [of the Ode's interpretation], their words proliferate and their interpretations are superfluous. The meaning [of the Ode] is diffused [in their interpretation] and does not agree with the *Preface*.

The interpretation offered by Zheng's *Annotations* is not there in the original Ode. When we test it against the Ode and *Preface*, we do not find this meaning anywhere.[71]

Arguments of this kind presuppose the authoritative character of the *Preface*. Although the charge of having overlooked or falsified the insights of the *Preface* was not usually in and of itself enough to discredit one of the Mao *Commentary* or Zheng's interpretations, such a charge did count against them. Probably at least three-quarters of the "Discussions" of the Airs of the States in the *Fundamental Significance* include as one of their arguments against the *Commentary* or Zheng interpretation and in favor of the interpretation that Ouyang proposed an explicit or implicit reference to the authority of the *Preface*.

At the same time, Ouyang by no means accepted the *Preface*'s authority uncritically. He did not hesitate in his interpretations of the Odes to reject the *Preface* as mistaken. In his discussion of the "Lin zhi zhi" Ode (Mao #11) for example, he says: "The *Preface* contains many errors concerning the [Odes of] the Two Souths [Zhounan and Shaonan]."[72] In such cases, Ouyang believed, the *Preface* represented Confucius's views imperfectly. Once, the understanding of the Odes had been intact and available, passed on from Confucius to Zixia in the expectation that it would be transmitted on down the generations. Then the traumas of late Zhou history and the Qin bibliocaust intervened, and perhaps a naturally entropic movement as well, and the tradition was lost and scattered and confused. Some of the Prefaces to the various Odes did indeed reflect the teachings of Confucius and thus could be used in the kind of argument outlined above. Others, however, represented corruptions, which came into being when later classicists fabricated explanations, either through arrogance (*zixin*) or because they were embarrassed not to be able to explicate those points that had no surviving tradition associated with them.

Ouyang thus claimed that there were two possibilities for the classicists. They could "search out the intentions of the poet, and penetrate the aims of the Sage," in which case their work would be fundamental, or they could "discuss the office of the Music Master and baselessly create theories where the traditions have been lost," in which case their contributions would be peripheral.[73] The former case applied to the authentic Prefaces and those interpretations of "Mao and Zheng" that faithfully developed upon them; the latter was the situation where the Prefaces were inauthentic, or where Mao and Zheng distorted the sense of an authentic Preface.

Ouyang's picture of the received exegetical tradition was of one heterogeneously but distinctly composed of interpretations that were wholly authentic and interpretations that were wholly mistaken. On the one hand, this view of the history of the received exegetical tradition had conservative implications, for it served to protect the authority of the "authentic" elements of the tradition from contamination by the inauthentic. Some elements of the tradition were corrupt, to be sure, but those that were not were to retain all the prestige and authority that accrued to the tradition as a whole in the medieval era. The corrupted, dangerous elements in the tradition were sealed off from the authentic elements; their criticism need not tarnish the authority of the rest. On the other hand, there was no way of knowing ahead of time which of the Prefaces were authentic and which bogus. Any of the individual Prefaces could turn out to be inauthentic, although presumably not all of them. The problem then became How did one recover the original intentions that animated the Odes? Did the Prefaces and the exegetical tradition generally help or hinder the interpreter in reading the Odes? Ouyang Xiu gave two largely contradictory answers to these questions.

Iconoclasm

We can distinguish two opposing themes in Ouyang Xiu's teachings concerning the reading of the Odes. On the one hand, scattered throughout his essays, letters, and the *Fundamental Significance* itself are various obiter dicta asserting that the Odes, indeed all the classics, were largely if not entirely susceptible to direct understanding by a careful reader. In these comments, Ouyang seemed to claim that the exegetical tradition was dispensable, if not actually an impediment to the understanding of the classics. On the other hand, again in various obiter dicta but most especially in his more sustained reflections on the difficulties of interpretation, Ouyang Xiu made a case that the received exegetical tradition could not be transcended and indeed could be modified only in a gradual, incremental fashion.

Most accounts, traditional and modern, have tended to emphasize the first, iconoclastic element in Ouyang Xiu's hermeneutic. This is not surprising, since this skeptical strain in his thought seems to exemplify and prefigure two of the most distinctive features of Song classics studies: the impulse to subject the tradition to a critique and the hope to transcend it altogether. Moreover, statements in which Ouyang asserted the possibility of dispensing with the tradition abound in his work. We can distinguish a number of key themes.

First, Ouyang stressed what was to become one of the characteristic themes of the Song hermeneutic of the *Odes*, its insistence upon the natural, "easy" character of that text. In effect, this meant that the Odes were not to be read (as in the *Correct Significance*) as a special kind of discourse that perfectly modeled moral and historical reality, but as ordinary speech. In the authoritarian hermeneutic of the *Correct Significance* commentary, the aims behind the Odes were accessible only through the authoritative exegetical tradition; they were emphatically not something that the reader could infer independently. In the more democratic, egalitarian view adumbrated by Ouyang Xiu and his successors, the Odes were understandable because they stemmed from the "human emotions" (*renqing*) the reader and the authors of the Odes shared in common: "Human emotions are the same today as they were in antiquity. If those who seek the significance of the Odes seek it according to [their own] emotions, they will not go far wrong."[74]

In a similar way the language of the Odes was not opaque and "subtle" (*wei*), as it was in the earlier hermeneutic, for the desire to express oneself and the act of expression itself are as natural as the emotions and intentions they reveal. Although the language of the Odes may have been indirect, it was not unnatural: "The ancients were simple and straightforward, not perverse or deliberately obscure."[75]

The hermeneutic consequence was that the aims or intentions that lay behind the Odes could be inferred from the language of the Odes themselves, often without recourse to the exegetical tradition: "Those [portions] of the classics that can be understood without reference to a commentary are seven or eight parts in ten, while those which are confused and obscured by the commentaries are five or six in ten."[76] Ouyang thus spoke in the *Fundamental Significance* of "seeking the significance through the text [of the Ode]" (*ju wen qiu yii*); of "testing" (*kao*) various theories and interpretations against the "significance of the Ode" (*shiyii*), the "text of the Ode" (*shi-wen*), or the "logic or organization of the text" (*wenli*). He commented in various contexts that the poet's intention in a given Ode "can naturally be seen" (*ziran kejian*), and wrote of the "Jingnü" Ode that "its text is perspicuous and its significance brightly and clearly easy to see."[77]

Ouyang moreover rejected interpretations that, in the interest of ascribing to an Ode some intention or significance, were not able to give a reasonable and plausible reading to its manifest content as well. Especially in the *Fundamental Significance*, he derided as "farfetched" (*yu*) readings that fragmented or dispersed the textual sense of the Ode—readings that demanded the Ode be understood in such a way that unity of reference or person could not be maintained throughout. To speak in such a way, or even to compose poetry in such a way, Ouyang argued, would have been too indirect and improbable.[78] Ouyang foregrounded the textual sense of the Ode—that is, the manifest sense of the Ode when read according to the "normal" conventions of reading—and rejected those interpretations that did not do justice to that manifest content.

It is not surprising that modern interpreters and historians have tended to see this as the most significant dimension of Ouyang Xiu's thought. This iconoclastic strain in his thought not only was essential as a means of liberating classics studies from the stultifying orthodoxy of the *Correct Significance*, but also was closely connected with the generation of the new general hermeneutic. It would be a mistake, however, to exaggerate Ouyang's iconoclasm; as I will show below, there was also a deeply conservative element in his thought.

Moreover, we may doubt that the iconoclasm of statements like those discussed above accurately reflected Ouyang Xiu's own exegetical practice. His interpretations of the Odes were by no means uninfluenced by the traditional reading of that text. Many of Ouyang's interpretations explicitly claimed the authority of the *Preface*, and we know that in a majority of cases—167 out of 311 to be exact—Ouyang considered the traditional, Mao–Zheng traditions to be correct, or at least not to have been decisively refuted.[79] Finally, as we saw above, even where Ouyang departed most radically from the traditional interpretation, he still stayed within the assumptions that shaped the medieval reading of the Odes. Ouyang Xiu's hermeneutical horizon was defined by a received tradition that could not simply be transcended by fiat or an act of will. His iconoclastic claims failed to take account of the pervasive influence of that tradition and underestimated its tenacity.

Conservatism

A second dimension to Ouyang's theory, however, explicitly affirmed the claims of tradition upon interpreters. This theme was given its most interesting and sustained development in the work entitled "Postface to the *Supplement to the Chronological Table of the Odes*" ("*Shipu* buwang houxu").[80] The "Postface"—as I will call it—was an apologia, composed at the end of a long engagement with the commentaries of

Zheng Xuan, first in the essays of his thirties, then in the *Fundamental Significance* composed in his middle age, and finally in the *Chronological Table of the Odes* of his later years. In the "Postface," Ouyang attempted to explain and above all to justify his treatment of the interpretive tradition and of Zheng Xuan in particular and to outline the conditions under which traditional teachings concerning the Odes and the classics generally could be discarded and revised.

Ouyang begins by specifying the reasons that compel the interpreter to acknowledge the superior authority of the received tradition. First, the received tradition provided the only link with the original, authentic understandings of the classics, understandings associated in Ouyang's system with Confucius. Not only the correct interpretations of the classics but the classics themselves suffered grievously in the disorders of the late Zhou and the trauma of the Qin book burning; what survived to Ouyang and his contemporaries were just "fragments and remnants of the bibliocaust."[81] Separated as they were by "hundreds and thousands of years" from the world in which the classics were written, contemporary interpreters, Ouyang claimed, had little or no hope of understanding them directly. Ouyang did not think that the *Preface* preserved the teachings of Confucius perfectly or that Mao and Zheng always expanded faithfully on the *Preface*; nevertheless any potential link with the past appeared precious when contrasted with the entropic disorder and confusion that threatened to extinguish the understanding of the classics altogether.

The exegetical tradition centered on the *Preface* and Mao-Zheng was thus indispensable if only because it was the sole link between the interpreter and the past. But Ouyang also believed that the interpretations of the exegetical tradition were in large part correct. First, the traditional interpretations represented the efforts of many intelligences; they had the sanction of collective wisdom: "Since the Han, fragments have been collected, lost meanings expounded, and mistakes corrected. That the general outline [of the teaching concerning the Odes] was thus obtained and transmitted to the present day: how could this have been accomplished through the efforts of a single individual!"[82] The received tradition thus represented a collective accomplishment of the kind that no single intelligence could hope to duplicate or to do without.[83]

To this general reason for believing in the value of the exegetical tradition, Ouyang added another argument in favor of Mao and Zheng in particular.

There are many places where I doubt Mao and Zheng, but I would not dare to lightly revise them. Their teachings are not only to be found in their *Notes* and *Commentary*. It is a matter for regret that we cannot see all of their books and cannot survey all their points [*zhi*]. Now not having seen their books yet to want to pass judgment on their correctness or incorrectness is the same as not yet having heard someone's argument and to want to decide on the merits of their lawsuit. Is this something that one could resolve himself or cause the parties to accept?[84]

Although in places Mao and Zheng may seem to make unsupported, improbable, or just wrong claims, the student cannot for all that hasten to dismiss them ("lightly to make revisions"), since the lost works of Mao and Zheng may have contained support for claims that seem doubtful. The damage suffered by the exegetical tradition here served paradoxically to support the idea that it was authoritative and indispensable.[85]

Still, Ouyang acknowledged that the received tradition was revisable, for it was deeply flawed: confused, corrupted, and partial. It thus was necessary to specify not only the sources of the authority of the exegetical tradition but also the circumstances under which the tradition could legitimately be revised.

As for the arguments of earlier scholars—if they are not self-contradictory when examined in detail and if they are not found to be injurious to principle or harmful to the classic when tested against the words of the Sage [i.e., Confucius], and if, moreover, it is not absolutely necessary to change them, then what justification could there be for vainly creating heterodoxies and entering into polemics?[86]

Ouyang specifies two conditions for the revision of the tradition. First, the traditional interpretation had to be shown to be invalid because it contradicted itself.[87] Second, the formulation of a new interpretation required the positive guidance of an authoritative teaching: "the words of the Sage" (i.e., Confucius).[88] Thus there were two possible kinds of criticism of an authoritative exegetical tradition. The first criticized that tradition but did not venture to form a new interpretation to replace it; the interpreter left a "blank" (*que*).[89] The second kind of criticism, which we must suppose to be rarer than the first, not only criticized the exegetical tradition but also formulated a new interpretation on the basis of some other canonical authority.[90]

The formulation of the "Postface" has the merit of taking into account the authority of the received exegetical tradition on the one hand and of allowing for the possibility of its criticism and revision on the other. But like the iconoclastic maxims discussed above, this relatively conservative vision of the interpreter's role failed to do justice to the complexities of Ouyang Xiu's own hermeneutic practice. Ouyang Xiu by no means limited himself to the criterion of self-contradiction in his criticisms of the *Preface*, Mao, and Zheng; rather, he criticized the traditional interpretations not only when they contradicted themselves, but also when they contradicted various of Ouyang's understandings and beliefs concerning history, society, prosody, and the like. Nor did he limit himself, in suggesting new interpretations of the Odes, to those cases where he could rely upon the received teachings of Confucius for guidance. The hermeneutic method outlined in the "Postface" offered an account that did not mirror Ouyang Xiu's own practice.

The Disjunction Between Theory and Practice in Ouyang's Hermeneutic

Thus neither the iconoclastic nor the conservative version of Ouyang Xiu's hermeneutic theory can do justice to his own interpretive practice. How are we to understand this blindness, this inadequacy, on the part of so insightful an interpreter as Ouyang Xiu? And how are we to understand the disparity between the two theories, conservative and iconoclastic, that Ouyang articulated?

The hubris of Ouyang's iconoclastic theory is perhaps relatively easy to explain. In wrongly supposing that he had transcended his tradition, Ouyang illustrated the Gadamerian principle that every interpreter is limited by a "horizon" of expectations and prejudices. This horizon simply cannot be abolished by fiat and is not so much transcended as modified or replaced by another such constitutive, enabling set of assumptions.[91] But if such horizons are ubiquitous, they are also invisible. The hermeneutical horizon is not available for reflection—at least not until it is challenged by the encounter with a text or until one becomes methodologically aware of it through theory. Ouyang Xiu's hermeneutic horizon was constituted by assumptions like that of the uniformly paradigmatic character of the intentions inscribed in the Odes, and these assumptions remained undefeated if not unshaken by his encounter with the Odes.

Ouyang's conservatism, and the disjunction between his iconoclastic and conservative theories, was a more complex phenomenon. Perhaps we may simply understand Ouyang's conservatism as a function of aging. He Zeheng has pointed out that whereas the writings of Ouyang that deal with the authority of tradition in his youth and to some extent in his middle years tend in both practice and theory to be iconoclastic and radical, his later writings show a shift to a relatively conservative attitude that was less confident about the interpreter's ability to surpass the tradition and more positive about the value of that tradition.[92] James T. C. Liu has pointed out how in his political career Ouyang showed a similar mellowing; the ardent and idealistic supporter of Fan Zhongyan's 1044 reforms had become, by the time Ouyang and Han Qi (1008–75) and Fu Bi (1004–83) acceded to power in the 1060's, a cautious pragmatist.[93] It may well be that in the writings of his later years, Ouyang came to doubt the confidence of his earlier theory and practice.

There may have been other concerns as well. We know that Ouyang was conscious of the privilege that future generations would enjoy of judging his work.

In his later years Ouyang edited the pieces that he had composed over his lifetime, and he exerted himself bitterly in this. His wife stopped him, saying "Why do you torment yourself so? Are you still afraid of being scolded by your elders [*xiansheng*, literally those born before]?" Ouyang laughed, "It's not the scolding of my elders that I fear, but rather the laughter of posterity [*housheng*, literally those born after]."[94]

With his most creative years behind him, Ouyang may have instinctively sought to shield his own work from the iconoclasm of future generations ("As I remember, so will I be remembered"). In the "Postface," he laid down the principle of a hermeneutic less radical than the one he had initiated, a hermeneutic that would preserve not only the traditional exegesis of Mao and Zheng to which Ouyang still felt attached but also his own work on the Odes. As it turned out, however, it was not the theory of the "Postface" but the example of the interpretations and argumentation of the *Fundamental Significance* that was to be influential in the decades to come. The iconoclastic and critical motion that Ouyang Xiu initiated would not stop until it had rejected not only the interpretive tradition that Ouyang sought to preserve but also Ouyang's own partial criticism.

CHAPTER SEVEN

Subjectivity and Understanding

Although we think we govern our words, . . . certain it is that words, as a Tartar's bow, do shoot back upon the understanding of the wisest, and mightily entangle and pervert the judgement. So that it is almost necessary, in all controversies and disputations, to imitate the wisdom of the mathematicians, in setting down in the very beginning the definitions of our words and terms, that others may know how we accept and understand them, and whether they concur with us or no. For it cometh to pass, for want of this, that we are sure to end there where we ought to have begun, which is—in questions and differences about words.
—Francis Bacon, *The Advancement of Learning*

The eleventh-century transformation of classics studies involved on the one hand the loosening of the authority of the classical exegetical tradition and on the other the emergence of a new, general hermeneutical practice that attempted to rediscover the original force and significance of the classics. The preceding chapter focused mainly on the first element of this transformation in classical studies, that is, with Ouyang Xiu's struggle with the problem of the exegetical tradition and its proper function and weight in the hermeneutics of classical texts. This chapter treats the formulation of the Song transformation's second element, the new general hermeneutic of engagement and subjectivity as it developed in the hermeneutical maxims of three of the founding fathers of eleventh-century Neoconfucianism, the brothers Cheng Yi (Cheng Yichuan; 1033–1107) and Cheng Hao (Cheng Mingdao; 1032–85) and their uncle Zhang Zai (1020–77).[1]

The criticism of the received exegetical tradition and the formulation of the new general hermeneutic of subjectivity were complexly interrelated developments. As we saw in the preceding chapter, Ouyang Xiu's reflections on the problems of interpretation were largely concerned with the role and criticism of the received exegetical tradition and had relatively little to say about how to read the Odes as such. At the same time, his criticisms of the Mao-Zheng interpretations were founded on a new way of reading that foregrounded the literal sense of the text as utterance. In the teachings of Cheng Yi and his contemporaries, the situation was reversed. A new hermeneutic was expounded and promoted, and relatively little was said concerning the exegetical tradition as such. But the concern to develop a new hermeneutic stemmed in large part from a widespread perception that the exegetical tradition was no longer an adequate guide for understanding the classics.

The Breakdown of Exegetical Authority in the Eleventh Century

We saw in Chapter 6 that by the last decade of his life Ouyang Xiu had modified his youthful iconoclasm, so that his hermeneutic teachings explicitly asserted the value and indispensability of the exegetical tradition upon which he had always relied in his commentaries. Ouyang Xiu may have moved from iconoclasm to conservatism in his later years because he foresaw that the abolition of the authority of the exegetical tradition would result in an unrestrained criticism that swept away both what he considered to be genuinely valuable in the tradition and also his own contributions to the interpretation of the classics. But although Ouyang attempted to cast his criticisms of "Mao and Zheng" in a form that did not subvert the authority of those elements of the tradition he wished to affirm, he had initiated a process he could not in the end contain. The generations of classical scholarship that followed Ouyang's—that is, the cohort born around 1020 that included Zhang Zai, Wang Anshi (1021–86), and Liu Chang (1019–68); and more significantly those born in the 1030's, including not only the Cheng brothers but also the Su brothers, Su Shi (Su Dongpo; 1037–1101) and Su Che (1039–1112)— proved those fears to have been justified.[2] In the writings of these scholars, we find an attempt to formulate a hermeneutic of the classics that largely dispensed with the guidance of traditional exegetical authority.

The perception that the received exegetical tradition was deeply flawed and not a sufficient guide to understanding transformed the interpretation of the classics. One response was to press ahead with the foundationalist critique of the received exegetical tradition. In studies of the Odes, the next step in this direction was taken by Su Che, the younger brother of the famous poet Su Shi, in his *Shi jizhuan* (Collected commentaries on the Odes). The significance of the *Collected Commentaries on the Odes* was that it brought into the mainstream tradition of integral commentary the insights concerning the stratified character of the *Preface* first adumbrated by Cheng Boyu in the Tang. Su distinguished between the Upper and Lower Prefaces, retaining the former as a guide to interpretation and discounting the latter.[3] He believed that although the Upper Preface probably represented the authentic teachings of Confucius, it need not have been written by Zixia; any of Confucius's disciples who were knowledgeable about the Odes could have composed it. Moreover, he recognized that the *Preface* was attributed to Zixia because of *Analects* 3.8: "Zixia discussed the Odes with Confucius [at *Analects* 3.8], and Confucius praised him. So those who studied the Odes in later generations attributed [the *Preface*] to him."[4]

As for the Lower Preface, the classicists of the Han "wanted to explicate [the Upper Preface] and so added on to it, confident as they were in the rightness of their explanations."[5] The repetitions and prolixities of the Lower Preface show that it did not come from a single hand; rather, it represented the compilation of a tradition by Wei Hong (first century C.E.). Although Su rejected the Lower Prefaces, he was not forced for all of that into any substantially new interpretations of the Odes; the Upper Prefaces, which in his view remained authoritative, still specified readings that were essentially conservative and traditional. Su Che did not, for instance, follow Ouyang Xiu in his readings of those Odes that would be called "debauched" by the Southern Song; he treated them in the traditional fashion as uniformly normative and drew no distinction between the poem's persona and its author.

In his rejection of the latest, and thus presumably most fallible, layers of the exegetical tradition and in his attempt to found understanding upon some more primitive and uncorrupted authority, Su Che was motivated by the same foundationalist vision that we saw at work in the hermeneutic of Ouyang Xiu. Although Su's intentions were not radical, his analysis had subversive effects that, like Ouyang Xiu's attempt to distinguish between the authentic and inauthentic Prefaces, outran the intentions of its author.

Another response to the breakdown of the exegetical tradition, never greatly developed, was to accept and even to celebrate the notion that the meanings of the classics could not be specified by a single interpretive orthodoxy. Here again, Su Che was exemplary. In an early letter, Su said that "the Way of the Sage may be likened to the remote mystery of the mountains, the sea, the marshes, or the fens." Into these enter woodsmen, hunters, and prospectors, who find there great trees, rich game, and precious jewels. Each supposes that he is able to exhaust the riches of the mountains and the sea, but the mountains and the sea are always full and can never be exhausted. The classics are similarly inexhaustible; indeed they were purposely made in such a way as to stimulate a diversity of opinion by Confucius himself.

He established the Six Classics and set people to seeking [the Way] there. He hoped that it would be understood only after deep thought. Thus he did not make his doctrines explicit, and caused everyone to employ their talents to seek them. Thus it is said that "The humane will call it humane, and the wise will call it wise."[6] . . . Now let those who are humane devote themselves to its humanity and those who are wise devote themselves to its wisdom, and let those who are great reflect on its greatness but not forget its lesser aspects, and those who are petty delight in reaching its minor features while submitting themselves to the great, each exhausting his strength as he relies upon his talents in order to reach to those points that are most subtle and intricate. Then the empire will devote itself to the teachings [of the classics] without fatigue.

Later ages did not understand this intention. They thought it a tragedy that there was a multiplicity of differing doctrines and that students found them difficult to understand, and they therefore brought up the subtle words of the Sages and analyzed them according to the private opinions of one man. And so the scholarship of commentaries and subcommentaries dominated the empire. As a result, students became steadily more lax, and the teachings of the Sages steadily more obscure.

Now let everyone base himself on the differences and agreements of the commentators, and allow each person to read widely and look everywhere, to distinguish rights and wrongs, and to discuss permissibility and impermissibility, inferring from the finer and the more commonplace to the most delicate and subtle. Then our discussions will be even more profound, and we will hold [to the Way] even more securely.[7]

In this piece, which may have been a response to the imposition by Wang Anshi of his own interpretations as a state orthodoxy in the 1070's, Su Che drew upon a tradition that allowed for the notion different personalities would find different meanings in the classics and that did not classify those personalities into a hierarchy of moral perfection and incompleteness.[8] Su was willing to accept, even to celebrate the possibility that the classics had no single correct meaning, but rather significance that varied according to the needs, interests, and abilities of the interpreter. Such an approach took it for granted that the orthodox exegetical tradition could not exhaust the meaning of the classics.

Interesting and significant though these developments may have been, the most important response to the breakdown of exegetical authority was neither the foundationalism nor the interpretive pluralism represented by Su Che; indeed it consisted not in any program for the resolution of the problems associated with the received exegetical tradition, but precisely in a turn away from those problems and toward a new dimension of hermeneutic concern. This turn was exemplified by Zhang Zai, Cheng Hao, and most especially Cheng Yi— thinkers who were not really interested in the development of or even the criticism of the exegetical tradition, and whose indifference spoke more eloquently of the disrepute into which the tradition had fallen than would the most vociferous criticism. Cheng Yi and the others were not interested in telling their students which commentaries to follow or even in criticizing those commentaries; rather, they wanted to tell them how to read.[9]

Significance, Literal Significance, and Intentions

Before the Song, there was no general hermeneutic of the classics; rather, there were characteristic, largely independent traditions of problems and approaches associated with each of the classics. Cheng Yi and his contemporaries developed their ideas about reading and understanding in the course of comments about specific texts, to be sure, but they also spoke in general terms about how to read; in their recorded conversations, for the first time, *dushu* "reading books" becomes a frequent topic. Moreover, when the eleventh-century Neoconfucians talked about reading books, they tended to use a single hermeneutic vocabulary. This vocabulary and the hermeneutic as a whole had much in common with the Mao tradition.

Like the traditional hermeneutic of the Odes, the new general hermeneutic of the Song took as its ultimate goal not the manifest content of the text but the impulses and personalities that lay behind it. As in the earlier hermeneutic, these original impulses were to be reflected upon and internalized by the student. Just as in the earlier hermeneutic, this was to result in the transformation of the very personality of the reader.

The Neoconfucian general hermeneutic of the eleventh century focused above all upon the specification of the subjective attitudes the reader was to bring to the text. On the one hand, Cheng Yi and those who thought like him cautioned against the approach to the classics they associated with the *Correct Significance* commentaries, both as that hermeneutic was exemplified in the *Correct Significance* itself and as it was displayed in the characteristic method of those who devoted themselves to that work. On the other hand, they attempted to specify in positive terms the attitudes they thought would make possible an authentic relation with the classics. In both cases—in both their negative and positive programs—they tended to fall back upon a pair of terms discussed above in connection with the hermeneutic of Ouyang Xiu, *yi* "intentions" and *yii* "significance."

As we saw in Chapter 6, the *yi* was the intention of an author or a speaker, defined either relatively narrowly as the aim behind a given speech act or utterance or more generally as the intentions that led, say, to the composition of one of the classics. In Warring States language theory, and medieval and early Song hermeneutics, *yi* "intention" was a more limited notion than *zhi*, which embodied and suggested a whole disposition of the personality. In the thought of Cheng Yi, the notion of the *yi* was expanded to include much of what had been implied by the older term: "Those who read ought to observe the intentions of the Sages in making the classics, as well as their ultimate concerns [*suoyi yongxin*] and the reasons why they were able to become Sages and we have not" (*Jinsilu* 3.39).

The reader was to seek the "intentions" that lay behind the text—not the general intentions or dispositions ("aims" or attitudes) referred to as *zhi* in the earlier theory but "the intentions of the Sages in making the classics." From an understanding of this sort of intention, however, the reader was to grasp the rest of what the earlier concept of *zhi* comprised, that is, what Cheng called "the ultimate concerns" of the sage/author (*shengren suoyi yongxin*). Although the text was in a proximate sense the result of an intention to say or do something, that intention was in its turn a consequence of its sagely author's moral concerns and general orientation toward the world. And from an understanding of the general orientation of the author, the student was to infer the character of the Sage, since the Sage's ultimate concerns were a function of his character. Thus the reader was, in a series of metonymic moves, to restore from the intentions relatively narrowly defined all of what had been implied by the earlier term *zhi*.

Yii "significance," on the other hand, was used to refer to the meanings that words had in and of themselves apart from their contexts or the intentions of their authors. Unlike *yi* "intention," which belonged to texts or passages but never to individual words, *yii* could be and often was a property of individual characters. *Yii* combined with a variety of terms to form compounds in the language of the eleventh-century Neoconfucian hermeneutic. For instance, Cheng Yi spoke of the "significance of the classic" (*jingyii*),[10] and Ouyang Xiu often referred to the "significance of the Ode" (*shiyii*).[11] The most common of these compounds, and for us perhaps the most interesting, was *wenyii* "literal significance." The relation between the literal significance of a text and the intentions of its author was a constant theme of the Neoconfucian hermeneutic of the eleventh century, both as an abstract question and as a matter of practical hermeneutical concern.

Before we can turn our attention to the relationship between literal significance and intention, however, there is a problem we must resolve concerning the reference of the term *wenyii*. In both of the other two compounds mentioned above, we understand the unit to which significance attaches, even if we are not entirely sure what the expression as a whole means. But to what level of the text does *wen* apply?

Cheng Hao's gloss on a famous passage in *Mencius* is instructive here. The passage in question is the one in which Mencius commented upon the correct way to expound the Odes: "Those who speak of the Odes should not let their literary qualities [*wen*] harm the words [*ci*], nor take the words in such a way as to harm the aim [of the poet]."[12]

Mencius's use of *wen* in this passage can be illuminated by reference to another passage where he says of the *Spring and Autumn Annals* that "the affairs [it treats] are those of [Duke] Huan of Qi and [Duke] Wen of Jin; and its form [*wen*] is that of a history."[13] By *wen*, Mencius seems to have meant the form or genre of a text, with its attendant conventions. In the case of the first quotation above, the danger to which Mencius referred had to do with what we should call the "literary" features associated with the form of the Ode. Thus Mencius goes on to cite as a negative example a reading that would take the hyperbole of Ode #258

> Of the masses of people who remained
>   of the Zhou,
> There is not one left.[14]

to mean that literally none of the Zhou people survived the drought that is the subject of the Ode. Mencius's point was that the Odes' way of being a text—their "textuality"—was such that they would occasionally say things that were not literally true. In such cases one had to pay attention not to the literal wording of the passage but to the author's aim in making the Ode and the particular statement in question.

If this reading is correct, then Mencius was making a point about the relation of literal and intended meaning, a subject that greatly interested Cheng Yi and his contemporaries. Cheng Hao's gloss on the passage, however, did not seize on this theme but on another: "In 'one should not let their *wen* harm the *ci*,' *wen* is [used as it is used in] *wenzi* ["characters"]. One character chosen out—that is *wen*. When they form sentences, then that is *ci*. It will not do to explain the Odes character by character."[15] For Cheng Hao, the contrast was not between figures of speech and intended meanings but between parts and wholes. Words (*wen*; "characters") had meaning only in sentences (*ci*), and it was not possible to correctly interpret the characters or words that made up a given Ode apart from their contexts in whole sentences.

Cheng's reading seems to depart from the sense of the original Mencian passage; on the other hand, the meaning of that original passage is by no means certain. The point is less about Mencius than about the eleventh-century thinkers with whom we are concerned: for Cheng Hao at least, *wen* meant "individual graph" or "character," at least in certain contexts. Since *yii* "significance" was simply the meaning that characters possessed in and of themselves apart from their intended meaning in a given situation, it seems that the *wenyii* of a text consisted of sum of the significances or meanings of its consituent individual characters.

One important aspect of the exegesis of the classics and of texts generally in China had always been the glossing of characters; that is, glossing both the actual words—"the vocabulary"—of the text and the graphs used to write those words. There are problems with archaic or unfamiliar words in the reading of any ancient text, and there were and are also a host of problems with Chinese texts that derive from their use of logographs: rare and variant forms, "loan characters," graphic corruptions, taboo characters and the like, as well as the problem confronting the beginning student of recognizing even the standard characters for words that he already knows. The explication and understanding of "the characters" was an essential first step in the study of any text.

It might seem that understanding the "significances of the characters" meant understanding the meanings of the individual characters of a passage only—"mastering its vocabulary," as we should say. But sentences and larger units as well also had *wenyii*. Western language theory, with its focus on syntax natural to inflected languages, has tended to see the meaning of a sentence or passage as entailing something more than simply a summation of the meanings of its constituent words, that "something" being provided by the grammar of the sentence. Chinese language theory tended, on the other hand, toward an accumulative rather than a combinatorial view of sentence meaning that did not problematize the notion of grammar. Rather, it conceived of sentences as strings of "names" (*ming*). There was thus no contradiction in thinking of *wenyii* or "literal significance" as something that could be a property of sentences or passages but that was constituted by the meanings ("significances") of individual characters.

I have been translating *wenyii* as "literal significance" rather than "literal meaning" in order to preserve the distinction between "intention" (*yi*) and "significance" (*yii*) that, in my opinion, was crucial to eleventh-century Neoconfucian hermeneutical thought. In some ways, however, "literal meaning" would be a more appropriate translation for *wenyii* than "literal significance." Like the Chinese term *wenyii*, "literal meaning" can be understood both in terms of its historical, etymological background and in terms of the system of contrasts and associations in which it functions. Historically speaking, the term "literal" is cognate with "letter"; it implies a letter-by-letter fidelity to and understanding of the text that is analogous to the character-by-character understanding presupposed by the Chinese *wenyii*. *Wen* itself means "graph" or "character" ("letter"). In terms of the semantic system of relations in which it is meaningful, "literal" once again resembles *wenyii* in that it both contrasts with and serves as the foundation for another type of meaning.

But a difference is important here. The English term "literal meaning" (and its analogues in other European languages) implies a contrast with a figurative meaning that is essentially metaphorical and typically displaced to another ontological plane of truth. The contrast between "literal meaning" ("literal significance") and "intention," on the other hand, opposes manifest meaning and an original, historical intention that serves to animate and unify the text.

The Relation Between "Intention" and "Significance"

For those of Cheng Yi's generation who reflected upon the problems of reading and interpretation, the *wenyii* presented a problem, and the relation between literal significance and the intentions of the text was conceived in a variety of ways. For some thinkers like Ouyang Xiu, the *wenyii* was relatively important. As we saw in the preceding chapter, Ouyang Xiu contrasted an originating, unifying intention with a complex and potentially confusing significance. At the same time, the contrast as articulated by Ouyang did not entirely favor its first term. To be sure, intentions served the controlling function in Ouyang's hermeneutic of specifying and defining the possible significances—the possible interpretations—of a given term, image, or text. Moreover, they provided purchase for a reading that resisted the subversive implications of the literal significance or manifest content of the Ode.

As we saw, however, in our discussion of what I called the iconoclastic theme in Ouyang's thought, one of the most important ways in which to approach those intentions was precisely through the (literal) significance of the text itself: those interpretations of "Mao and Zheng" that, though sanctioned by tradition, nevertheless failed to do justice to the manifest literal significance or meaning of the Ode were rejected. Thus Ouyang Xiu argued concerning the Mao-Zheng interpretation of "Shu yu tian" (Mao #77) that in it "the literal significances of the first and last stanzas are not of a kind [i.e., do not agree], and so it can be seen that this [interpretation] does not represent the original intention [*benyi*] of the poet."[16] And as the title of his work suggests, Ouyang was perhaps interested in intentions in the final analysis largely as a means to the specification of the correct, "fundamental" significances of the Odes.[17]

In the teachings of both Zhang Zai and Cheng Yi, the distinction between *yi* "intention" and (*wen*)*yii* "(literal) significance" became fully thematic, indeed one of the central problematics of their hermeneutical thought, but their views on the topic contrasted sharply. Zhang Zai tended to discount the importance of the literal significance of a text: "The *Documents* is most difficult to read [because] it requires a mind that is sufficiently capacious. If [on the other hand] you want only to understand the literal significance of the text [*wenyii*], that is not difficult."[18]

Or take this quotation, which may come from either Cheng Yi or Cheng Hao: "For those who are devoted to study, the important thing is not to be hindered by the text [*wenzi*]. Even if one misunderstands the literal significance [*wenyii*], there is no harm so long as he is conversant with its principle [*daoli*]."[19] This rather cavalier attitude toward the literal meaning of the text was to earn the "Song scholars" the opprobrium of the historically minded philologists of the Qing, and indeed it is unclear what sort of existence the "principle" of a text can have, or how it could be understood, apart from its concrete expression.[20]

The opinion that was in the event to prove most influential, however, was the compromise position articulated by Cheng Yi. In this view, both the literal significance of the text and its animating intentions were deserving of the attention of the student, if not in the final analysis of equal value: "Whenever one is reading a text [*wenzi*], he must first understand its literal significance [*wenyii*]. Only then can he seek its intention. There has never been a case where someone saw the intention [of a text] without having first understood its literal significance."[21]

In this passage Cheng Yi defended the usefulness of the literal significance against those like Zhang Zai who denigrated it. As the literal meaning or significance of a text, the *wenyii* was a legitimate and necessary object of concern and the indispensable means by which the intentions were to be grasped. At the same time, however, Cheng Yi took it for granted that it was the intention, not the literal significance of the text, that mattered. Cheng Yi thus envisioned reading as a kind of two-stage process. In the first stage, the student mastered the literal significance of the text—its philological and historical problems. The specification of this literal significance depended at least in part upon judgments about the intentions of the maker of the text, those intentions serving to limit and specify the plurality of significances any text could have. But the intentions were not important simply as a means by which to limit and specify significance; rather, as in the earlier hermeneutic of the Odes, the motivations of the text (its intentions or aim) were the ultimate goal of reading, to be reflected upon and internalized by the student.

Enmired

The new general hermeneutic of subjectivity enunciated by Cheng Yi and others in the eleventh century was a reaction against the prevailing hermeneutic orthodoxy. In the view of Cheng Yi, classics studies in his day had become empty and formalized, leading (at best) to success in the imperial examinations rather than to Sagehood. Thus Cheng Yi was concerned not only to explain to his students the approach he felt they should take to the classics—what we might call his positive hermeneutic—but also to caution them against the dangers of what he called "chapter and sentence" (*zhangju*) exegesis.

When Cheng Yi and his associates discussed chapter and sentence exegesis, they spoke of the danger of becoming *ni*.[22] This term, which originally meant "mire" or "to be enmired," had a volitional sense as well: "to cling (uncritically) to something," as in the compound *nigu* "to cling uncritically to what is old." In a *Jinsilu* passage, for example, Cheng Yi says:

In reading books, one must not cling to [*ni*] a [single] significance [*yii*] [simply] because [the characters] are the same or similar. Otherwise every word will be a hindrance. One must observe the intention of the context and of the direction [of the piece]. For example, "beauty" in [the saying] "He whose goodness is extensive and solid is called a beautiful man," and "beauty" [as it is used] in the *Odes* are different things.[23]

It is clear that in this passage becoming "enmired in the significance" meant insisting upon or clinging to a view of language where words were univocal in their meaning and trying to formulate understandings that would embrace all their occurrences.[24] Such readers remained "stuck" at the level of what we might call dictionary meanings, unable to see the animating intentions of the contexts in which individual words get their meanings.

In another passage from the *Jinsilu*, however, to "cling to the literal significance" (*ni wenyii*) seems to mean something more than being limited to an accumulative, dictionary understanding of a text.

Those students who do not cling to the literal significance [often] turn away from it completely, whereas those who understand the literal significance [often] become enmired and inflexible [*zhini er bu tong*].
For instance, [in telling the story about] when Zizhuo Ruzi was a general, Mencius intended only that one ought not to rebel against his teacher. But some people have insisted upon trying to understand from the story how to serve one's ruler. Or when Wan Zhang asked about Shun's repairing a granary and digging a well: Mencius just replied with the general idea [*dayi*—"the general intention"]. But some people have insisted on trying to understand how Shun came

out of the well or how he came down from the granary. That kind of study just wastes the mind's energy.[25]

Cheng Yi mentions the danger of "departing from" the literal significance as well as that of becoming enmired in it, but both examples he gives are of the latter failing. Both take the *Mencius* as a point of departure. The second of the two has to do with the myth of Shun, second of the legendary Sage-kings of antiquity, a prototype of all those who accede to high office by reason of their virtue and a particular favorite and concern of Mencius (the passage to which Cheng Yi is referring here, 5.A.2, is one of a series in which Mencius clarifies various points concerning Shun's story). In one legend, Shun demonstrates his filial and fraternal piety even in the face of attempts by his father and brother to burn him in a granary and to bury him in a well. When he is asked about these stories, Mencius "replies giving the basic idea"—the point of the stories—which is to illustrate Shun's filial and fraternal piety and his sincerity. To speculate on details not contained in the story—how Shun escaped from the granary or the well—is to suppose that the story has a life of its own apart from the point that it is intended to impart. This seems clearly to be a case of becoming "stuck" (*ni*) at and not progressing beyond the level of literal significance.

The other example that Cheng Yi gives of someone being inflexible and enmired in the literal significance is more complex and more interesting. In the story as it is given at *Mencius* 4.B.24, Zizhuo Ruzi is sent by Zheng to make a raid on Wei, and Yugong Zhisi is dispatched by Wei to intercept him. On the expedition, Zizhuo Ruzi falls ill, unable even to grasp his bow. Upon learning from his charioteer that they are being pursued, he announces, "I am a dead man." But Yugong Zhisi, Zizhuo Ruzi's pursuer, had been the student of Zizhuo Ruzi's student and is thus obliged to spare his teacher's teacher. Upon overtaking the Zheng party, he therefore fires at Zizhuo Ruzi four arrows whose heads he had first knocked off. Having thus discharged his obligation to his teacher as well as "his lord's business," he returns to Wei.[26]

It is not clear at first why Cheng Yi insists that in citing this story "Mencius intended [to make clear] only that one ought not to rebel against his teacher" and not to say anything about "how to serve one's ruler"; if we take the story to address both of these concerns, the ethical issues are more complex and perhaps more interesting. When, however, we consider the context in which this story is embedded, we see that Cheng Yi is correct in maintaining that Mencius's intention was simply to illustrate a point about the student-teacher relationship. There are two narratives at *Mencius* 4.B.24, one concerning Yi the archer and his death at the hands of his student Peng Meng, and the other the story about Zizhuo Ruzi and Yugong Zhisi related above. As the translations of James Ware and D. C. Lau make clear, Mencius tells the Zizhuo Ruzi story in order to support his claim that Yi himself had a share of blame in his fate; Zizhuo Ruzi provided a counterexample of someone who chose his students well.[27] In this case, then, the error of those who would "cling to the literal significance" was not of failing to interpret but rather of interpreting too much. Their readings were not chastened and unified by an understanding of Mencius's intention in telling the story.

The focus on intentions thus served to control the kinds of interpretations that might be made of a text. This function of the focus on motivations had a long history in the hermeneutic we have been exploring, beginning with Mencius's use of the term *zhi* to control the readings of the Odes (see Chapter 3) and including Ouyang Xiu's similar use of *yi* "intention." But it would be a mistake to suppose that the denigration of *wenyii* "literal significance" had to do only with its potential for generating superfluous meanings and that the chief function of the *yi* in the Neoconfucian hermeneutic was to specify meanings. That impulse to specify meaning was for the most part marginal for the thinkers we have been discussing (Ouyang

Xiu was exceptional in this regard). Rather, the point of focusing on intentions and the associated discounting of literal significance was that a focus on the latter led the reader to approach the text—so the Neoconfucian hermeneuticians thought—in a niggling, anxious, and ultimately futile manner that ruled out the possibility of an authentic, consequential engagement there.

Application and Understanding

Cheng Yi hoped to be transformed by the classics. That transformation was to be achieved first by reflecting upon the texts of the classics as deeds of words—that is, in terms of their intentions—and second by internalizing those intentions. This kind of reading could not be accomplished through, indeed was thwarted by, a niggling attention to the literal significance of the text. Rather, the student had to approach the text in a spirit that sought always to realize its transformative potential. These goals were to be accomplished by, and flowed from, a commitment on the part of the student to the classics, a commitment in which the student took the classics seriously, as having a real bearing upon his existential situation rather than simply as being the objects of speculative exegesis.

Cheng Yi insisted that one who read without being transformed had not really read the classics: "People today do not know how to read. . . . Take reading the *Analects*. If before, when he has not read [the *Analects*], he is this person, and if after reading he is still this person, then he does not know how to read" (*Jinsilu* 3.30).

A problem in both the Western and the Chinese traditions concerns the relation between application in the sense of an essentially contemplative self-understanding and application in the sense of action—that is, of action or behavior that is changed.[28] It is certainly possible to imagine a situation in which we understand or perceive the application of some text to our own situation but have not succeeded in changing our life or behavior or character. Part of the attraction of the *Odes* as a classical text was the obviation of this problem that it promised, and Cheng Yi borrowed an element of this tradition surrounding the *Odes* in the following passage from the *Jinsilu* (3.38): "With the *Analects*, there are those who after reading it feel nothing at all. There are those who after reading it find one or two passages there that they like. There are those who after reading it know [enough] to be fond of it. And there are those who after reading it are not aware that their hands are dancing it and their feet tapping it out." This passage gives a staged progression of levels of accomplishment in reading, culminating in a type of understanding described in terms borrowed from the "Great Preface."[29]

It may seem that Cheng Yi's statement involves a notable misprision of the *Preface* passage he quotes, for whereas that passage describes the process by which a text (the Ode) was generated, Cheng was clearly concerned with the reading of a text. It is tempting to see here the contrast between the creative phase of a civilization (i.e., the dynamic and creative vitality of the Hundred Schools period and of the Western Zhou) and the scholastic spirit of an age that conceived reading, rather than writing, to be the paradigmatic activity. Leaving aside the fact that the *Preface* was itself the product of the Han academy, we can trace a deeper ambiguity in this formulation. There is a sense in which the earliest theory of the Odes as represented by the *Preface* dispenses with, or rather does not happen upon, the distinction between creation and repetition or recitation—an identity concisely illustrated by the ambiguity of the term *zuoshi* "to create an Ode," but also "to recite an Ode," the two senses being for all practical purposes indistinguishable in many early contexts.[30]

It was this idea of reading (or recitation, for the two were closely linked) as reenactment that inspired Cheng Yi's statement. The best readers were those who internalized and applied the text so well that the distinction between understanding and application—between knowledge and action, in another, more famous formulation—disappeared, and the reader was inspired by the text in a manner that obviated the possibility of a lag or failure in its implementation. Thus was the old promise of the Odes and the music with which they were associated rejuvenated in a new general hermeneutic.

Easiness and Difficulty

Just as the focus on *wenyi* "literal significance" was linked in the new hermeneutic with a constrained and niggling approach to the text, so the focus on intentions was associated there with a reading that was playful and relaxed. In the teachings of the Chengs and Zhang Zai, this orientation was expressed in the injunction to be "easy" (*yi*): "Whenever one [seeks to] understand a text, let him only make his heart easy [*yi qi xin*]; then he will naturally see the principle [there in the text]. [This] principle [in the text] is nothing other than the principle of man [*renli*]. It is very clear, like a smooth and level road" (Cheng Yi; *Jinsilu* 3.25).

As with so many other aspects of the new general hermeneutic, the notion that a calm and easy attitude was the sine qua non of real engagement with the text was given a relatively early and particularly salient development in discussions of the *Odes*. The *Odes* was a difficult text, which presented a host of potentially distracting and frustrating philological problems. At the same time, the Odes had, somewhat paradoxically, historically been associated with the ideal of "easiness" both in the moral accomplishment of their authors and in their effects upon readers. These themes are well exemplified in two quotations from Zhang Zai.

Zhang [Zai] said: The aims of the poets were as straightforward and easy as they could be, and so they did not say anything difficult or forbidding. If one seeks [the meaning of the Odes] in a straightforward and easy way, then one's thoughts will range far and wide. The more difficult and uncomfortable [the spirit in which one approaches the Odes], the more shallow [one's interpretations]. In general, what [the poets] talked about was what was before their eyes; the significance [of the Odes] is contained therein.[31]

Zhang [Zai] said: In seeking to understand the Odes, the important thing is a straightforward easiness. One must not be too overcautious. One should seek to match the poet's emotional nature—his gentility, his equipoise, and his maturity. Now if one is too overcautious, his heart will be constricted before [he begins] and he will be unable to see the poet's emotions.[32]

The reader's easiness reproduced the "easy" moral accomplishment of the authors of the Odes (who said the right thing spontaneously) and foreshadowed the easy transformation of the reader's own personality. This is one aspect of the utopianism of Neoconfucian thought: by a simple subjective change to being "easy," one could, it was claimed, enter into an authentic relation with the text that would result in the most advanced moral accomplishment. In the thought of Zhu Xi a hundred years later, the discovery of the recalcitrance of the self to such a simple change would result in a more complex vision, as would the further erosion of the (unacknowledged) exegetical consensus that permitted the claim that all the Odes were easy to understand.

Savoring the Text

Cheng Yi believed that understanding came about "naturally," so long as the student was unimpeded by fixed views or by an anxious and pedantic attention to questions of the literal meaning of the text and its discursive exposition. Thus in the first instance one came to understand the text by removing the subjective obstacles that artificially impeded understanding. At the same time, there were positive steps that the student could take in order to put himself in touch with the animating intentions of the text. Perhaps the most important term in this respect is *wanwei*: literally, "to play with and savor" the text.

Although the term came to mean simply "to reflect on something thoroughly," an exploration of its etymological background will reveal its more profound implications and associations. The first element of the compound, *wan*, has two connected meanings. First it means *xinong* "to play (with something)." To *wan* is to turn something—perhaps, as the jade radical at the character's left suggests, a gem or precious trinket—over in the hand. The kind of knowledge that such a gesture provides is tactile, physical, palpable—intimate without being visual as such—and involves a sense of the heft, the resiliency, or the three-dimensional thingness of an object.

This kind of intimate knowledge is relevant to the second sense of the term *wan*. This the *Cihai* dictionary defines as *yanxi* "to study or practice," and it quotes the following passage from the "Great Appendix" to the *Yijing*: "That in which he joys and *wan*s are the remarks [attached to] the lines."[33] Legge has for *wan* in this passage "study";[34] and a more recent translator renders it as "rolls [in his mind]."[35] The two senses are of course related: in this hermeneutic, one is to study or learn a text by trying its nuances, "turning it over in the mind," much as one might turn over or toy with a bauble.

A similar range of meanings is found with the second term of the compound, *wei*. First, and most commonly, it means "savor" or "taste." Like many Chinese nouns, it can also have a verbal sense: "to taste." But in Cheng Yi's usage, it often means something very like "meaning"; indeed, it became one of those privileged terms—like *yi* "intention," *zhi* "aim," or *li* "principle"—for the ultimate rather than the proximate significance of a text.[36] As with "intention," words provide the indispensable means of access to understanding: "Take the words of the Sages and savor them."[37] But as in the intention / literal significance contrast, it is possible to be seduced by language: "Later students were adept at reciting the words but forgot the savor [*wei*]."[38]

The point to notice is the peculiar coexistence of accessibility and difficulty in the notion of *wei*. The *wei* is difficult because it can be missed—it is not necessarily on the surface. This notion, that there is a second understanding to which we must be directed or to which we must direct ourselves, is fundamental to the notion of a hermeneutic and to exegesis, no matter how that hermeneutic may insist upon the transparency of the text. The notion of *wei* as the deferred object of understanding has this much in common with all notions of meaning, and in particular with the ideas concerning intentions and aims that populate early linguistic and hermeneutic theory in China.

At the same time, the notion that it was the savor of the text that reading sought implied a peculiarly non-problematical relation between the reader and the text. The taste of something—of food or drink—is there for us in a particularly immediate way. We do not have to strive, still less somehow to discard our naive ways of tasting, in order to savor something; rather, we have only to allow it to speak to us, to allow itself to reveal itself to us. The only thing that can prevent savor from revealing itself is the sort of anxious and preoccupied attitudes castigated by Zhang Zai and Cheng Yi. By the same token, a relaxed and unconflicted attitude that "plays" (*wan*) allows the savor of something to reveal itself. The analogy from European culture that is immediately called to mind is the careful, appreciative exploration of a fine wine by a connoisseur, where the oenophile plays with the wine in the mouth in order to appreciate all its subtleties and nuances, especially those that do not immediately reveal themselves. When applied to the reading process, the two terms suggest the sort of reflective and careful attitude that I will translate as "savoring the text."

Wanwei and Recitation

Cheng Yi often insisted that his students "savor the text." But what did this mean for Cheng Yi in practical terms? We can distinguish two dimensions to the process of *wanwei*, one relatively intellectual and inward, the other more overt and "behavioral." Let us begin with the latter.

The *Jinsilu* (3.44) ascribes to Xie Xiandao (Xie Liangzuo, 1050–ca. 1120) the following passage concerning Cheng Yi's older brother, Cheng Hao.[39]

> Xie Xiandao said, "Mr. Mingdao [i.e., Cheng Hao] was good at discussing the Odes. He never engaged in the explanation of chapters nor the explication of verses,[40] but rather would just freely and easily explore the savor [of the text], crooning it from beginning to end. He was thereby able to make people understand.
> "[Regarding Ode #33, which says,]
>
>> I look at that sun and moon;
>> Long and longingly I think [of you].
>> The road is far;
>> How will you be able to come?
>
> [Cheng Hao said,] 'Longing earnestly!'
> "[Regarding the last verse of the same Ode, which says,]
>
>> You gentlemen do not know of my
>>   virtuous conduct;
>> I have not been wicked or greedy.
>> Why are you not good?
>
> [he said,] 'In the end, it returns to correctness.'"
> [Xie] further said, "Bochun [i.e., Cheng Hao] often discussed the Odes. He never made even a single philological gloss. Sometimes he would simply repeat one or two characters, emphasizing [them] as he read [the Ode] over. This would enlighten people."[41]

The interpretation of this passage is made more difficult by its colloquial elements. The passage as a whole, however, seems to consist of two versions of the same saying, separated by two comments of Cheng Hao's on the "Xiongzhi" Ode (Mao #33). Both versions of Xie Liangzuo's description of Cheng's exegetical practice have the following structure:

1. Cheng Hao was fond of discussing the Odes / often discussed the Odes.
2. He never engaged in the traditional exegesis of the Odes, which consisted largely of the detailed explanations of individual characters.
3. On the contrary, he simply read the Ode over, and
4. His auditors then understood the Ode.

The interesting thing about this passage for our present purposes is what it can tell us about Cheng's practice of "exploring the savor" of the text and about his hermeneutical practice generally. It seems that exploring the savor of a passage was not necessarily an "internal," private activity, but something that could be done out loud, for other people. Although Cheng may have made his texts clear by giving the sort of brief comments we find here (or, if we accept Wing-tsit Chan's reading of the passage, by changing one or two characters in a passage, presumably to easier, more familiar ones), in the main he communicated and perhaps in a sense derived his understanding of the passage in question simply by reading it aloud—that is, by modulations of tone and emphasis. He thus restored to the text the animating and defining presence of the living voice, removing ambiguities and opening the way to understanding.

That the recitation of the Odes was not only a means for communicating understanding but also a means for achieving understanding is suggested by the numerous passages, both in Cheng Yi's works and in those of other writers, that recommend recitation to the student.[42] Recitation was in its turn closely linked for these thinkers with memorization: "Take the words of the Sages and explore their savor; put them in your heart and memorize them."[43] Zhang Zai made the point even more strongly: "You must memorize the classics. Even if you had the wisdom of a Yao or a Shun, to read [the classics] over silently is no better than receiving directions from a blind person or a deaf person. Thus if you can remember them, you can explain them, and if you can explain them, you can practice them. So when beginning to study, you must recite and memorize."[44]

Wanwei and Reflection

From other passages, it is clear that *wanwei* also involved a kind of intellectual reflection upon the text. Consider, for example, *Jinsilu* 3.36:

> If those who read the *Analects* take the disciples' questions as their own questions and take the Sage's replies as something they themselves have heard today, then they will naturally get something [out of the text]. If one is able to search deeply in the *Analects* and the *Mencius* and reflect upon their savor, then one's cultivation will complete itself and one's *qi*-endowment will become excellent.

In this passage, the phrase "to search deeply . . . and reflect upon their savor" (*shenqiu wanwei*) resumes the admonition to imagine the disciples' questions as one's own and Confucius's answers as something that one has heard today. To do so involves not just an imaginative projection into the situation of the inquiring disciple but also the effort to imagine the relevance of those questions to one's own situation—to understand, as we might say, the existential force of the questions. This injunction to discover the application of the dialogues to one's own concerns is resumed and made explicit by the admonition to treat the Sage's words as something one has heard; the addition of "today" (*jinri*) particularly emphasizes the notion that the words of the Sage are to have application to one's own real, present situation and not merely to some abstract or speculative concern. The practice of savoring the text thus involves the exploration of its meaning, including its significance for the existential situation of the reader. Preserving the concrete dimension of Cheng Yi's language, we might say that savoring the text involves finding and exploring the connections between the text and one's own experience.

The theme that savoring a text entails its application to the existential situation of the reader is further developed in *Jinsilu*

3.37: "All those who read the *Analects* or *Mencius* must thoroughly reflect upon their savor, taking the words of the Sages and applying them to themselves. One cannot just take them as so much talk. If people can just read these two books applying them to themselves, they will receive much benefit throughout their lives."

Again in this passage we find *wanwei* "to explore savor" in a relation of apposition that allows us to better understand the meaning of the phrase, but here the term is negatively as well as positively defined: the reader must not treat the text "as so much talk." This would trivialize the text; it would be to treat it as the coin of everyday discourse, which was not intended for and did not receive the kind of reflective and sustained attention that the classics deserved. Moreover, in Chinese as in English, to treat the text as so much talk means to leave it in the realm of just talk. Both of these senses are connected; as we noted above, for Cheng Yi an integral element of an understanding of the text's meanings in their fullness is an appreciation of their consequences. Indeed, one could say that this is the only real meaning the text has. Cheng Yi contrasts throughout an understanding that could be called "pragmatic"—that is, consequential—with one that fails to grasp and actualize the consequences of the text. Such pragmatic understandings can be accomplished only through a real familiarity and extended engagement with the text. The relation is not one-way, but dialectical or circular: the application of the text is made possible by taking it seriously, but "taking it seriously" entails the attempt to apply the text.

Savoring the text thus involved recitation and memorization on the one hand and reflection upon its nuances and implications on the other. It was the centerpiece of a hermeneutic that employed neither an authoritative exegetical tradition nor a methodological "decision procedure" to bring the reader into a right relation with the text. Rather, it taught that this aim was to be achieved by approaching the text in the correct frame of mind, the easy and unconflicted reflectiveness named by *wanwei*.

The new general hermeneutic adumbrated by Cheng Yi and his fellows both drew upon and transformed the medieval hermeneutic of the Odes. Like that hermeneutic, it aimed to transform the personality of the student in a way that finessed many of the most persistent difficulties associated with the mobilization of the emotions and the implementation of the teachings contained in texts. This was to be accomplished by internalizing the motivations of the text: the *zhi* in the earlier Odes hermeneutic, the *yi* in the Song case. Reading was to transform the subjectivity of the reader. But in the Song hermeneutic, a transformed subjectivity became not only the effect of but also the means to effective reading. For Cheng Yi, the adjustment of subjectivity was conceived in largely negative terms: as the removal of the obstacles that a niggling approach to the text presented to its understanding, and the achievement of that state as the solution to the difficulties of understanding and being moved by the text. By the time of Zhu Xi a century later, the difficulties of that "simple" injunction to be easy had revealed themselves, and in his hermeneutic a more complex and psychologically insightful view emerged.

CHAPTER EIGHT

Zhu Xi's New Synthesis

Reading is secondary. Principle [*daoli*] is complete in every person; it is not something that can be added on from outside. This being the case, when the sages insist that one must study a given book, it is because although one possesses this principle, he must experience it. What the sages speak of was gained by experience.

—Zhu Xi, "The Way to Read"

T he twelfth century was a turning point in the history of classics studies generally and in the studies of the Odes in particular. On the one hand, the criticism, pioneered by Ouyang Xiu, of the received exegetical tradition continued; in the field of Odes scholarship this resulted in the discrediting of the foundation of the received, orthodox tradition, the *Preface to Mao's Odes*, and the acknowledgment that certain of the Odes—notably the so-called "debauched Odes" (*yinshi*)—expressed longings, joys, and sorrows abhorrent to the puritanical strain in Confucian morality. At the same time, the new hermeneutic of engagement adumbrated by Cheng Yi and other eleventh-century thinkers was given a detailed and more complex formulation. The great Neoconfucian teacher Zhu Xi (1130–1200) played an important role in both of these developments: as in so many other areas of Confucian thought, Zhu Xi's views on the nature and composition of the Odes and his hermeneutic teachings came to constitute a new orthodoxy.[1] In this chapter I first describe the process by which the medieval view of the Odes was criticized and ultimately overthrown in the Song. Then I turn to Zhu Xi's hermeneutic, and finally I offer some tentative conclusions concerning these two phenomena and their possible connections.

The Discovery of Depravity in the Odes

As we saw in the previous two chapters, in the middle and late eleventh century thinkers like Ouyang Xiu and Su Che undermined the authority of the *Preface* by pointing out its essentially composite and heterogeneous nature. Ouyang and Su did not for all that wish to discard the *Preface*, and the conclusions they drew from its criticism were relatively conservative ones. The effect of their criticism, however, was not at all conservative, and within a few decades a very different view of the *Preface* and of the Odes was being developed. The first surviving examples of the next stage in the criticism of the *Preface* appear in the writing of Chao Yuezhi (1059–1129). Chao argued in his four "Essays on the *Preface to the Odes*" that none of the *Preface* could have been composed by the poets themselves or by Zixia or Master Mao.[2] Rather, it was probably put together by Wei Hong from materials perhaps ultimately deriving from Zixia and Master Mao.[3] As a sample of his argumentation, let me give the fourth, possibly fragmentary section of his "Essays on the *Preface to the Odes*":

Mencius, Xunzi, Zuo [Qiuming], Jia Yi, Liu Xiang,[4] and all the Han Confucians often discussed the Odes, and yet there is not a word in any of them concerning the *Preface*. Then the creation of the *Preface* was late indeed.

Mencius said: "In the 'Kai feng' Ode [Mao #32], the fault of the relative is minor." Yet the *Preface* says "In Wei dissolute mores were prevalent. Even the mother of seven sons could not rest content in her house [because she desired to remarry after her husband's death]."

[According to the *Preface*] this was the mother of seven sons, not a proper wife to her husband nor a proper mother to her sons. What fault could be greater than that? Are Mencius's words wrong? If Mencius's words are not wrong, then the *Preface* is mistaken.[5]

Chao employs a two-pronged strategy against the *Preface*. On the one hand, he argues on purely historical grounds that the *Preface* cannot be a pre-Han document because it is not mentioned in the works of late Warring States and early Han Confucianists. On the other hand, he argues on doctrinal grounds that one of the interpretations of the *Preface* is invalid by showing that it contradicts the relatively more authoritative teachings of Mencius.

It is noteworthy that this first, flat rejection of the *Preface*'s claims to interpretive authority appeared in an essay rather than in an integral commentary on the *Odes*. Typically, such insights were expressed first in relatively "free" genres like the essay or poetry before being assimilated and worked out, often several generations later, in the interpretations of an integral commentary. In a similar way, perhaps the first explicit avowal that certain of the Odes inscribed non-canonical attitudes appeared not in a work of integral exegesis but in an essay authored by Chao Yuezhi's elder cousin, Chao Buzhi (1053–1110). In the Preface (*xu*) to his *Continuation of the Chuci* (*Xu Chuci*), this well-known song (*ci*) writer and protégé of Su Shi said in defense of Qu Yuan and his poem that "not all the Odes were made by sages or worthies. . . . The Three Hundred Pieces are mixed [*za*], but they cannot be discarded."[6]

The language of Chao's "Preface" closely resembles that of Ouyang Xiu's poem to the "Odes-studying monk" (see Chapter 6). The language of that poem was in turn associated not only with skeptical questions about the uniformly normative character of the Odes but also with the denial of such implications.[7] The significance of Chao Buzhi's comment lies in its relatively more "serious" context and in its frank acknowledgment that "not all the Odes were made by sages or

worthies"; in this Chao makes explicit what was only tacit in
Ouyang Xiu's poem. It may be significant that, like Ouyang
Xiu, Chao Buzhi was a writer of *ci* songs and thus perhaps
quick to recognize a love song when he saw one. He also surely
was aware of the criticisms of the *Preface* being leveled by his
cousin and others around this time. Indeed, that the first sustained attack on the authority of the *Preface* as a whole and the
first explicit acknowledgment that not all the Odes inscribed
paradigmatically normative attitudes were produced by two
cousins is appropriately emblematic: it does not seem possible
to assign to either the criticism of the received tradition or the
emergence of new, more "empirical" readings of the Odes a
simple priority; these two dynamics reinforced one another in
a complex, dialectical relation.

The Southern Song

The criticism of the *Preface* did not end with the acknowledgment that some of the Odes inscribed attitudes inconsistent with Confucian morality. In the writings of certain figures who came to maturity in the first decades of the Southern
Song (1127–1278), this claim was developed and supported by
arguments that anticipated those of the great critical scholars
of the Qing and Republican eras in insight and sophistication.
In addition, the rejection of the *Preface* in its entirety and the
acknowledgment that some of the Odes were "debauched"
moved into the exegetical mainstream and were developed in
works of integral exegesis on the Odes.

The most important figures in the early Southern Song revision of Odes studies were Cao Cuizhong and Zheng Qiao.
Cao Cuizhong (*jinshi* 1124) was the son-in-law of Li Guang
(1077–1155), a high official and disciple of Liu Anshi
(1048–1125). Cao's refusal to receive the notorious Qin Guan
led to Li's dismissal from office.[8] Thereafter the two lived in
retirement, Li Guang devoting himself to studies on the

Changes and Cao to his annotation of the *Odes*. The bibliographical chapter of the *History of the Song* (*Songshi yiwenzhi*)
lists a *Fangzhai shishuo* (Fangzhai's explanation of the Odes) in
30 *juan*, but the work is no longer extant.[9]

According to Wang Yinglin, Cao Cuizhong was interested
in Three Schools scholarship.[10] Although Cao gives no sign in
the surviving fragments of departing from the orthodox view
that the Odes were all normative, he does criticize the *Preface*,
and his sophisticated account of the composition of that text
resembles modern theories developed by biblical scholars in
the West and by critical historians like Gu Jiegang in China
about the growth and elaboration of traditions.

Cao claimed that the *Preface* was the product of a long process of transmission and elaboration by Han scholars: "You
must know that when the *Mao Commentary* first circulated,
there was not yet a *Preface*. Once Mao had ascribed the *Preface*
to Zixia, then his school passed it on one to the other, each
adding to it the teachings of his teacher, until Wei [Hong]
wrote it down. Later, others added to it yet again. It did not
come from a single hand."[11]

To bolster his argument that the *Preface* was created after the
Mao Commentary, Cao pointed out that the two texts sometimes disagree, as in the case of the "Gaoyang" Ode (Mao
#18).

Regarding

> On the lamb furs,
> Five many-thread tresses of white silk

the *Mao Commentary* says: "The ancients used white silk thread to
decorate their clothes; they did not fail to conform to the forms. The
great officers wore lamb coats at home." It says this and nothing
more. Yet the *Preface* says "Those in office were frugal and upright.
Their virtue was like a lamb's." Moreover, the interpretation of
tuishi ["they withdraw for their meal"] to mean "they reduced their
rations" began with [Zheng] Kangcheng [i.e., Zheng Xuan]. Mao
did not intend that.[12]

If it proves anything, the fact that two texts disagree shows only that they are not from the same hand; there is nothing in the simple fact of disagreement to indicate which is earlier and which later. It would be possible, for instance, in the case under discussion to draw from the discrepancies between the *Preface* and the *Commentary* the conclusion that the *Preface* was the earlier text (indeed Qiu Guangting reached this conclusion in the tenth century).[13] It may be that the fact of disagreement between the two texts simply served to confirm a predisposition on Cao Cuizhong's part to see the *Preface* as late. In this and in his other two examples, however, the *Preface* is shown to be more prolix and moralizing than the *Commentary*, and this seems to have indicated to Cao that the *Preface* was the later text. Moreover, his account, quoted above, of the manner in which the *Preface* was composed describes the sort of institutional context in which traditions tend to elaborate and to become more schematically moralizing. The argument thus suggests modern accounts of the elaboration and development of traditions, especially those transmitted orally, as well as the methodological principle in the history of traditions and texts that (all else being equal) the "fuller"—more elaborated and prolix—of two parallel texts is probably the later. If, however, Cao did hold to this background picture of how traditions grow and change, he did not make it explicit. Even in this relatively sophisticated and insightful argument, the crucial assumptions remain only tacit.

In the work of the great critical historian and scholar Zheng Qiao (1104–62), much of what had been only implicit or hinted at in earlier studies of the Odes was fully developed. Zheng treated the Odes in several of his works. He frequently discussed them in his magnum opus, the *General Treatise* (*Tong zhi*), and he composed at least one work of commentary on the Odes, the *Refutation of Absurdities Concerning the Odes* (*Shi bian wang*). There are also passages on the Odes in the *Discussion of the Profundities of the Six Classics* (*Liujing aolun*), a work of questionable authenticity that may nevertheless reflect some of Zheng Qiao's thought.[14]

Zheng Qiao was famous for his vehement criticism of the *Preface*, which he pronounced the work of a "rustic ignoramus."[15] He marshaled a host of arguments to show that the *Preface* was the work of the Eastern Han scholar Wei Hong, among which we can distinguish three types.

First there were historical arguments. If the *Preface* was really by Zixia, then why did it appear in the state of Zhao, rather than in Qi or Lu, the home of Confucius and his disciples? The *Preface* refers to the loss of the words of certain of the Odes;[16] this shows that it must have been composed after the Qin bibliocaust. The statement, made in the Preface to the Ode "Shangshang zhe hua" (Mao #214) that "in antiquity, officers held their offices hereditarily" could not have been made before the Qin, when offices ceased to be so.[17] These arguments show a keen critical sense of a type that had not hitherto been applied to the criticism of the *Preface*.

There are, moreover, arguments that show a real understanding of the way that texts like the *Preface* were pieced together from earlier works.

Whenever the author of the *Preface* had a text on which to rely, he would specify the person [to whom the Ode was supposed to refer], and when there was no such source, he simply said what the intention [of the Ode] was.

[The *Preface*] takes the Ode "Hou ren" [Mao #151] to satirize Duke Gong [of Cao; r. 651–617]. Before Duke Gong was Duke Zhao [r. 660–652], and so [the *Preface*] takes the "Fuyou" Ode [Mao #150] to satirize Duke Zhao. In fact, there is no record of [the accomplishments or failures of] Duke Zhao [in the historical sources], but he was unlucky enough to come close to Duke Gong in the royal genealogy, and so was used by Wei Hong to fill out his account.[18]

But Zheng did not, if the following passage is authentic, simply suppose that the *Preface* was cobbled together out of written sources.

Some say that the *Preface* is detailed and circumstantial and not something that Wei Hong could have created [out of whole cloth]. [I] say, if you mean that Wei is supposed to have made it up out of nothing, then even Confucius could not have done it, but if you suppose that it was made by repeating [*song*] [older] teachings about the Odes, then even Wei could have done it easily. The "intentions" [that he gives] were the teachings of Mao and of generations of teachers of the Odes; Wei simply glossed and expanded upon them.[19]

This represents the third and most interesting argument that Zheng Qiao marshals against the traditional view of the Odes. These arguments are based on an account of how the misunderstandings he aims to refute might have arisen as the Odes came to be increasingly central to Confucian textual and doctrinal culture. Some of these arguments were already familiar: for instance, he points out the attribution of the *Preface* to Zixia must stem from *Analects* 3.8, where Confucius praises the acuity of that disciple in understanding Confucius's interpretation of the Odes. Others were more original.

Zheng recognized that in a situation where the exegesis of texts has become institutionalized, there will be a powerful impetus to create meaning or "significance" (*yii*): "Scholars take it as their task to seek out significance."[20] As a result, they overinterpret. For example, in the case of the "Guanju" Ode (Mao #1), scholars overinterpreted the image of the osprey, which was simply something that the poet saw: "That the osprey is on the island in the middle of the stream stands for [*yu*] the fact that the good and beautiful girl cannot be had. What need is there to take the osprey as the girl? What sense does it make for Mao to claim that it symbolizes the joy of the girl in the virtue of her lord or that there is nothing in which they were inharmonious?"[21]

Similarly, the names of the three divisions of the *Odes*, the *feng*, the *ya*, and the *song* had been overinterpreted.

When characters were created, it was on the basis of the shape or form [of the object represented]. Now *feng*, *ya*, and *song* were all sounds [i.e., they were all types of music]; they had neither shape nor form and so lacked characters. In each of these cases, another character was borrowed. For instance, the character for *feng* originally represented the *feng* that means "wind," as in "wind and rain"; whereas the character [borrowed] for *ya* originally represented the *ya* that means "crow." . . . But whoever made the *Preface* would insist on searching for meaning in these borrowed graphs![22]

Zheng also realized that Confucius's comments on the "Guanju" at *Analects* 3.20 and 8.15 concerned its music and not the meaning of its words.

When [Confucius] said, "The coda of the 'Guanju'—how floodlike does it fill the ear!" he was speaking of the splendor of its sound; and when he said, "The 'Guanju'—joyful but not abandoned; sorrowful but not harmfully so!" he was speaking of the harmonious qualities of its sound. . . . The Han established erudites to discuss the Odes, who concerned themselves only with passing on their moral significance [*yiili*]. Thus when Wei Hong came to make the *Preface*, he took "joyful" to mean "joyful to get a good girl" and "not abandoned" to mean "was not debauched by her beauty"; and he took "sorrowful" to mean "sorrowing at isolation" and "not harmfully so" to mean "without harm to the good." If one explains the "Guanju" in this way, then what is the point of "how floodlike does it fill the ear"?

Thus Zheng could say, "When the music of the Odes was lost, then [discussions of their] moral significance arose!"[23]

But certainly the most significant and consequential aspect of Zheng Qiao's scholarship on the Odes was his blunt comment, made in connection with the Ode "Jiang Zhongzi" (Mao #76), that "these are the words of a debauched eloper; they have nothing at all to do with the business of Duke Zhuang [of Zheng] and Shu Duan."[24] This was the clearest statement to date of the claim that not all the Odes represented the words and thoughts of Confucian paragons. It was perhaps the first attempt to apply this insight to the actual interpretation of the Odes. But Zheng Qiao, for all his critical acumen and erudition, was not particularly interested in the Odes either as literature or as elements in the moral curriculum; it remained for others to work out the hermeneutical consequences of this realization.

By the middle part of the twelfth century, the notions that the *Preface* could not serve as a guide to the interpretation of the Odes and that some of the Odes expressed non-normative attitudes were widely held. Cheng Dachang (1123–95) devoted the ninth, tenth, and eleventh of his "Essays on the *Odes*" to a detailed attack on the authority of the *Preface*.[25] Wang Zhi (1127 or 1135–89) composed an integral commentary on the Odes entitled *A Summary of Teachings on the Odes* (*Shi zong wen*) that rejected both the Upper and Lower Prefaces, without, however, differing from them in all its interpretations. The spirit of the age was summed up in the weary worldliness of a remark of Lin Guangchao (1114–78): "There is more than one intention [*yi*] [expressed] in the Odes. . . . Just as with the *Zuo Tradition*, the good things are few and the bad things are plentiful."[26] This was not a happy discovery. As in so many things, Lin seems to say, the world had turned out to be more unpleasantly complex than he had been led to believe. There was no single, normative intention or personality unifying the Odes. Rather, one confronted the fragmenting and disturbing possibility that many of them had been written not by sages but by morally depraved people. The privileged focus of the reading of the Odes was threatened, if not lost.

Of course, not everyone in twelfth-century China agreed with the radical criticisms of the *Preface* and the traditional view of the Odes that it embodied, and works of essentially conservative scholarship continued to be written. One of the most popular and influential of these works was the *Notes on Reading the Odes in a Family School* ([*Lüshi*] *Jiashu du Shi ji*) of Lü Zuqian (1137–81).[27] Lü Zuqian's work is of interest not only because it contains Lü's own more or less traditional interpretations of the Odes, but because it also quotes from an early work on the Odes by the man who was to make of the insights of the Song iconoclasts a new orthodoxy, the great Zhu Xi.[28]

Zhu Xi

It is well known that Zhu Xi changed his mind about the Odes; he himself commented on a number of occasions about his struggle to free himself from the tyranny of the traditional interpretation of the classic.

When I made my first commentary on the *Odes*, I followed the Minor Prefaces. When the explanations did not make sense, I made up justifications for them. Later I felt unsatisfied [with these explanations], and the second time I glossed the *Odes*, although I still retained the Minor Prefaces, I also disputed them from time to time. But in the end, I still could not see the poet's intention. Finally, I realized that I had to dispense with the Minor Prefaces altogether, and then everything went smoothly. I washed away all traces of the old explanations, and the intentions of the Odes lived again.[29]

By the time he composed the present text of the *Collected Commentaries on the Odes* (*Shi jizhuan*), Zhu Xi had become convinced that the interpretations of the *Preface to Mao's Odes* not only could not serve as a guide to the Odes but actually presented obstacles to understanding them. What is more, he had come to agree with Zheng Qiao that certain of the Odes, most especially some of the Airs collected from the states of Zheng and Wei, were indeed "debauched": the products not just of bad historical moments, but of personalities who had themselves been corrupted by the misrule of their society.[30]

Zhu Xi salvaged the exemplary status of the Odes by developing the view first broached in the *Hanshu* that the Odes had been collected from among the people by emissaries of the court: "I have heard that of what are called 'Airs' among the Odes, most come from the songs and ditties of the villages and backways. They are what men and women sang to each other, each articulating their feelings [*qing*]."[31] As such, the Odes must necessarily contain some poems at least expressing attitudes that are not uniformly normative; these "debauched Odes" (*yinshi*) poems had been included in the collection by Confucius, its compiler, in order to serve as negative examples.

[*Analects* 2.2 says:] "As for the three hundred Odes: if one saying can cover them, it would be 'No swerving in your thoughts.'" Many people say that all the thoughts of the authors of the Odes were unswerving in this way. This is wrong. As for the Lauds, of course there is no swerving. But among the Changed Airs and Changed Elegantiae, there are depraved and debauched places. Still, it is only "no swerving in the thoughts" that can sum up the significance of the Three Hundred pieces. There are of course many worthy maxims in the Odes, but this one is the most important. The reason that Confucius included both [normative and debauched Odes] when he edited the collection is because he wanted to make apparent the good and bad mores [behind the Odes]. The Sage taught people in this way as well.[32]

Given the heterogeneity of the Odes, how were they to be read? Zhu Xi maintained that the function of the debauched Odes was to warn the reader against potential errors and to inspire self-reflection. Still, he did not recommend that they be intensively studied: "When reading the Odes, read for the general meaning [*dayi*]. Take, for instance, the Odes of Wei: of course those among them that discuss the events of the day ought to be studied carefully. [But] what is the point [literally 'the interest' *yisi*] of digging into the debauched Odes of Zheng? If in one day you read five or six, that will be fine."[33]

Although Zhu Xi acknowledged that the Odes contained certain poems expressing non-normative attitudes, his hermeneutic was not for all that oriented toward those Odes. Rather, he focused, and he urged his students to focus upon, those Odes that could foster and elicit correct emotional and moral responses.

Zhu Xi's Hermeneutical Teachings

The most important source for Zhu Xi's hermeneutic teaching is the great collection entitled *Zhuzi yulei* (Master Zhu's conversations categorically arranged).[34] In this vast work, comments and conversations of Zhu Xi are organized ("classified") on a topical basis into some 140 chapters, covering the whole gamut of Neoconfucian concerns. Of particular interest for the history of hermeneutics are the tenth and eleventh chapters, which are entitled "Dushu fa" (The way to read). These two chapters together contain some 245 sections, many of which contain two or more comments or anecdotes.* They allow a detailed, complex, and discursive exposition of Zhu Xi's hermeneutic on a scale unmatched by anything earlier in the tradition.

Zhu Xi's hermeneutical teachings can be daunting in their complexity and scope. True to his pedagogical intent, however, Zhu Xi frequently attempted to sum up his teaching in relatively short and memorable formulas or précis. In what follows, I discuss Zhu Xi's hermeneutic by focusing on one such formula and discussing, as necessary, related concepts.

In its most concise form, what I call Zhu Xi's three-part program runs as follows: "Read less, and recite [what you do read] until utterly familiar. Turn it over [in your mind], and apply it. Don't imagine things or calculate gains [to be realized by study]. Make these three constants" (10.35). Each of the teaching's three parts either consists of or contains a four-character phrase of the type so common in Chinese proverbs, sententiae, and literary texts, and each of the first two of these four-character phrases is composed of two grammatically parallel bisyllabic expressions. The teaching's form was intended to facilitate its memorization and retention: the student

---

*I refer to these sections by citing first the chapter number and second a number designating their order within the chapter; "11.1" thus refers to the first section of the eleventh chapter.

was to make of the teaching a kind of slogan, reflecting upon it, repeating it over, and drawing out its implications.[35]

"Read Less, and Recite Until Utterly Familiar"

The first element of Zhu Xi's three-part program was the admonition to *shaokan* "read less." In its various guises, this simple piece of advice was one of the most frequently repeated of Zhu Xi's hermeneutical dicta.

Regarding books, one ought to read less, but to learn them very well.   (10.37)

In reading, you must reduce the amount covered but increase the effort you apply. If you are able to read two hundred characters, read only one hundred, and make a ferocious effort to understand those one hundred.   (10.39)

In reading, one must not be greedy, but must rather seek mastery [*jingshu*]. If today you are able to read one page, then read only half a page; and use the energy [saved] to read the first half page twice.   (10.40)

It is worth heeding Zhu Xi's injunction here, to pause to consider carefully the implications of this terse dictum. Reading less is not always easy; all the constraints and pressures of modern life conspire to hurry us over the texts we read. This is true not only of texts in the workaday world, but even of those literary or religious texts that are the typical objects of hermeneutical attention. To treat the text as something other than an instrument or means, as something other than the object of a kind of technology of reading, is to resist all those forces in the modern world that conspire to subordinate every activity to a calculus of costs and benefits.

These same forces were at work in Zhu Xi's world as well. Those who were engaged in study, either with the goal of passing the imperial examinations or in connection with the Neoconfucian project of self-cultivation, confronted an overwhelming mass of material. Students (like many of Zhu Xi's) preparing to take the imperial examinations were expected to have studied not only the Confucian classics, but also the dynastic histories and poetry.[36] Those engaged in the Neoconfucian program of self-transformation for its own sake faced an even more daunting agenda. True, Zhu Xi took up and promoted Cheng Yi's suggestion that the Four Books could provide a relatively concise, privileged access to the teachings of the classics; for those whose circumstances or occupations limited the time they could devote to study, such a truncated curriculum might suffice.[37] The serious student was, however, committed in Zhu Xi's view to go on from the Four Books to the mastery of an enormous amount of material. In addition to the Thirteen Classics themselves, the student was to study the exegetical tradition (11.206), including even the commentaries of Wang Anshi (11.197), and both the "standard" dynastic histories and Sima Guang's epitome (11.234).[38] Confronted with this mass of material, Zhu Xi doubtless spoke for his students when he said: "There are so many books! If you just read along, when will you ever finish? You must make a great effort, for not even one item can be omitted. Even those texts that ought already to have been read have not been, not to mention all the others" (10.32).[39] Little wonder then that in a fashion which seems to us quite modern, the men of the Song approached these problems technologically, availing themselves of examination aids and précis or experimenting with "speed reading."[40]

In the face of these pressures, Zhu Xi insisted that his students reduce, rather than increase, the amount of material covered in a day. Besides advising his students to "read less" (10.35–37), he told them to "reduce the scope" (*xiao zuo kecheng*) of their studies (10.39) and not to be "greedy for quantity" (*tanduo*) (10.40–42). He emphasized the need to read "carefully" (*zixi*) (10.74–79), and he often stressed the necessity of understanding the text sentence by sentence, section by section: "In reading books, one must concentrate. If you are reading this sentence, then understand this sentence. If you are reading this section, then understand this section. You must see right to the bottom of this section [*jiande ci yi zhang chele*] before going on to the next section" (10.52).

He further insisted upon the value of review, claiming: "When you read a text, you must do so carefully and in detail [*zixi*]. Even if it is something you have read before, when reviewing it, you must do so carefully and in detail. Read [only] two or three sections every day. Not the places where you have questions [*yichu*], but rather the places where you have none: that is where you should put your energies" (10.74). There must have been something surprising and counterintuitive about this advice to respond to the overwhelming burden of the tradition by reading less. Indeed it is difficult to escape the conclusion that Zhu Xi was being deliberately provocative in his insistence that his students slow the pace of their progress in this way.

These admonitions must be understood in terms of one of the structuring themes of Zhu Xi's hermeneutic teaching: the contrast, sometimes explicit but always presupposed, between two types of reading. One type was superficial, dry, and futile; the other engaged, possessed of an "inexhaustible interest,"[41] and transformative. Zhu Xi habitually identified the first relation to the text as typical of "people today" (*jinren*);[42] I will call it "modern reading." The second, more desirable reading was not as a rule named, but we will not be unfaithful to the ideal nor to the vocabulary associated with it if we deem it "deep reading."[43]

It would be difficult to exaggerate the importance for Zhu Xi and his disciples of the contrast between deep and modern reading or the clarity with which it was drawn. To read deeply was to be engaged productively in study, the central activity of the Neoconfucian project. Given the view of reading that originated in the medieval hermeneutic of the Odes, reading well—reading deeply—was not just a means to moral transformation; it was itself constitutive of that end. Although the deep reader encountered moments of difficulty and even confusion, and although deep reading demanded from the student hard effort and determination, still it was presented by Zhu Xi as an experience of ease, intellectual excitement, and personal renewal. The student who read deeply and well was changed by that very experience, experiencing the sensation of "godlike" power and elation that was Neoconfucianism's most seductive promise.[44]

Modern reading, on the other hand, was both fruitless and subjectively uncomfortable and discouraging.[45] In contrast to the deep reader, who discovered a wealth of interest in the text,[46] the hapless modern reader found the text "dry" and uninspiring.[47] Unlike the deep reader, who as it were peeled away the layers of the text (10.80), "penetrating to the bottom" of the sentence, passage, or work, the modern reader "floated" (*qingfu* [10.14], *fanfanran* [10.39]) over the surface of the text; he could find no purchase in the texts that were supposed to inspire him and change his life.

"Reading less" was important because to do otherwise—to rush through ("over") the text—ensured that one's experience would be inauthentic and superficial. In reading slowly and less, on the other hand, the student read as the deep reader read. Such a practice did not itself constitute deep reading in the same way that its opposite ensured a superficial experience of the text, but reading less allowed for the possibility that engagement would take place, creating as it were a space in which deep reading could occur, in which understanding could come.[48] To read less (and thus slowly and more carefully) was a kind of existential bet on the part of the aspirant deep reader, who had through an effort of the will to resist his anxious desire to rush through the text, in the hope that by reading as the deep reader read he would experience the text as the deep reader did.

Linked with "read less" in the first part of Zhu Xi's three-

part program was the injunction to *shudu* "recite [the text] until utterly familiar." Reading less was important because it allowed the student to sink into the text, to explore its depth and
complexities. Zhu Xi sometimes portrayed this process as a
passive one, in which the reader could only "await" understanding.[49] But there were steps a reader could take to facilitate
understanding; perhaps the most important of these was to recite (*du*) the text until it was utterly familiar (*shu*). The mastery
of the text that resulted from this process was prized because
it facilitated reflection upon the meaning of the text, because
it was closely identified with the idea of the internalization of
the intentions of the Sages, and because it allowed for the
ready reproduction of the text, a goal prized both as a symbol
and for its practical utility.

The term *shudu* is, like *shaokan* "read less," a compound
composed of an adverb and a verb. The first term, *shu* (also
pronounced *shou* in some contexts), can be variously translated as "cooked" or "processed," "ripe" (as of fruit),
"sound" (as of sleep), or "very familiar" (as of people or
texts). In this expression, the term is used adverbially to mean
something like "thoroughly" or "until done." *Du*, the second
element of the compound, is the first word in the title of chapters 10 and 11 of the *Yulei*, the "Dushu fa." This title derives
from the phrase with which Zhu Xi began so many of his
comments, *dushu* "(in) reading books." In such contexts, *du*
meant simply "to read"; it was synonymous with other terms
like *kan* (elsewhere "look") and *guan* (elsewhere "observe").
Often, however, Zhu Xi meant by *du* the practice of reading
aloud, chanting, or reciting: "When reading books [*dushu*],
the important thing is that you must read them aloud [*du*]; it
will not do simply to think [*si*] [about the text]. When you read
aloud [literally, 'when you read in your mouth' (*kouzhong du*)],
then your heart will be at ease and the principle of the text will
reveal itself. I myself began my studies in just this way; there
is no other" (10.120).[50]

Thus *du* was recitation in contrast to silent reading. In Zhu Xi's view, silent reading was typical of modern readers, whereas oral recitation of the text was characteristic of the ancients as well as of deep readers. The distinction between moderns and the ancients was a flexible one in Zhu Xi, often more mythic than historical. In the case of oral recitation, however, Zhu Xi located the transition to modernity with some precision: sometime after the Northern Song, with the advent of readily available and inexpensive printed editions, it came about that the classics were no longer transmitted (*xiang-shou*) by recitation without reference to a written text (*ansong*) (10.66). Before that time, books were relatively rare and hard to obtain; they were prized, recited, and memorized (10.67). As with the transition to modern reading generally, the transition from the oral recitation of texts to the silent reading of printed editions implied and was connected in Zhu Xi's mind with a series of associated dichotomies: public, communal recitation versus private reading; sectarian piety and doctrinal orthodoxy versus speculative exegesis and facile iconoclasm; external voice versus internal thought.

The recitation and internalization of the text were closely linked in Zhu Xi's thinking with its memorization; indeed one of the most important marks of knowing a text well was the ability to "remember" it (*ji, jide*). For a number of reasons, Zhu Xi and his disciples highly prized the ability to effortlessly recall a studied text. It freed the student from the written page and enabled him to reflect upon the words of the classic at any time (10.69), and it was understood to be the concrete proof of the successful internalization of the text's intentions. Remembering texts was also important in the imperial examinations. These examinations placed a premium on the ability to recognize and recall passages from the classics and their authoritative commentaries, and the preparation for them involved committing large amounts of material to memory. Zhu Xi's disciples often complained to him about their inability to remember the texts they read or asked him how they could improve their memories,[51] and it was in connection with the memorization of texts that Zhu Xi made some of his most audacious claims.

> Long ago, Master Chen Lie was upset that he had no memory [*wu jixing*]. One day he read in the *Mencius*: "As for the way of study it is just this: seek the heart-mind that you have lost."[52] Suddenly enlightened, he said, "I have never recovered my own heart-mind. How could I remember the books I have read?" Thereupon he closed his gate and did quiet sitting, never reading, for a hundred-some days in order to recover his heart-mind. Thereafter when he went to read, he lost nothing even after just one perusal.   (11.110)

In this passage, the ability to remember is the very emblem of an authentic engagement with the text. The claim that this goal could be reached as a result of a single, Zennish transformation must have been alluring, and it suggests the intensity with which the goal was desired.

It is interesting, given this intense interest in being able to recall texts, that Zhu Xi rarely spoke about or advocated "memorization" (*bei*) as such.[53] Indeed he sometimes condemned the practice.[54] It is not difficult to see why: "memorization" seemed to aim only at a mechanical reproduction of the words of the text, whereas "mastering" (*shudu*) the text involved internalizing its intentions.[55] The structuring contrast is one with which we have become familiar; in comparison with the intentions of the text, its actual wording (*wenyii*) was contingent and almost trivial. Memorization of important texts like the classics was like studying with the aim of passing the exams, a travesty of real study; rather, the ability to remember what one had read was to be a side effect of a deep and authentic engagement with the text.

Zhu Xi made the point through the example of a merchant who, although he could not read, knew all his accounts by heart.

> Once there was an old man who was illiterate. But he remembered every detail of his accounts for years back. He would repeat them over, and when they were written out and he would repeat them

again, there was never an error. This was because he was conscientious and concentrated [*zhuanyi*]; he did nothing else, and so he remembered. Scholars today are unable to remember what they have read. They habitually rely upon brush and ink and characters, and so they forget more and more. (11.182)

Because the merchant cared intensely about his money, he remembered his accounts; a student similarly concerned with the texts he studied would remember them too.[56] The ability to remember, like the deep reading for which it stood, was a function of the subjective attitudes of the student.

The first part of the three-part program was concerned with the mastery of the text. By limiting the amount of text studied, the student allowed himself to become utterly familiar with the text. Reciting it over and over to himself, he did not so much memorize it as internalize it; his ability to remember the text was a function of, rather than a means to, his familiarity with the text.

"Turn It over in Your Mind, and Apply It"

Like the first part of the three-part program, the second element was also made up of two grammatically parallel bisyllabic expressions. The first of these two expressions, *fanfu* "to turn (something) over and over," appears relatively rarely in Zhu Xi's hermeneutical dicta. In one passage, we find it combined with the key term of Cheng Yi's hermeneutic, *wanwei*, in the phrase *fanfu wanwei* "to turn (the text) over and over (in your mind), and reflect upon its savor" (10.34).[57] Elsewhere it appears paired with *shudu* "to recite until familiar."[58] Like *wanwei*, *fanfu* implied a close consideration of the text akin to coming to know the three-dimensional heft and "thingness" of an object.

Tiyan "apply it (to yourself)," on the other hand, was one of a family of compounds beginning with the word *ti* "embody" that reappear throughout Zhu Xi's teachings. These terms have been discussed by Tu Wei-ming in an article enti-

tled "'Inner Experience': The Basis of Creativity in Neo-
Confucian Thinking."[59] Most of the terms Tu discusses, including *tiyan* (10.137), *ticha* (10.138), and *tiren* (10.141), also
appear in the "Dushu fa." In his article, Tu shows that in these
expressions *ti* means "to embody" and thus implies "involving the whole person," and he suggests that *tihui* means to
"understand experientially."[60] Indeed Zhu Xi draws a contrast
between *tiyan* and a reading that simply focuses "on the paper" (10.139–40).[61] *Tiyan* was a kind of understanding that
went beyond the superficial to involve the whole person; it
had to do with the application of the text to the reader's own
existential situation.

This exploration of the text was threatened by the fixed
ideas and prejudices of the modern reader. In the expanded
version of the three-part program given at 10.36, *fanfu tiyan*
is contrasted with *zuanyan lishuo* "to dig away (at the words
of the text) and to set up interpretations." To *zuanyan* "to dig
away" was to bore into a hard substance like jade or stone; the
associations were of effort and of penetration into an ever
more narrow and confining space—into a corner, as we
should say.[62] Such readings came about as a result of the modern reader's having "established" (*lile*) an interpretation (*shuo*,
jianjie) or opinion (*yi*) to which the text was made to conform.[63]

These prejudicial views could be of two kinds: "Nowadays
scholars have two sorts of defects. One is to follow their own
private opinions [*siyi*]; one is to subscribe to long-held interpretations" (11.173).[64] By the latter defect, Zhu Xi seems to
have meant the uncritical acceptance of traditional or received
teachings. He often cautioned his students that they should
not accept teachings, even his own,[65] simply on the authority
of the interpreter: "Otherwise, if someone says that sand can
be cooked like rice, then we will also say that sand can be
cooked like rice; but how can it be eaten?" (11.167) But the
student's own insights (*siyi*, "private views or intentions")

could also obscure the original intentions of the text.[66] In either case, the student "first set up his own view" (*xian li ji yi* [11.123]), and "forced" (*qianjiu*) the text to conform to it (11.165, 11.167). This was a kind of solipsism, Zhu Xi argued, in which the words and views of the ancients were all interpreted in terms of one's own ideas.

Reading is like asking someone about something. If you want to know about that matter, you must ask that person. Nowadays, people do not ask the person who knows, but simply judge according to their own ideas [*jiyi*], saying "It must be like this."   (11.166)

People today usually have an idea in their mind before they begin and make use of what other people say in order to expound their own ideas [*yisi*]. When they come to a place that does not agree, then they bore and chisel to make it agree.   (11.164)

In order to avoid the limiting effects of having first set up an interpretation, Zhu Xi advocated that his students *xuxin* "void the mind." The expression *xuxin* had a long history in Chinese hermeneutics. The proximate source for Zhu Xi was probably the teachings of the Northern Song master Zhang Zai (1020–77), where the voided mind represented the solution to the problem of the breakdown of exegetical consensus. For Zhang Zai, the mind emptied of all prejudices and egotism was capable of distinguishing the authentic and transformative elements in the classics from later interpolations and corruptions.[67]

The concept of emptying the mind or the empty mind was, however, not original with Zhang Zai; indeed we find it in texts as old as the *Xunzi* and the *Zhuangzi*. For instance, Xunzi says in his treatise "Dispelling Obsessions" (Chapter 21, "Jie bi"): "That which does not allow what is already stored away [in the mind] to injure that which is about to be received is called the mind's emptiness."[68]

Dubs suggests Daoist antecedents for this notion, mentioning the well-known passage in the *Laozi* that advises, "The government of the Sage consists in emptying the people's minds and filling their bellies."[69] This is the *Laozi* in its Machiavellian mode; the passage proposes not a program for educating the people but one for keeping them ignorant. A better Daoist antecedent would be the *Zhuangzi*, where in the treatise entitled "Worldly Business Among Men" (chap. 4, "Renjian shi") is the following:

Unify your aim [*zhi*]. Rather than listen with the ear, listen with the heart-mind [*xin*]. Rather than listen with the heart-mind, listen with the energies [*qi*]. Listening stops at the ear, the heart-mind at what tallies [with the thought]. As for "energy," it is the tenuous [*xu*] that waits to be roused by other things. Only the Way accumulates the tenuous. The attenuating [*xu*] is the fasting of the heart-mind.[70]

In a note to this passage, Graham says that when the *qi* ("the purified fluid") has become perfectly tenuous (i.e., *xu* "void," "empty"), the *xin* will be "emptied of conceptual knowledge."[71] In the (probably later) "Old Fisherman" chapter, *xuxin* appears clearly linked with learning. Confucius, who in this story serves as a foil for the Daoist fisherman, implores that worthy to share his wisdom: "From my childhood I have cultivated learning, by now for sixty-nine years, and found none from whom to learn the ultimate doctrine. What can I do but keep the space open in my heart [*xuxin*]?"[72]

For Zhu Xi, too, emptying the heart was connected with removing prejudicial views that could impede understanding. But for Zhu Xi, voiding the mind was less a matter of emptying the mind of all its presuppositions than it was of holding them in check. Thus Zhu Xi cautioned against "pressing on" (*po, xiangqian*), by which he seems to have meant not only the anxious impulse to race ahead in the text he cautioned against when he advised students to "read less" (11.171), but also the premature imposition of one's own views (11.173). To "pressing on," he contrasted "stepping back" (*tuibu*).

When people today read, they begin by setting up an opinion [*lile yi*], and only then do they finish reading. They take the words of the ancients in and [understand] them according to their own ideas/intentions [*yisi*]. To read like this is simply to expand upon one's own intentions; how can one see the intentions of the ancients? You must step back [*tuibu*]; do not supply the intentions yourself [*zizuo yisi*]. Take the words of the ancients and place them before you. See where their intentions really go. If you reflect in this way, then you will grasp the intentions of the ancients. As Mencius says, one must "meet [*ni*] the aim [*zhi*] [of the poet] with one's intention [*yi*]." Now "meet" [*ni*] means "await." It is as if you were waiting for someone on the road. When he hasn't come, you must patiently wait; eventually he will arrive. If when he hasn't yet arrived you are upset and anxious and go ahead to look for him, then that is not "meeting the aim with one's intentions" but using one's intentions to grab the aim. If you do this, you will just be twisting [*qianshuai*] the words of the ancients to accord with your own intentions. (11.130)[73]

Zhu Xi's ideal of the "empty heart" did not require the interpreter to be without *yi* ("opinions"). Rather, the interpreter was to resist the impulse to prematurely impose his opinions upon the text; he was to explore the intentions of the text, granting them a kind of provisional life. As with reading less, the ideal was one not of being without concern or compulsion but of holding those anxieties in check. The calmness of Zhu Xi's interpreter was not the calmness of vacuity (the *xu* of *xuxin* notwithstanding) but the calmness of powerful energies held in a delicate balance. Unbiased understanding was as much an accomplishment of the emotions as it was of the intellect.

"Don't Imagine Things or Calculate Gains"

Like his Northern Song masters, Zhu Xi believed that the key to reading well was less a matter of hewing to this or that exegetical orthodoxy than one of the subjective attitudes that readers brought to the text. The heart (*xin*) was to be calm, settled, and concentrated,[74] and this equanimity on the part of readers would allow them not only to understand but more important to be moved and transformed by the classical texts they studied. At the same time, Zhu Xi's world was more complex than that of Cheng Yi or Zhang Zai. Not only had controversies like that over the *Preface* subverted the (unacknowledged) consensus concerning the correct interpretations of the classics, but Zhu Xi and his disciples discovered that the subjectivity of the reader, treated in the Northern Song as the solution to the hermeneutic problem, was one of its sources. It turned out that the subjectivity was recalcitrant and not transparent to the will of the student. It was not easy to be easy.

Zhu Xi discussed a number of dangers to the calm and centered subjectivity he sought,[75] but the most important and the one he most frequently discussed was the concern with "results" (*jihuo*) he addressed in the third part of the three-part program: *bubi xiangxiang jihuo* "don't imagine things or calculate gains." As we saw above, Zhu Xi's attitude toward ends or results contained ambiguities and ambivalences. We noted, for instance, Zhu Xi's doubts concerning the practice of memorizing texts, even as he held out to his students as one result of reading deeply and well the promise that they would be able to "remember" what they had read. Similarly, although Zhu Xi maintained that "reading is secondary" (10.1–2) and not an end in itself, he nevertheless insisted that a deep reader should "linger over the text as if he does not want to leave" (10.46) and that the desire to finish the text was one of the chief obstacles to real understanding. The admonition not to "imagine things or calculate gains" seems at first to be of a piece with this insistence that the only authentic (and thus productive) reading was one in which the reader utterly and totally immersed himself in the text, motivated solely by its "inexhaustible interest" rather than by any hope of eventual gain.

When we look at the concepts linked in the "Dushu fa" with this admonition, however, a more complex picture emerges. The three-part program given in 10.35 is restated in somewhat expanded form in 10.36; in that context the third element of the program is *maitou lihui, buyao qiuxiao* "devote yourself to understanding [the text] and do not seek results."

And at 10.29, we find the same idea in yet another form: "Above all, one must not prematurely demand results [*xian zexiao*]. If once you demand results, you will have thoughts that are anxious and upset; you will become all knotted up inside."

The Odes were exemplary here. The most ambitious claims were made for this text: its powers of inspiration and transformation were supposed to transcend the difficulties of ordinary texts. But, paradoxically and frustratingly, it turned out that this "easiest" of all texts was fraught with difficulty, and not only in its formidable philological problems. More important, even when understood, it did not inspire (*xing*) the student as it was supposed to.

Xu Yu asked [regarding *Analects* 8.8: "Be stimulated by the Odes, established by ritual, and perfected by music"], " 'Establishing oneself by ritual' is [a task] to which one can apply his strength, but the Odes are hard to understand now, and moreover their music is lost—how can one be 'stimulated' by them?"

[Someone] asked, "You, Master, have presented us with your commentary on the Odes, and you have moreover taught us saying, 'You must read the text until it is utterly familiar [*shudu*].' I have read one or two of the Odes until I was utterly familiar with them, but I remained unmoved [*wei you ganfa*]."[76]

The anxiety over whether study would lead to real results was deepened and aggravated by the disciples' conviction that their inability to be affected derived not from the inherent difficulties of the texts, nor yet from the difficulty of intellectually understanding them.[77] Rather, as Zhu Xi stressed, the problem derived from the subjective orientations the disciples themselves brought to the text: the key to an authentic relation to the classics lay paradoxically and frustratingly unused within their own hands. The promise of the Northern Song hermeneutic here revealed its darker side: if all one needed to do to be transformed by the classics was to change the way one

approached them, then the failure to understand was simply
the result of one's laziness or lack of commitment.

This disappointment was by no means limited to the Odes:
the disciples often found in the enterprise of "study" (*xue*) that
their experience did not correspond to that of the Master.
Committed either because they were studying for the examinations or because they were embarked upon the Neoconf-
fucian project of personal and social transformation to an ar-
duous and extended course of reading in the classics, their
commentaries, and the histories, the disciples often felt that
they were simply going through the motions, tied to texts
that, far from inspiring and transforming them, simply bored,
or worse still, confused them. The tension between this experience of disappointed ennui and the transformative elation
Zhu Xi assured them was theirs for the asking inspired hope
on the one hand and lacerating self-doubt on the other.

Zhu Xi's hermeneutic addressed this concern of his disciples in a number of ways. First, there were the promises he
made for his program of deep reading. Read less, Zhu Xi told
his disciples, and you will be able to read more, as well as to
remember what you have read. "The important thing with
texts is to thoroughly understand three or five places; thereafter [the text will] 'fall apart at a touch of the knife.' What
students must avoid is floating over without deeply entering
[the text]" (10.14).[78] Such promises must have been intended
among other things to curb the disciples' anxiety over the
seemingly contradictory demands of Zhu Xi's hermeneutic
and the daunting tasks before them. By giving up their desire
to gain something from reading, he told them, they would
reap a rich reward.

A more important response was, I think, one touched on
already. In the discussion of the first step in Zhu Xi's three-
part program, we encountered the notion that the injunction
to read less was, among other things, the advice to read as the

deep reader did, as a kind of existential bet. To read in this way was to stave off, through an act of the will, the anxious and dangerous impulses to rush ahead in the text, and to adopt the stance of the deep reader.

It is not surprising, given this complexity, that Zhu Xi conceived of reading as a process involving a measure of tension, even of conflict. Zhu Xi disparaged the Northern Song ideal of *congrong wanwei* "freely and easily savoring the text" (10.23), and he often spoke of study as a struggle requiring courage and determination on the part of the student. Reading was like a fight with staves (10.24) or the pursuit of bandits (10.27); the reader must be like a general (10.25) or a harsh official who is "merciless" (*bushu, mei renqing*) in his determination (10.25–26). As I suggested above, the calmness of Zhu Xi's reader was not the calmness of emptiness or ataraxy, but the calmness of powerful forces held in balance, as Zhu expressed in a striking image: "In reading texts, be like some great ship that spreads its sails before the wind, traveling a thousand *li* in a single day" (10.28).

The unspoken but unquestioned assumption that the correct subjective attitude was the key to an authentic relation with the text placed Zhu Xi's hermeneutic firmly within the Song mainstream. At the same time, it differed from that of his Northern Song masters in one crucial respect: whereas they saw the injunction to make the subjectivity "easy" and unconflictual as the solution to the hermeneutic problem, for Zhu Xi (and even more so, for his disciples), this was the problem. They had discovered that it was not always easy to be easy; that the subjectivity, seemingly the one domain in which the student had perfect freedom and autonomy, was in fact prey to unforeseen constraints that foiled and disappointed the reader. Just as in the first great creative period of Chinese hermeneutics in the Warring States period, here again the deepening of Chinese hermeneutics was related to a more complex vision of the personality.

Conclusion

The relation between the two themes of this chapter, between Zhu Xi's hermeneutic and the critical scholarship in which he had a part, is complex and does not lend itself to simple or easy formulations. On one level, Zhu Xi's response to the discovery that not all of the Odes inscribed paradigmatically normative attitudes was simply to suggest that readers ignore the "debauched" Odes and go on reading the normative ones as they always had—that is, by internalizing the attitudes they embodied. On a deeper level, however, we may wonder at the consequences. One effect of the diminished faith in the motivations inscribed in the Odes may have been a softening of the *yi* "intention" / *yii* "significance" dichotomy that had preoccupied the Northern Song. Not only does *yii* begin to appear in contexts where formerly we would have found *yi*, but the "intentional" character of *yi* becomes blunted in compounds like *yiyii* ("intention and significance," "meaning") or *yisi* ("intention and thought," "interest").[79] Both *yi* and *yii* would continue to be important for the subsequent history of Chinese hermeneutics, but the contrast between the two had lost its fascination.

Another effect may have had to do with the "adoption" of the subjectivity of the deep reader. The traditional promise of the Odes had been to provide a kind of model—a *zhi* "aim" in the medieval hermeneutic, an *yi* "intention" in the Song version—around which the personality of the reader was to form itself, a view summed up in Zhang Zai's claim that texts *weichi cixin* "support 'this heart'" (11.103).[80] For Zhu Xi, however, this promise was no longer enough. The student's mind could be "supported" by the text only when his mind had been readied, composed, and made receptive, and this process of making the mind ready involved "borrowing" the attitudes and approach of the deep reader—of one who had already been supported by the text. The attitudes adopted by the reader—the bet made by the reader—were confirmed by the text. Thus the process was not circular, but neither was it so firmly grounded in a faith in the text as had been the medieval or even Northern Song hermeneutics.

The story of the hermeneutics of the Odes did not end with Zhu Xi. In subsequent centuries, scholars offered new solutions to the traditional problems of hermeneutics or proposed altogether new ways of thinking about the tradition. In the early Qing, for instance, Wang Fuzhi (1619–92) argued that although a single meaning may have been intended by the authors of the Odes, that intention need not limit the meanings which readers find in the text.[81] Later in the dynasty, scholars associated with the "evidential research" movement directly challenged the subjectivist biases of the Neoconfucian hermeneutic, arguing for the primacy of philological and analytic considerations in deciding the meaning of the classics.[82] Emphasizing methodology in a way that some have thought foreshadowed the modern scientific method, certain Qing scholars were led eventually to treat the classics as historical documents rather than as sacred scriptures.[83] The Qing reevaluation of the classical tradition was as momentous in its own way as the rise of historicism in the West, and it had far-reaching hermeneutical consequences. Still, the Neoconfucian "way of reading" first adumbrated in the eleventh century and given its authoritative formulation by Zhu Xi remained central to the tradition as a whole, and it influenced even those who felt themselves obliged to argue against it.[84]

The Neoconfucian general hermeneutic thus constituted a kind of orthodoxy in late imperial China. Influential as such orthodoxies may have been, it is important to acknowledge that accounts which (like this one) focus on them will tend to overlook, discount, or ignore altogether other approaches which were denied or marginalized in their own day, or which have simply been lost through the vicissitudes of history. A full account of Han studies of the Odes, to take an example from the earlier period, would have to consider not only the Three Schools eventually supplanted by the Mao school, but also the traditions represented by the new materials recovered at Fuyang and Mawangdui excavations.[85] Moreover, it is entirely possible that there were other regional esoteric traditions of which we have no trace. We must therefore be wary of treating as natural or inevitable a triumph that was historically contingent and partial. Finally, outside the approach we have been calling "Confucian," Buddhist and Daoist interpreters applied to their own canons approaches that seem often to have proceeded from premises radically different from the ones outlined here.[86]

For all these reasons it would be premature to speak of a typically Chinese hermeneutic in opposition to a Western one. Rather, there was a panoply of approaches in traditional China to reading, study, and exegesis, of which the one discussed in this study was only the most influential. These approaches may well have had no single feature in common, unless it was the conviction of the cardinal importance of beginning with the text.

Reference Matter

Notes

For complete author names, titles, and publication data for the works cited here in short form, see the Works Cited, pp. 295–307. The following abbreviations are used in the Notes:

CSPG   *Correct Significance* commentary on the Preface to the "Guanju" (*Maoshi zhushu, Guoxue jiben congshu* ed.)
FS   Ouyang Xiu, *Fundamental Significance* (*Shi benyii, Sibu congkan* ed.)
YS   Zhu Xi, *Shizhuan yishuo* (*Siku quanshu zhenben* ed.)

BOOK EPIGRAPHS: Stevens, pp. 358–59; Bishop, pp. 188–89; Dong, 3.9a.

CHAPTER ONE

1. The early lore concerning natural omens and portents survives in the oldest strata of the *Changes* (*Yi*) and in the Odes. On the role of the remnants of folk religion in these texts, especially the former, see Kunst, pp. 62–81. On the oracle bones of the Shang, see Keightley.

2. One recent writer defines doctrine as "communally authoritative teachings regarding beliefs and practices that are considered essential to the identity or welfare of the group in question . . . [and] . . . indicate what constitutes faithful adherence to a community" (Lindbeck, p. 74). Lindbeck is speaking of Christian doctrine, but the notion of a doctrinal culture can be extended to include legal traditions and, I would argue, traditions like Confucianism as well. A doctrinal culture has a number of features. First, it begins from and constantly returns to certain foundational teachings, usually but not necessarily a text or texts. These foundational teachings are the most important source of authority in the tradition. Doctrinal exposition and controversy focus on issues of interpretation of the foundational teachings; they thus tend to be hermeneutic in character. Moreover, the interpretation performed in such a culture is not disinterested or purely historical; rather,

it is consequential. In a legal tradition, for instance, the results of interpretation (as certified by the courts) are considered binding both upon the interpreters themselves and upon the rest of society. In a religious tradition, interpretation may aim at discovering the laws of God or at bringing about the moral transformation of the interpreter. In all cases, however, interpretation is not value-free, but committed to the project of the tradition as a whole. Finally, a doctrinal tradition tends to write its own history. The most important sources for its understanding are not works written "outside" the tradition, but rather the historical discussions that are part and parcel of doctrinal argument.

3. The literature on classics study is enormous. Like most doctrinal traditions (the Western legal tradition is a good example), it was constantly engaged in the interpretation and reinterpretation of its own past; the best sources for the history of classics study are thus works in that tradition. Still, a number of studies attempt to provide overviews of the history of the tradition. I have found the following particularly useful: Fan; Honda; Jiang Boqian; Kageyama; Ma; Morohashi, *Keigaku kenkyū josetsu*; Pi, *Jingxue lishi* and *Jingxue tonglun*; and Taki. Jiang Shanguo; Morohashi, *Shikyō kenkyū*; Xu; and Zhu Ziqing have useful information on the history of Odes scholarship specifically.

4. An emphasis on the constitutive role of the reader is typically associated with "reader-response" criticism, whose most famous representatives are Roman Ingarden, Hans Robert Jauss, and Wolfgang Iser, but in fact it characterizes a wide range of contemporary criticism. See Culler, pp. 31–43.

5. Of course, the relationship between the codes by which texts are read and those texts themselves is complex and problematical. Explicitly stated hermeneutics in particular are perhaps never innocent: rather, they always attempt to legislate reading, to rule out certain possibilities and to make others seem necessary or even inevitable. And even a tacit hermeneutic may be out of step with the texts it seeks to understand. Still, by and large the texts of a culture are written in the expectation that they will be read according to the dominant hermeneutic of their time and place; they anticipate and solicit certain kinds of reading.

6. See, e.g., the discussions in Bleicher, pp. 1–5; and Mueller-Vollmer, pp. ix–xi. "Hermeneutics" does not directly translate any term appearing in traditional Chinese texts. The equivalent typically used today in Chinese, *quanshixue*, is a neologism that does not appear in, say, Morohashi's *Dai Kan-Wa jiten*. *Jingxue*, while of venerable pedigree, refers only to the study and exegesis of canonical texts, and not to theorizing about such exegesis or to the study of non-canonical texts. The traditional expression that seems to correspond most closely to the English "hermeneutics," *dushu fa*, does not appear until the Song dynasty and is also of relatively limited application, meaning something like "the way to read."

7. Grant, *Letter*, surveys hermeneutics and exegesis in the ancient and early Christian worlds.

8. On the early history of the discipline of hermeneutics in the West, see Mueller-Vollmer.

9. For the nineteenth- and early-twentieth-century advocates of hermeneutics, see Mueller-Vollmer. Bernstein, esp. pp. 109–14, gives an account of the renaissance of what I am calling programmatic hermeneutics in the 1970's and 1980's.

10. The last point is crucial. Its first great advocate, Wilhelm Dilthey, presented hermeneutic "understanding" (*verstehen*) as an alternative to the "explanation" supposed to be characteristic of the natural sciences (Mueller-Vollmer, pp. 23–28). This concern to advocate for the human sciences a method or approach appropriate to them remains characteristic of such contemporary partisans of programmatic hermeneutics as Paul Ricoeur and Richard Rorty. Perhaps because the natural sciences never enjoyed the intellectual prestige in traditional China that they do in the modern West, this kind of programmatic hermeneutics was never promoted as an alternative methodology there.

11. Ricouer, pp. 43–44.

12. Heidegger, pp. 36–37.

13. Ibid., pp. 61–62.

14. Gadamer, pp. 235–74, esp. pp. 267–74.

15. This definition rules out purely instrumental interpretation like that of the oracle bones in Shang China, as well as "historicist" scholarship in which the text no longer has an authoritative character.

16. Culler, pp. 279–80.

17. *Xunzi*, "Quanxue," 1.4a–4b. There are many editions of the Mao text of the Odes; I have chiefly used the texts contained in the Harvard-Yenching Concordance series *Maoshi yinde* and in the *Maoshi zhushu*. See Chapter 5 for details on the latter work. Of the major translations and research aids, I have relied chiefly upon Legge, *She King*; Waley, *Book of Songs*; Karlgren, *Book of Odes* and *Glosses on the Book of Odes*; and Shirakawa.

On the role of the Zhou court musicians in the collection and preservation of the Odes, see Shirakawa, p. 1; and also the brief but suggestive comments of Hawkes in his *Ch'u Tz'û*, p. 1, and in his review of Diény, p. 153. The Han dynasty Music Bureau (*Yuefu*) may have performed an analogous function; on its structure, activities, and history, see Loewe, pp. 340–51.

18. Dobson, "Linguistic Evidence," pp. 322–43. The question of the dating of the Odes is complicated by their oral-formulaic character; even the latest of the Odes may contain formulas and themes that are quite old. By the same token, Odes that may refer to some historical event and were perhaps composed shortly thereafter often were modified in their subsequent transmission. On the latter phenomenon, see C. H. Wang, pp. 95–96.

19. The lauds connected with the ducal house of Song are associated in the received text of the *Odes* with the Shang kings deposed by the Zhou; hence the title of the section, "Shang song" (The lauds of Shang). The descendants

of the Shang kings were invested with the state of Song; the *Guoyu* account of how the lauds of Shang were returned to that state is cited in Legge, *She King*, p. 632.

20. The translations "Lauds" and "Elegantiae" are from Achilles Fang's "Introduction" to Ezra Pound's translation, p. xiv.

21. Several of the Lesser Elegantiae contain explicit avowals of why and how they were made. For example, Ode #191:

> Jiafu has made this poem [song]
> To detail the king's calamities.

Most of these explicit avowals of auctorial intention imply that the Ode was made and "presented" (*chen*) by a member of the court in order to influence state policy.

22. See, e.g., Shirakawa's discussion (pp. 456–58) of how elements of the "Guanju" (Mao #1), in its present form a love song, were originally associated with the sacrifices of the family cult.

23. In the introductory remarks to his "Glosses on the Kuo-feng Odes," Karlgren cites as reasons for believing that the Odes must be the products of "well-trained, educated members of the gentry" their strict meter, their very regular rhymes, and their sophisticated and "upper-class" diction (pp. 75–76). Gu Jiegang had reached similar conclusions in the 1920's: see his "Lun *Shijing* suolu quanwei yuege," pp. 639–57 (cited and discussed in Schneider, pp. 177–78). Although the Airs as we have them were thus authored, even "literary" productions, I think that most scholars would agree that their characteristic themes and imagery (as well as the music to which they were presumably performed) must have originally derived from folk songs.

24. Knoblock has argued that the application of the term "Confucian" is anachronistic before the Han establishment of the state cult of Confucius. But the reverence for Confucius shown by figures like Mencius and Xunzi seems to me to justify the term. Knoblock also argues that "In ancient China there was no 'school' of Confucius." Certainly there was no single school of Confucius; but as Knoblock's own discussion shows, there were a number of competing schools all claiming to represent the authoritative teachings of Confucius as passed on to one or another of his disciples (see Knoblock, pp. 52–53). On the politics of the Confucian schools, see Chapter 2.

25. Waley, *Book of Songs*, p. 21.

26. Karlgren, *Book of Odes*, p. 61.

27. See Pope, pp. 89–229, for a survey of the history of the interpretation of the *Song of Songs*.

28. For the concept of the *Odes* as a "snapshot" of the repertoire of the Zhou court musicians, I am indebted to Prof. Michael Fuller of Harvard University, who developed the concept in a course on the *Odes* he taught at Harvard during the spring term of 1986.

29. This insight, which perhaps first appears in the thought of Zheng Qiao (see Chapter 8), has been developed in this century by Zhu Ziqing and He Dingsheng, among others.

30. There is, for instance, another Ode among the Airs (Mao #35), also traditionally entitled "Gufeng," which employs the same language and imagery as Mao #201 *and* the same persona of an abandoned wife. See Watson, *Early Chinese Literature*, pp. 219–22, for a discussion of the possible relations between the folk and literary elements in such complaints and satires.

31. Hightower, "The *Han-shih wai-chuan*," p. 267.

32. See Knechtges. As Knechtges shows, it often proved impossible to keep these two elements in balance, and the didactic element in Han rhapsodies was often ignored by its object, the emperor. See, e.g., p. 40, on the rhapsodies of Sima Xiangru.

33. Of course, rhyme and meter could serve to fix the texts of the Odes only after they had acquired prestige by virtue of their association with the Zhou court and with Confucius; before that time, and especially so long as they remained close to the oral-formulaic tradition that generated them, they must have been quite fluid. Moreover, variations in the Odes quoted in various pre-Qin sources tend to be the phonetic variants one would expect to find in such an orally transmitted text, and in any event they do not reflect a desire to "improve upon" (i.e., moralize) the text.

34. Of course folk songs, including love songs, were collected in later China—the so-called Music Bureau poems (see note 17 above) are a good example—but they were not canonized like the Odes.

35. See Chapter 3 for a fuller discussion with citations.

36. See Heidegger, p. 185. The Confucian *zhi* could, however, be thematic in a way that the Heideggerian "projection" (*entwerfen, Entwurf*) is not.

37. See the discussion of Cheng Yi's comments on this topic in Chapter 7.

38. Karlgren (*Grammata Serica Recensa*, #962), classifies *zhi* "aim" in the same series as *zhi* "to go."

39. See the discussion of Mencius 2.A.2 near the end of Chapter 4.

40. Although both the "lyric" that emerged in the first centuries C.E. and the Odes were called *shi*, their formal features were very different.

41. See Owen, *Traditional Chinese Poetry and Poetics*; and Pauline Yu, *The Reading of Imagery*, for detailed expositions of the presumptions associated with the *shi* lyric genre. James J. Y. Liu gives a survey of what he terms "deterministic and expressive" theories of literature in *Chinese Theories of Literature*, pp. 63–87.

42. See Cahill.

CHAPTER TWO

EPIGRAPH: quoted in Kelber, p. 1.

1. Soulen, p. 114.

2. Grant, *Historical Introduction*, pp. 105–17. Not all scholars agree that "Q" represents a written source; Grant (ibid., p. 116), for instance, doubts this.

3. For a recent account of some of the many revisions and criticisms of the Graf-Wellhausen hypothesis proposed in the hundred years since its appearance, see Noth, esp. chap. 4 and the Translator's Supplement.

4. Form criticism began with the work of Hermann Gunkel on Genesis and the Psalms. In New Testament studies, the seminal works were by Martin Dibelius and Rudolf Bultmann.

5. For a criticism of this method, see Gerhardsson, esp. pp. 9–15.

6. See, e.g., the description of competing Mohist and Confucian sects at *Han Feizi* 19.7b.

7. *Mencius* 3.A.4.

8. Another sign that the rhetorical forms of Confucianism derive from teaching is that Confucian doctrine is characteristically referred to as a "teaching" (*jiao*).

9. Like *Analects* 11.26 and 16.13, discussed below. All references to the *Analects* are to the traditional numbering as given in Yang, rather than that of the Harvard-Yenching Sinological Index Series *Lunyu yinde* or of Waley, *Analects*. I have relied upon Waley's work and Lau, *Analects*, in preparing my translations.

10. By "motivated" I simply mean structured and in a sense determined in content or form by the usually moralizing concerns of a tradition. Of course, every discourse is in some sense motivated, if only by choices about what is of interest or value. But it is possible to distinguish materials or elements that can adequately be accounted for by the concerns of their transmitters from those that are not. This distinction resembles that drawn by Karlgren ("Legends and Cults") between "free" and "systematizing" texts; the latter are "motivated" in my terms, and the former are not or at least less so. Karlgren's optimism that texts can be cleanly classified into one or the other of these categories was criticized in a review by Eberhard; the controversy is summarized in Wheatley, pp. 151–52.

11. On the "criterion of dissimilarity," see Perrin, pp. 405–6. See also Breech for a recent study emphasizing this approach.

12. It has been claimed that by the sixth or fifth centuries B.C.E. the *Changes* (*Yi*) had come to be read as a "philosophical text" (see Shchutskii, pp. 192–93). But almost all of the *Zuo Tradition* references that Shchutskii cites appear in the long, rhetorical speeches that were almost certainly the creations of the text's late-fourth-century redactors. It is noteworthy in this connection that the *Yi* is not mentioned at all in the *Mencius*, once only (in what may be a late interpolation) in the *Analects* (see Dubs, "Did Confucius Study the Book of Changes?"), and only rarely in the *Xunzi*. If the *Yi* was indeed treated as an authoritative doctrinal text during the Warring States period, it was marginal to the mainstream Confucian tradition. The Documents are quoted twice in the *Analects* (2.21, 14.40) and referred to once or perhaps twice (7.18, 11.25[?]).

13. It is not impossible that some of Confucius's dicta were written down by his immediate disciples; see *Analects* 15.6 for a passage portraying such an incident. On the other hand, chap. 15 certainly contains late material.

14. See Cui; and Creel, *Confucius*, p. 291.

15. Various scholars include other chapters in this earliest group. For example, Arthur Waley would include chaps. 8 and 9, and D. C. Lau chaps. 9 and 11 through 15. Lau (*Analects*, pp. 227–33) gives reasons for ascribing a late date to chaps. 1, 2, and 8. My strategy here is to be as strict as possible, taking only those chapters unanimously accepted as early. Among other important studies of the dating of the *Analects* are Takeuchi; Tsuda; and Kimura.

16. Translation adapted from Lau, *Analects*, p. 130. The Ode quoted is #34 ("Pao you kuye").

17. Note, however, that the version recorded in the "Kongzi shijia" in the *Shiji* (p. 1925) omits both the quotation from the Odes and Confucius's reply. See Riegel, "Poetry and the Legend," p. 16, for a discussion of this passage. Riegel's demonstration of the ways in which earlier texts, especially the Odes, served to structure the various narrative traditions concerning Confucius is insightful and convincing. On the question of the interpretation of 14.39, however, I am persuaded to differ with him by the parallels cited in the next note.

18. See *Analects* 18.6 and 18.7 for similar examples of Confucian additions to Daoist stories critical of or mocking Confucius. Although it is not necessarily the case that such modifications must have taken place in a context of oral tradition, the point remains that the elements of the tradition were, at the time when passages like these were being created, still essentially fluid, not yet fixed as texts.

19. *Mozi*, "Gongmeng" chapter. Translation adapted from Shih-Hsiang Chen, p. 13.

20. Waley, *Book of Songs*, #224 (Mao #282).

21. *Analects* 3.1; see also 3.6, 3.10.

22. The claim first appears in Sima Qian's biography of Confucius (*Shiji*, p. 1936).

23. He Dingsheng, pp. 124–25.

24. It provided the starting point for the *Mao Preface* exegesis of the "Guanju." See Chapter 4 below.

25. Or, with Ezra Pound, "When Music Master Chy began the ensemble finale of the fishhawk song, came wave over wave an ear-full and how!" Quoted by Achilles Fang in his "Introduction" to Pound, p. x.

26. In both of these passages, Confucius refers to the "sounds" (*sheng*) of Zheng, rather than to, say, the "Airs" or "Odes" of that state. This term usually refers in later texts like the *Preface* or the "Record of Music" ("Yueji") either to instrumental music or to the human voice. At 17.10, Confucius advises his son to "do" (*wei*; presumably, to "study") the Zhounan and Shaonan. But this is probably a late passage; see note 55 below.

27. See, e.g., *Analects* 1.15, 3.8, 9.27, 9.31, 12.10, 14.39. In references to "the Odes" or "the Ode," the concern is also with the language of the Odes; see 8.3, 13.5, 16.13, 17.9, and especially 8.8, where "the Odes" are contrasted with music. *Analects* 11.6, where Nan Rong is said to have thrice "repeated" (*fu*; = *fu* "recite"?) "[the lines about the] white jade scepter," is a unique case.

28. Compare 3.3, 7.13, 8.8, and 17.11 for other examples of the association of music with moral perfection.

29. Waley (*Analects*, pp. 242–43) also points out that Mohists called the third part of the Odes the "Daxia" rather than the usual "Daya."

30. Waley, *Book of Songs*, #86. The last line does not appear in the extant texts of the Odes.

31. This passage is almost certainly the source of the traditional attribution of the *Preface to Mao's Odes* to Zixia.

32. On the criterion of dissimilarity, see above.

33. The competition among various competing Confucian schools is described in the "Xianxue" chapter of the *Han Feizi* (19.7b) and reflected in comments made in Xunzi's treatise "Contra Twelve Philosophers" ("Fei shier zi"; *Xunzi* 3.13a). For a discussion and translation of Xunzi's comments, see Knoblock, 1: 219–20, 229. Some of these schools may have claimed to be in possession of esoteric teachings of Confucius; see my discussion of *Analects* 16.13 below.

34. Zixia was prominent among the disciples of Confucius supposed to have founded schools. Others included Zizhang, Ziyou, and Zengzi, as well as Confucius's grandson, Zisi, and Zigong*ª* (not the Zigong of *Analects* 1.15, but another disciple of Confucius's supposed by Xunzi to represent the authentic Confucian orthodoxy). See Knoblock, 1: 52–53.

35. Ode #55; translation from Waley, *Book of Songs*, #42.

36. The *Analects* passages in which the Odes are quoted or discussed in this way are 1.15, 2.2, 3.8, 8.3, 9.27, 9.31, 12.10, and 14.39. With the exception of 3.8, all of these passages are from the second or third stratum of the *Analects*. I am inclined to suppose that 3.8 derives from the same milieu, for the reasons discussed above. On the other hand, given its context and structure, 14.39 is probably later than most of these other passages.

37. I think it possible that the historical Confucius quoted from the Odes in this fashion, but it should be kept in mind that these passages probably stem from a milieu relatively remote from Confucius's and are unlikely to reflect authentic historical traditions concerning the Master. Subsequent references to "Confucius," then, should be understood to mean the Confucius portrayed in these passages, a figure with only a tangential and problematical relation to the historical Confucius.

38. Waley, *Analects*, p. 191*n*1. See Riegel, "Poetry and the Legend," pp. 15–16, for a reading of this Ode.

39. On the meaning of *xing* in the *Mao Commentary* and as an element in the Odes, see Shih-Hsiang Chen, pp. 16–41; and below.

40. Compare 8.2, which contains the grammatically parallel expression *xing yu ren* "to be stimulated by humaneness."

41. On this controversy as it was developed by Zhu Xi, see Chapter 8.

42. Waley, *Analects*, pp. 44–46. Waley (p. 88) translates 2.2 in such a way as to make it explicit that the phrase *si wu xie* applies to Confucius's own teachings (rather than to the Odes).

43. This is also the view of James J. Y. Liu (*Language*, p. 95), who says that Confucius was indulging here in "a species of punning."

44. The practice also appears in the *Discourses of the States* (*Guoyu*), a text closely allied to the *Zuo Tradition*, but in no other pre-Qin work. See Tam, p. 1. Tam conveniently brings together and translates all the *Zuo Tradition* passages that include incidents of the chanting of the Odes.

Although the *Zuo Tradition* depicts the events of the years 722–468 B.C.E., it probably did not assume its present form until around 300 B.C.E. See Karlgren, "Authenticity," pp. 64–65; Maspero, pp. 137–208; Hsu, pp. 184–85; and C. S. Gardner, pp. 11–12n8. Even if the Odes recitation narratives are taken to reflect the concerns of the Warring States Confucians rather than the historical realities of the Spring and Autumn period, they are significant for what they can show us about the assumptions concerning the Odes and their meanings current at that later date. My translations from the *Zuo Tradition* are based on Legge, *Ch'un Ts'ew*.

45. This narrative appears in the *Zuo Tradition* attached to Year 23 of the reign of Duke Xi. The phrase "assist the Son of Heaven" comes from the second stanza of the "Liuyue."

46. Tam, pp. 14–15. For a discussion of this and other forms of performance, see Yuen Ren Chao, pp. 52–59 (cited in Tam, p. 15).

47. Mao #183. In the text of the *Zuo Tradition*, the title of this Ode is given as "Mianshui." Du Yu considered it a "lost Ode," but as Wei Zhao pointed out, *mian* is probably a corruption of *he*. See Tam, p. 165n4. Translation from Waley, *Book of Songs*, #280.

48. See, e.g., chap. 66 of the *Laozi*, which begins in Waley's translation (*Way*, p. 224), "How did the great rivers and seas get their kingship over the hundred lesser streams?"

49. For example, the stories concerning Qing Feng at Xiang 27 and Xiang 29, and concerning Hua Ding at Zhao 12.

50. Modified from Waley, *Book of Songs*, #133.

51. The *Mao Preface* associates it with an expedition by King Xuan (r. 826–781 B.C.E.) against the northern tribes.

52. Cited by Tam, pp. 61–62.

53. Holzman, p. 33.

54. See the discussion of *Zuo* Xiang 27 below for examples of *guan*, *qun*, and *yuan*. *Guan* is often used in the *Analects* to refer to the hermeneutic observation and analysis of character. See, e.g., *Analects* 1.11, 2.10, 4.7, 5.10, 8.11, and 12.20.

55. The Zhounan and Shaonan are the first two sections of the "Airs of the

States," traditionally associated with the transformative virtue of the early Zhou. They are mentioned nowhere else in the *Analects*, although 9.15 mentions the *ya* and the *song*. Neither the *Zuo Tradition*, the *Mencius*, nor the *Xunzi* show any preference for the two *nan* chapters; this preference seems to have been a relatively late development.

56. Part of the interest of the passage probably had to do with the sorts of claims to authority—including, perhaps, claims of secret teachings—that I suggested motivated 1.15 and 3.8.

57. Chen Gang recalls another good "reader" from an earlier stratum of the tradition, Fan Chi (*Analects* 2.5).

58. See Hawkes, *Ch'u Tz'û*, p. 6; and DeWoskin, pp. 93–94. Hawkes speculates that the music of the south was "mournful, erotic, and languorous in slow tempi and somewhat hysterical and excited when . . . fast."

59. *Liji xunzuan* 19.16b. Translation adapted from DeWoskin, p. 94. Note the similar passage at *Mencius* 1.A.2.

60. This has been confirmed by the set of bells belonging to Marquis Yi of Zeng datable to 433 B.C.E., which was excavated in Hubei in 1978. See DeWoskin, p. 25, for the tonal implications of this find.

61. See also *Analects* 15.11: ". . . Banish the sounds of Zheng and keep smooth men at a distance. The sounds of Zheng are depraved [*yin*], and smooth men are dangerous."

62. DeWoskin, p. 92.

CHAPTER THREE

1. Graham, *Later Mohist Logic*, pp. 15–18.

2. Interestingly, however, the term does not appear as the name of a virtue in the *Analects*.

3. Lau (*Analects*, p. 234) cites 1.2, 1.6, and 6.26 as other cases where *ren* ("humaneness") is used for *ren* ("human").

4. Adapted from Karlgren, "Book of Documents," p. 21. See also on this passage, Karlgren, *Glosses on the Book of Documents*, #1437 (p. 187). For the possibility that the "Pan Geng" may have been composed in connection with the transfer of the Zhou capital in 771 B.C.E, see Wheatley, pp. 13–14. On this chapter, see also Creel, *Origins*, p. 448; and Waley, *Analects*, p. 53. An eighth century B.C.E. date would, of course, be very early.

5. I borrow the term from Schwartz, pp. 263–78.

6. On this passage, see Riegel, "Reflections on an Unmoved Mind."

7. It may be important that *zhi* does not appear in a hermeneutically significant context in an indisputably early passage of the *Analects*. In most of its appearances in the early chapters, *zhi* is a verb (i.e., 4.4, 4.9, 7.6) or is not hermeneutically significant (4.18). The one exception, 5.26, is the antepenultimate section in the chapter and may very well be a later addition. In the *Yijing*, *zhi* never appears in the oldest (*jing*) layers of the text, but is quite common in the later *tuanzhuan* and *xiangzhuan*.

8. Waley, *Analects*, p. 86.

9. Takeuchi Yoshio (pp. 219–25) notes as markers of lateness the use of *fuzi* as a term of direct address (on which see Lau, *Analects*, p. 224); the obvious reliance upon 5.26 and 5.8; the promotion of Zeng Xi, who is not mentioned elsewhere in the Analects but who is referred to three times in the *Mencius*; and the "Daoist" content of the passage. To these we might add the sophisticated narrative technique of the piece; the context of the story (the last section in a late chapter); and the reduction of the character of Zilu to his stereotypical temerity. A *terminus ad quem* for the tradition is provided by the *Lunheng* of Wang Chong (27–ca. 97 C.E.), who makes reference to the story (Forke, 1: 520, and 2: 335). The *Analects* passage seems to provide the model for *Hanshi waizhuan* 7.25 and 9.15 (Hightower, *Han Shih Wai Chuan*, pp. 248–49 and pp. 303–4), and, I will argue below, for the narrative of the meeting at Chuilong given at Xiang 27 in the *Zuo Tradition*. In the latter case especially, however, the resemblances are subtle, and there is no guarantee that this particular version of the story existed in its present form when the *Zuo Tradition* narrative took shape.

10. See Wing-tsit Chan's discussion of interpretations of this passage in his *Source Book*, p. 38.

11. This detailing is typical of the narrative as a whole, which is certainly one of the most sophisticated in the *Analects*; note, for instance, how the business with the lute that precedes Zeng Xi's response serves to postpone and thus highlight the story's climax.

12. Zeng Xi does not appear elsewhere in the *Analects* (he is the only one of the personae of 11.26 not taken over from 5.8), but he is mentioned three times in the *Mencius*: at 4.A.19 and 7.B.36, where he is the recipient of exemplary filial piety on the part of his son, the famous Zengzi; and at 7.B.37, where he is mentioned as an example of one of the *kuangzhe* ("unrestrained ones"?) given a lukewarm endorsement by Confucius at *Analects* 13.21 and by Mencius at 7.B.37. In the same passage, these *kuangzhe* are characterized in terms of their aims (*zhi*), which are said to be *jiaojiao ran* "grandiose," "magniloquent." In the *Lunheng* of Wang Chong, Zeng Xi is mentioned along with Gu Sou, the father of Shun, as an example of an unkind or unworthy parent (Forke, 2: 137). Compare also *Hanshi waizhuan* 8.26 (Hightower, *Han Shih Wai Chuan*, pp. 280–81).

13. The notion that a person's character was most accurately represented by desires and tastes is also visible in a passage from the second stratum of chapters: "The Master said, 'Look at what he uses, observe what he comes from, examine what he finds peace in. Can a man hide? Can a man hide?'" (*Analects* 2.10) As so often is the case in the *Analects*, the tripartite structure of this passage is the structure of completion. To "look at what he uses" is to look at the means a man employs in pursuit of his ends; this is the manifest text of his actions. To "observe what he comes from" is to examine the circumstances and stimuli to those actions; it is to put them into context. To "examine what he finds peace in" is to discover the ultimate motivations

that will shape all his actions in whatever circumstances, and one discerns those motivations by observing what makes him happy.

14. The poetry of Tao Qian is exemplary in this respect. See Owen, "The Self's Perfect Mirror."

15. Waley, *Book of Songs*, #92.

16. Ibid., #269.

17. See *Zuo* Xiang 30 and Zhao 7 for the story of his fall and demise.

18. We are told that Zhao Meng "observes" (*guan*) the aims of the Zheng grandees and that Bo You expresses resentment or "complains" (*yuan*). It seems clear that the Odes recited by the other Zheng grandees are intended to *qun* "express solidarity." Only *xing* "stimulation" is missing from the *Analects* 17.9 catalog of the uses of the Odes.

19. *Mencius* 2.A.2.xvii. Mencius conceived of moral accomplishment in terms of the "full actualization of [the heart's] moral capacities" (Schwartz, p. 266).

20. We might wonder what that doctrinal milieu was. We should be wary of treating this passage as transparent upon the historical reality it purports to depict. As with the other prediction stories in the *Zuo Tradition*, this story is intended to show that Confucian morality determines human history—that it can be predicted that good people will come to a good end, bad people to a bad end. This linkage derives not from some peculiar consistency in Spring and Autumn history, but rather from the didactic interests of the Confucian teachers in whose hands the anecdotes took their present shape, building, adding, emphasizing, and de-emphasizing certain elements as the stories were told and retold. It was in this context of doctrinal exposition and teaching that the mythology and hermeneutics of the Odes took shape; it was a product of the Confucian schools and their typical concerns.

The didactic interest of the narrator in showing that Bo You's character must soon lead to his demise (and that he is responsible for that demise) structures not only Zhao Meng's and Shu Xiang's predictions (which we might suppose could be amputated as being some redactor's retrospective gloss) but the main body of the narrative as well; hence the patently inappropriate nature of the Ode chanted by Bo You. Indeed the whole story is structured by these sorts of Confucian concerns; it clearly belongs to a tradition of didactic anecdote rather than to the genre of historical reportage.

I think therefore that whatever conclusions we might reach concerning the historicity of the meeting at Chuilong (and I see no reason to doubt that such a meeting took place), the recitation of the Odes portrayed here probably and the interpretations of Zhao Meng and Shu Xiang certainly are products of doctrinal elaboration—of the moral imagination. Although we cannot assign their addition to the narrative to a particular date (neither the prediction that "the family of Zi Chan will be the last to perish" nor the one concerning Bo You show that the piece is any later than the approximate date of the demise of Zi Chan's line [mid-fifth century B.C.E.?]), we may suppose that they are relatively late, perhaps stemming from the same general milieu as the later *Analects* passages.

21. Adapted from Waley, *Book of Songs*, #285.

22. Following Karlgren, *Book of Odes*, p. 225.

23. See Riegel, "Reflections on an Unmoved Mind," p. 450*n*4.

24. Waley, *Book of Songs*, #285.

25. Ibid., p. 320*n*1.

26. See, e.g., *Mencius* 2.A.4, where Confucius is made to say of Mao #155 that its author "knew the Way."

27. For other examples of this sense of *wen*, see *Mencius* 4.B.21, and *Zuo* Xiang 25.

28. As in the dictum attributed to Confucius at *Zuo* Xiang 25, discussed in Chapter 4.

29. For Xunzi's thought generally, see Dubs, *Hsüntze* and *The Works*; and Knoblock. Unless otherwise noted, all references to *Xunzi* are to the *Sibu beiyao* edition.

30. Even if the traditional view of the *Analects* as more or less historically accurate is retained, still he was concerned with the Odes largely as a handbook of rhetorical phrases and mentioned the other "classics" rarely if at all.

31. *Mencius* 7.B.3. The translation is from Legge, *The Works of Mencius*, p. 479.

32. See Karlgren, "The Early History," p. 19; and Knoblock, 1: 49.

33. See Knoblock, 1: 42–49, for the status of these various texts in Xunzi's day.

34. Xunzi quotes the Odes some 82 times, compared to Mencius's 30, a significant increase even allowing for the greater length of the *Xunzi*.

35. Knoblock, 1: 139. In a note to this passage (1: 270*n*39), Knoblock points out that "recitation" was associated with the Odes, although Yang Liang's note on the passage says that the classics referred to also included the *Documents*.

36. See note 34 above. Xunzi quotes from the *Documents* twelve times (Knoblock, 1: 43).

37. *Xunzi* 4.7a.

38. The other alternative was the strategy adopted by Zhu Xi, which asserted that Confucius had compiled the *Odes* and had included those Odes expressing sentiments and aims that were not normative as negative examples. For this theory, see Chapter 8.

39. See *Analects* 15.11 and 17.18. In both of these passages, however, Confucius refers to the "sounds" (*sheng*) of Zheng, rather than to, say, the "Airs" or "Odes" of that state. This term usually refers in later texts like the *Preface* or the "Record of Music" ("Yueji") either to instrumental music or to the human voice.

A famous passage from the *Zuo Tradition*, datable to after 375 B.C.E., tells how in 543 a son of the ruler of the southern state of Wu, one Duke Zha, made a visit to Lu, Confucius's home state and a territory renowned as the home of orthodox ritual traditions. According to the *Zuo Tradition*, Duke Zha took the opportunity to request a complete performance of the Odes; and the narrative contains his comments upon each section of the Odes in turn. The Airs of Zheng are singled out for criticism, although not specifically characterized as *yin*. Duke Zha says: "Beautiful! In intricacy they have gone too far. The people will not be able to endure, so Zheng will be the first state to vanish." (Translation adapted from DeWoskin, p. 22. The original appears at Xiang 29.) We can be quite confident from the context that Duke Zha was speaking of the Airs of Zheng in the present collection of the *Odes*. Moreover, since we are told that the Odes were sung to Duke Zha, we may also be sure that he heard their words, not just an instrumental performance. Still, it may have been the musical qualities of the Odes, rather than their words, that Duke Zha criticized; the term used to characterize the Airs of Zheng, *xi* "intricacy," is well suited to the criticism of rhythmic or melodic lines. See DeWoskin, pp. 24–25; and Picken, "The Shapes," p. 103.

40. *Xunzi* 4.7a.

41. Ibid., 19.13a. Compare 1.4b: "The Odes [show] where moderate sounds come to a halt."

42. *Xunzi* 1.4b.

43. Ibid.

44. Ibid., 14.1a. See also 14.1b: "So when one listens to the sounds of the Elegantiae and Lauds, his aims and intentions [*zhiyi*] will be broadened thereby." In this passage as elsewhere in the "Discussion of Music" ("Yuelun"), Xunzi is speaking of the Odes in their role of "refined music"—the ritually correct music associated with the Odes, which was threatened and indeed probably very largely displaced already in Xunzi's day by the "new music" against which Confucius is made to rail at *Analects* 15.11 and 17.18.

CHAPTER FOUR

EPIGRAPHS: *Er Cheng ji*, p. 1046; Zheng Qiao, p. 3.

1. It is not clear that the Qin actually intended to extirpate Confucianism or its texts; the First Emperor is said to have consulted with Confucian scholars concerning various matters and to have employed seventy "erudites" (*boshi*), some of whom were probably Confucians. See Wang Guowei, 1.1b–2a; and Hsiao, pp. 469–70. Still, the continuity of the Confucian tradition was disrupted by the Qin's policies and the unsettled social conditions accompanying the dynasty's rise and fall.

2. *Shiji*, p. 2692.

3. Schwartz, p. 239; Tu, "The 'Thought of Huang-Lao.'"

4. Tjan, 1: 84–89; Wang Guowei, 1.2a–28a; Qian, "Liang Han boshi jiafa kao," in his *Liang Han jingxue*, pp. 165–233.

5. Wang Guowei, 1.13b.

6. Fung, 2: 18.

7. These texts were supposed to have been written in the pre-Qin "tadpole" hand; hence the name *guwen*, literally "ancient script." Although the controversy at court over the relative merits of the Old Texts and the New Texts did not begin in earnest until the end of the Western Han, and although some of the stories associated with the discoveries of the Old Texts are certainly legendary, nevertheless it seems that alternative versions of the classics dating from the pre-Qin era indeed circulated during the second century B.C.E. On the controversy between the adherents of the Old and New Texts in the Han, see Tjan, 1: 137–45; Zhou; and Qian, *Liang Han jingxue*.

8. *Han shu*, p. 2410.

9. As, for instance, the story of the *Grand Master's Art of War* (*Taigong bingfa*) given to Zhang Liang by a mysterious old man in the *Shiji* (p. 2035). For other early stories about magical texts, see Seidel, esp. pp. 297–302.

10. The distinction between Old and New Text versions of the Odes was made even though it was never claimed that the Mao text differed in provenance from those of the three New Text schools—all were written down from memory after the Qin. Rather, the distinction had to do with the institutional affiliations and interpretive orientations of the schools.

11. See Chen Qiaocong and Wang Xianqian for collections of these materials. Jiang Shanguo, pp. 38–76, has a good discussion. See Hightower, "The *Han-shih wai-chuan*," pp. 252–53, on the difficulties involved in deciding to which school any particular quotation should be assigned and for translations of the biographies of Shen Pei, Yuan Gu, and Han Ying (pp. 268–78).

12. Hightower, "The *Han-shih wai-chuan*," pp. 251–53.

13. Ibid., p. 253. As an example of the sort of exegesis practiced by the Qi school, see the quotation from the *Shi wei fan li shu* discussed in Jiang Shanguo, pp. 47–51. On the thought of Yi Feng, see Hsiao, pp. 508–13.

14. Hightower, *Han Shih Wai Chuan*, is a translation of this work. Han Ying became an erudite during the reign of Emperor Wen (Hightower, "The *Han-shih wai-chuan*," p. 253).

15. Hightower, "The *Han-shih wai-chuan*," p. 264.

16. The text was also known in the Han as the *Maoshi guxun zhuan*. Like the *Preface*, the *Commentary* can be found in the *Shisan jing zhushu* edition of the *Odes*.

17. *Han shu* 88.

18. Zheng Xuan, *Shipu*, quoted at *Maoshi zhushu* 1.2.

19. Quoted in Karlgren, "Early History," pp. 12–13.

20. Ibid., p. 33.

21. Hu Pingsheng and Han Ziqiang, p. 19.

22. *Mawangdui Hanmu boshu*, 1: 17–27.

23. Like most early commentaries, the *Commentary* probably originally cir-

culated as a document separate from the *Odes*; in the translation below I have followed the usual arrangement, cutting up the *Commentary* and appending it to those lines of the Ode to which it seems to refer.

24. *Xing* differs from *bi* "analogy" in the traditional accounts in that "analogy" carries through the whole Ode, but *xing* appears only in a few lines, usually at the beginning of the stanza or Ode as a whole. *Xing* is thus characterized as a combination of *bi* and *fu* "direct presentation." See Shih-Hsiang Chen, pp. 16–20, for a summary account of some of the interpretations given *xing* in traditional criticism. C. H. Wang, pp. 6–22, summarizes some modern scholarship on *xing* and offers an interpretation based on the Lord and Parry theory of oral-formulaic composition. See also Pauline Yu, "Allegory, Allegoresis"; and Hu Nianyi.

25. *Shiji*, p. 3115. Pi, *Jingxue tonglun*, pp. 4–7, gives examples from a variety of other Han texts. But note the claim of Xue Shilong that these comments specified the circumstances not of the composition of the Ode but of its quotation or recitation (quoted in Wang Yinglin, *Kunxue jiwen* 4.3.224).

26. Note Sima Qian's comment that "the coda of the 'Guanju' is the beginning of the Airs" (quoted in Guo, 1:66).

27. *Siku quanshu zongmu tiyao* 15.1. A representative selection of the traditional controversy concerning the *Preface* can be found in chap. 99 of Zhu Yizun. Modern scholarship has tended to favor Fan Ye's claim that the *Preface* was authored in whole or in part by Wei Hong (1st century C.E.) (*Hou Han shu*, p. 2575). Representative studies include Gao, "*Maoshi xu* zai jiantao" and "San lun *Maoshi xu*"; Gu, "*Maoshi xu* zhi beijing"; Zhang; and Zheng Zhenduo. Conservative scholars have vigorously attacked the contention that Wei Hong authored the *Preface*; see, e.g., Huang Jie; Pan, "*Shixu* mingbian"; and Su Weiyue. The claim that Zixia authored the *Preface* is still maintained today; see, e.g., Zhu Guanhua.

28. This account, from a lost portion of the *Chronological Table*, is referred to by the Northern Zhou scholar Shen Zhong and quoted in Lu Deming's (556–627) commentary on the Odes. See *Maoshi zhushu* 1.4.

29. *Maoshi zhushu* 9.837.

30. Shen Zhong refers to a "Great Preface" in the comment cited in note 28. But the name was used with varying applications by different writers. See Jiang Shanguo, pp. 80–81, for a survey. Jiang says that Lu Deming began the practice of calling the Preface to the "Guanju" the "Great Preface" (p. 80). Cheng Boyu (Tang dynasty) says that the Preface to the "Guanju" was entitled the "Great Preface" in the *Wenxuan* of Xiao Tong (501–31) (quoted in Zhu Yizun, 99.1b); but modern editions of the *Wenxuan* have "Maoshi xu" as the title (*Wenxuan* 45.29b).

31. Zhu Xi, *Shixu bian*, 1b–2b. This arrangement is followed in Legge, *The She King*, "Prolegomena," pp. 34–37.

32. As, e.g., in the ubiquitous *Annotations and Explications of the Thirteen Classics* (*Shisan jing zhushu*) edition of the Odes.

33. As in Zheng Xuan's account, given above. So far as I know, the system-

atic division of the *Preface* into two strata was first advocated by Cheng Boyu in the Tang; it became one of the commonplaces of Song Odes studies. On Cheng Boyu, see Chapter 5. On Song developments of the idea of the stratified nature of the *Preface*, see Chapter 7.

34. Jiang Shanguo, pp. 79–83, has a good discussion of the various terminologies.

35. Only the titles and the Upper Prefaces survive for these six Odes; three of these are printed in the Mao editions of the *Odes* between Mao #169 and #170, and the other three after Mao #170, #171, and #172.

36. In the case of the Preface to the "Guanju," the Lower Preface would contain all the material commonly included in the "Great Preface," plus Pericopes 2–3 and 19–21.

37. Such reformulation is by no means incompatible with "traditionalism"—that is, with the premium placed in a doctrinal culture upon the quality of having been received ("traditional")—but it resembles indirect rather than direct quotation. Thus such teaching is neither limited by a text nor has it yet itself become a text.

38. The sense that the Upper Preface was a text to be accommodated and interpreted rather than simply a tradition to be restated or reformulated is reflected in the way that the Lower Prefaces handle the numerous contradictions between the *Commentary* on a given Ode and its corresponding Upper Preface (see Wei for examples). Probably the most striking examples are those in which the *Preface* reads as a satire or "jab" (*ci*) an Ode that the *Commentary* considers a poem of praise (e.g., the "Jingnü" Ode [Mao #42]). The Lower Preface disposes of these anomalies by claiming that the Ode "presents the ancient" (*chengu*) in order to abash the present; that is, the Ode does indeed praise an earlier prince but only to criticize a contemporary ruler. Thus whereas the Upper Preface and the *Commentary* seem unaware of one another, or at least unconcerned about the ways in which they may disagree, the Lower Preface is concerned to maintain the integrity of these two texts and to somehow synthesize and reconcile them. This synthetic impulse, along with the tendency to preserve and comment upon earlier texts without, however, clearly marking them off, will be seen below to be important to the rhetoric of the "Great Preface."

39. That they are printed as two paragraphs in Legge's edition reflects the Song distinction between Upper and Lower Prefaces, but there is no evidence of which I am aware that they were so treated before the Song.

40. A famous example of this phenomenon is the case of the *Shui jing zhu*; it was discovered by the Qing scholar Quan Zuwang (1705–55). See C. S. Gardner, pp. 20–21n8.

41. The distinction between pretextual, proto-textual, and textual rhetorics should not be schematically associated with a historical process, nor yet with a distinction between oral and written composition, although it is clear that both connections hold in a general way. The particular form of discourse a doctrinal expositor adopts is a function of the degree of authority of the

foundational text, social situation, and the like. *All* three forms of discourse are options from very early on.

42. The "Preface" may have *Yili* 4.10a and 6.12b in view here.

43. See Pericope 11 for what seems to be another version of the same contrast.

44. Parallels to Pericopes 5–7 may be found in the "Yueji" (*Liji xunzuan* 19.2a, 19.26a). For Pericope 5, see also *Mencius* 4.A.27.

45. The *gu* that begins this passage is a marker of transition to a new topic, and not a logical connective. See note 51 below.

46. See *Zhouli* 6.13a.

47. That is, they are called "Airs" (*feng*) because they sway (*feng*) their hearers.

48. Literally, they "received understanding from [*ming hu*] the records of gain and lost [i.e., success and failure]." Who exactly the "state historians" (*guoshi*) were supposed to be is not clear. While the *Preface* attributes some of the Odes to "historians" *shi* (e.g., the Ode "Jiong" [Mao #297]), most are ascribed to various historical figures of Spring and Autumn history or to anonymous authors among the people or grandees. For example, the *Preface* attributes the "Minlao" (Mao #253) to Duke Mu of Shao, and the "Huangniao" (Mao #131) is ascribed to "the people" (*guoren*). See the *Correct Significance* discussion of Pericope 13 (*Maoshi zhushu* 1.14–15), where it is asserted that the historians are mentioned because it was they who received the Odes and passed them on to the musicians, and that the term *shi* could refer to any literate person, not just to the historians proper.

49. That is, the "Linzhizhi" (Mao #11), the final Air of the Zhounan section. The Minor Preface to the "Linzhizhi" says: "The 'Linzhizhi' responds [*ying*] to the 'Guanju.' The transformations of the 'Guanju' were wrought, and no one in the world went against ritual. Even the rulers of unhappy generations were all trustworthy and generous, just as they had been in the age when the hooves of the *lin* were to be seen." The *lin* was the portent of an age of sagacious rule.

50. The "Quechao" (Mao #12) and "Zouyu" (Mao #25) are the first and last Airs of the Shaonan section. Zhou and Shao were the fiefs from which the transformative virtue of King Wen spread, assisted by the famous Duke of Zhou in the former case and the Duke of Shao in the latter.

51. For example, at Pericopes 8, 10, 19, and 21. For *gu* as a pseudo-connective linking independent units, see Lau, *Tao Te Ching*, pp. 172–73; and Henricks, pp. 511–12.

52. Although the rest of the Preface to the "Guanju" seems to presuppose that the Consort is Taisi, the wife of the great King Wen, here as in the case of the *Commentary* discussed above that identification was not made explicit. We must allow for the possibility the Upper Preface, insofar as it circulated as an independent document or tradition (that is, insofar as it was not fleshed out with the sort of teachings contained in the Lower Preface) in the second century B.C.E., did not make this specific historical identification.

53. Compare Pericope 3.

54. See the "Wangzhi" ("Kingly Institutions") chapter of the *Liji* (*Liji xun-zuan* 5.6b); and the *Hanshu*, p. 1708. See Chapter 8 for Zhu Xi's account.

55. See in this connection Pericope 6, where *dong* is used in connection with the emotions.

56. See note 42 above.

57. These materials also appear in the *Records of the Historian* (*Shiji*) of Sima Qian and in the *Xunzi* under slightly different titles and in slightly different forms. The "Yueji," which now forms one of the "chapters" of the received text of the *Liji*, was supposed to have been compiled at the court of the same Prince Xian of Hejian who patronized the Mao school of the Odes (see p. 83). That the "Preface" passage probably derived from the "Yueji" (or some ancestor thereof) is suggested first by the fondness of the "Preface" for quotation and second by the fact that the materials brought together in Pericopes 5–7 are scattered in the "Yueji." The "Preface" version brings them together, altering a character here and there to smooth transitions and rearranging them to form a more coherent and fluent account.

58. *Zuo* Xiang 25. The blunting of the sense of *zhi*, the reference to an authoritative text, and the attribution to Confucius all argue for the lateness of this passage.

59. On this term and its history, see Chapters 5 and 6.

60. Owen, *Traditional Chinese Poetry and Poetics*, p. 58.

61. *Zhuangzi*, "Tiandao," 13.36.

62. Ibid. Translation based on Graham, *Chuang-tzŭ*, p. 139; and James J. Y. Liu, *Language*, p. 9. The first chapter (pp. 3–37) of Liu's book is a discussion of the tradition of skeptical and paradoxical Chinese views on language and texts.

63. *Xici zhuan* ("The Great Appendix"), A.12 (*Zhouyi* 7.10b).

64. See, e.g., Xunzi's comments discussed in Chapter 3.

65. Hence the paronomastic definition that "music [*yue*] is happiness [*le*]." The two terms are written with the same graph.

66. *Zuo* Zhao 25.

67. The idea that the special virtue of the Odes is to act upon the *zhi* appears in a number of Han and pre-Han texts.

> So when one listens to the sounds of the Elegantiae and Lauds, his aims and intentions [*zhiyi*] are broadened thereby. (*Xunzi* 14.1b)

The superior men knew that those in power could not control the people through evil means, and so they chose the Six Arts to help and cultivate them. The *Odes* and *Documents* are to order [*xu*] their aims [*zhi*], the *Rites* and *Music* to purify their cultivation, and the *Changes* and *Spring and Autumn* to illuminate their understanding. The Six Arts are all great, and each is great in its own way. The *Odes* guide [*dao*] the aim, and so they foster substance. The *Rites* moderates and shapes, and so fosters cultivation. (Dong, 1.8b–9a; trans. adapted from Chow, p. 159)

Chow translates *dao* as "expresses," but I think the parallel with *jiezhi* "moderates and shapes" in the next line warrants the more active reading. The same holds true of the summary found in the "Tianxia" chapter of the *Zhuangzi*: "The *Odes* serves as a guide to the aim, the *Documents* to affairs, the *Ritual* to conduct, the *Music* to harmony, the *Changes* to the Yin and Yang, and the *Spring and Autumn Annals* to names and portions" (*Zhuangzi yinde*, p. 91; trans. adapted from Graham, *Chuang Tzu*, p. 275). The idea that the Odes were supposed to transform the emotional natures of those who studied them is also reflected in the following passage from the "Jing-jie" chapter of the *Liji*: "Confucius said, 'Upon entering a state, the teachings employed there can be known. If the people are mild, gentle, sincere and generous, it is the teachings of the Odes' " (*Liji xunzuan* 26.1a). On this passage, and for other Han and pre-Han texts concerned with the relation between the Odes and the *zhi* and the *qing*, see Zhu Ziqing, pp. 285–91, and *passim*; and Chow, pp. 155–60.

CHAPTER FIVE

EPIGRAPH: Berman, p. 131.

1. The *Correct Significance* texts and expositions of the Five Classics (the *Changes*, the *Documents*, the *Odes*, the *Record of Ritual*, and the *Zuo Tradition* with the *Spring and Autumn Annals*) form the basis of the *Annotations and Explications of the Thirteen Classics* (*Shisan jing zhushu*) of Ruan Yuan (1764–1849).

2. Ruan Yuan's edition of the *Correct Significance*, entitled *Maoshi zhushu*, also contains the philological glosses of Lu Deming (556–627). On Zheng Xuan, see note 8 below.

3. See, e.g., Pi Xirui's chapter "The Age of Disunion in Classics Study" ("Jingxue fenli shidai") in his *Jingxue lishi*, pp. 170–92; and Honda, pp. 183, 206.

4. For an account of some of the social conditions behind the eclipse of Confucianism during the third to the sixth centuries C.E., see Balazs, "Political Philosophy" and "Nihilistic Revolt."

5. Pi, *Jingxue lishi*, pp. 178–79, 182.

6. For a useful reconstruction of the classics studies of this period, see Jian.

7. *Beishi*, "Rulin zhuan" (Biographies of Confucians), p. 2709.

8. Zheng Xuan (Zheng Kangcheng, 127–200) was one of the most prolific and certainly the most influential of the Eastern Han classicists. He produced commentaries on most of the canonical texts of his day; however, only those on the *Odes*, the *Yili*, the *Liji*, and the *Zhouli* have survived intact. For a detailed discussion of the Zheng Xuan corpus and its problems, see Hung, pp. 74–134; and Pi, *Jingxue lishi*, pp. 141–42, esp. Zhou Yutong's note 20 on p. 146 of Pi's work. The most important source for Zheng Xuan's reading of the Odes is his *Annotations to Mao's Odes* (*Maoshi jian*), which is

included in and commented upon in the *Correct Significance of Mao's Odes*; but his *Shipu* (*Chronological Table of the Odes*) was also influential. The latter work is partially reconstructed in the *Zhengshi yishu*. Zheng's significance for the history of the interpretation of the *Odes* lies (1) in his preparation of a syncretic text incorporating certain Three Schools readings into the Mao text (thereby rendering those texts superfluous and precipitating their disappearance) and (2) in establishing and elaborating the interpretations of the Mao school. On his *Odes* scholarship, see Ōkawa.

9. That is, the *Yi Ritual* (*Yili*), the *Institutes of Zhou* (*Zhouli*), and the *Record of Ritual* (*Liji*).

10. Liu Yiqing, 4.2. According to the story, Zheng Xuan overheard Fu Qian discussing his ideas about the *Zuo Tradition* outside an inn; impressed with Fu's exposition, he presented Fu with the notes to his own unfinished commentary on the work and abandoned the project to him. See Mather, pp. 93–94.

11. Yen (Yan), pp. 64–65. Yan goes on in the same passage to ridicule contemporary pedants unable to make use of any source other than the commentaries of Zheng Xuan. See also Dien, pp. 51–54, on Yan's classics scholarship and on the distinction between Northern and Southern Learning.

12. *Wu qiu bei zhai Lunyu jicheng*, vols. 22–26, reprints the 1923 Kaitoku dō edition.

13. Pi, *Jingxue lishi*, p. 177*n*5.

14. Tang Yongtong, "Yan yi zhi bian," pp. 26–47.

15. Ode #241 "Huangyi"; trans. modified from Karlgren, *Book of Odes*, p. 196.

16. *Analects* 11.12.

17. See Tang Yongtong, *Wei Jin xuanxue lungao*; and Pauline Yu, *The Reading of Imagery*, pp. 41–42.

18. At *Analects* 3.16.

19. Pi, *Jingxue lishi*, p. 196.

20. See Hightower, "The *Han-shih wai-chuan*," pp. 259–64, for a discussion of some of these problems.

21. The following discussion draws heavily on the researches of these scholars.

22. It has been hypothesized that the first explications were originally notes on these discussions. Mo Runsun (pp. 357–58) argues that the *shu* of *yiishu* means *ji* "note"; *yiishu* would thus be "notes or records of discussions" (*yii=yi* "discussion"), either taken by students or spectators, or made beforehand by the expositor himself. Later writers imitated these notes, and the explication as a literary form was born. It is important to keep in mind, however, that the practice of the oral exposition of the classics must have continued after explications began to be composed in written form; and there would have been a complex and ongoing interaction between oral and written forms of exegesis.

23. Quoted in Wright, "T'ang T'ai-tsung," p. 241.

24. For a more detailed account of the classics scholarship of the Tang, including the composition of the *Correct Significance*, see McMullen, pp. 67–112.

25. This account is based on Morohashi, *Keigaku kenkyū josetsu*, pp. 61–68; and Pan, "*Wujing zhengyi* tanyuan."

26. Wu, p. 220.

27. Yu Zhengxie.

28. As McMullen (pp. 76–79) shows, both the Tang emperors and the literati as a group were relatively tolerant of departures from the *Correct Significance* orthodoxy. But although alternative interpretations were not suppressed, the *Correct Significance* succeeded in effectively dominating the world of classics studies for the next century (ibid., pp. 83–84).

29. For a passage without a Sequence, see Pericope 6. The terms I use to identify these sections of the *Correct Significance* commentary are my own; neither the "Sequences," the "Paraphrases" nor the "Topics" are explicitly identified as such in the text.

30. Although not invariably; see Pericope 10.

31. *CSPG* 4.1, 5.4, 7.1. Like the Sequences, these Paraphrases have antecedents in the history of exegesis. They closely resemble the *zhangju* "chapters and sentences" commentaries popular in the Eastern Han, of which the *Mengzi zhangju* (*Mencius [explicated] section by section and phrase by phrase*) of Zhao Qi (d. 203 C.E.) is a good and well-known example. For a brief description of this work and its aims, see Dobson, *Late Han Chinese*, pp. xix–xx.

32. The "Yueji" chapter of the *Liji* was a particular concern in this respect; see, e.g., *CSPG* 7.17–26.

33. But we must recognize that the elements of the system are bound together not by relations of logical entailment, but by some more capacious ideal.

34. For examples of this sort of expansion, see *CSPG* 8.5–8; 10.4–6, 7–8; 13–14; 11.5–7; 13.3–10; 14.8–12; 15.7–8; and 17.3–4.

35. *CSPG* 10.17–20, 11.7.

36. *CSPG* 15.7–8.

37. See Cikoski for an ambitious attempt to discuss early Chinese reasoning in these terms.

38. Handbooks of Chinese prosody contain long lists of such categories and their members. For an example, see Wang Li, pp. 153–66.

39. For a good discussion of this phenomenon as it appears in traditional Chinese poetry, see Frankel, pp. 165–67.

40. That is, rites and morality ground and must precede government (*CSPG* 12.4).

41. *CSPG* 10.16–17.

42. *CSPG* 17.14–16.

43. *CSPG* 11.7–8, 17.14–16.

44. It is not entirely clear who the *Correct Significance* thinks responsible for the arrangement of the Odes. The *Correct Significance* commentary attached to the title "*Mao's Odes*: The Airs of the States" says that the Music Master of the Zhou court was responsible for the order of the chapters within the "Airs of the States," but that their arrangement may have been altered by Confucius (line 24). I am not aware of any statement concerning the order of the Airs within the chapters.

45. *CSPG* 2.1–2. The *Correct Significance* is taking for granted here Zheng Xuan's interpretation of the "Guanju." Zheng reads the "Guanju" as praising the Consort's absence of jealousy, as manifested by her delight in getting for King Wen another virtuous wife—the "virtuous girl" (*shunü*). See Zheng's annotation of the second line of the "Guanju."

46. *CSPG* 2.2

47. Karlgren, *Grammata Serica Recensa*, #976.

48. The contrast with the typical moves of Western hermeneutics is instructive. There texts are "saved" from meaninglessness or triviality in an operation that is essentially metaphorical. The text is redeemed by showing it to refer to some larger significance. Here, on the other hand, it is not that the relation between King Wen and the Consort only seems to be a trivial matter (*xishi*); it *is* a trivial matter, but one that plays a crucial role in the more magnificent historical project of King Wen through a logic of organic growth.

49. *CSPG* 2.3–4.

50. See Pauline Yu's remarks concerning the role of the *Odes* in traditional Chinese culture (*The Reading of Imagery*, pp. 79–80), which she likens to the Western epic. Havelock's view of the early Greek epics as the vehicles of socialization and moral education in an oral culture is also suggestive in this connection.

51. Compare *Analects* 17.19: "I would like to be without words"; see also 1.3, 5.4, 6.14, 11.20, 12.3, 14.29, 15.40.

52. *CSPG* 6.10–11.   53. *CSPG* 6.11–12.

54. *CSPG* 6.1–2.   55. *CSPG* 6.6–9

56. Zheng Qiao believed that the performance traditions for all but a few of the Odes had been lost by the Jin (quoted in Jiang Shanguo, p. 325). In the Song, Zhu Xi published musical settings for twelve Odes in his *Yili jing-zhuan tongjie* (Comprehensive explanation of the *Yi Ritual* and its commentaries). These were supposed to have derived from the Tang Kaiyuan period (713–42), but this is by no means certain. See Picken, "Twelve Ritual Melodies." Howard J. Wechsler (pp. 117–18) says that the music of the Sui was used at the court of Tang Gaozu (r. 618–27); Taizong (r. 627–50) commissioned new music to be used at court ceremonies, which was called the "court music of the Great Tang" (Da Tang yayue). The *Correct Significance* speaks of the knowledge of the ultimate motivations of the authors of the Odes as something that (only?) the Zhou court Music Masters could know (see, e.g., *CSPG* 6.7, 6.12).

57. Metzger, p. 179.

58. Of course, Zhu Xi was profoundly influenced by the *Preface*, but I am speaking here of his own image of his hermeneutical situation, which was of someone who could understand the classics "directly." See Chapter 8.

59. *Mencius* 7.B.3. The translation is from Legge, *The Works of Mencius*, p. 479.

60. Pulleyblank, "Chinese Historical Criticism," pp. 143, 147. I believe Pulleyblank is too quick to dismiss Zheng Qiao (ibid., pp. 150–51), on whom see Chapter 8.

61. My account of these thinkers is based largely upon E. G. Pulleyblank, "Neo-Confucianism and Neo-Legalism."

62. Ibid., p. 89.

63. Ibid., p. 90.

64. The text, which does not appear in all collections of Han Yu's works, can be found at 9.1.3b–4a in the *Waiji* "Outer Collection" of the *(Yinzhu) Han Wengong wenji*. On this piece, see Murayama; and Katō.

65. Following Katō's emendation (p. 24).

66. Again following ibid.

67. The last comment is meant to show that the Han Confucian who composed the *Preface* relied upon the *Zuo Tradition* and the *Records of the Historian* for his accounts of the circumstances of the Odes.

68. Although Han Yu is mentioned by Chao Yuezhi, on whom see Chapter 8.

69. Zhu Yizun, chap. 103.

70. I have used the text given in the *Tongzhi tang jingjie*, pp. 9103–10.

71. *Maoshi zhishuo* 1a–2b.

72. Ibid., 7b–8b.

73. On this figure, see Wang Yinglin, *Kunxue jiwen* 4.3.218.

CHAPTER SIX

EPIGRAPH: Ouyang, *Ouyang Yongshu ji* 8.71.

1. The best account in English of Ouyang Xiu's life and thought is James T. C. Liu (Liu Zijian), *Ou-yang Hsiu*. This is a translation and revision of the same author's *Ouyang Xiu di zhixue yu congzheng*. For Ouyang Xiu's classics studies and historiography, see He Zeheng.

2. On Ouyang Xiu's literary writings, see Egan, *The Literary Works*.

3. The *New Tang History* (*Xin Tang shu*) and *New History of the Five Dynasties* (*Xin Wudai shi*). See James T. C. Liu, *Ou-yang Hsiu*, pp. 105–9, and *Ouyang Xiu*, pp. 47–60; and He Zeheng, pp. 105–66.

4. On Ouyang's innovations in the field of genealogy, see James T. C. Liu, *Ou-yang Hsiu*, pp. 112–13; and He Zeheng, pp. 194–97. Ouyang's *Jigu lu*

(Record of collecting antiquities) was the first compilation and study of stone and bronze inscriptions. See the description by Chikusa Masaaki in Hervouet, p. 199; and He Zeheng, pp. 177–89.

5. On Ouyang Xiu's classics studies generally, see James T. C. Liu, *Ou-yang Hsiu*, pp. 85–99, and *Ouyang Xiu*, pp. 19–46. For his *Changes* and *Spring and Autumn Annals* scholarship, see He Zeheng, pp. 37–49 and 77–87, respectively.

6. On the diversity of the eleventh-century revival of Confucianism, see Tillman, pp. 30–52.

7. For a somewhat different account, see D. K. Gardner, pp. 9–14. My "institutional" and "metaphysical" approaches correspond roughly to Gardner's "programmatic" and "philosophical" approaches; his latter category includes texts and approaches that I would classify as "personal/devotional."

8. On Sun Fu and Hu Yuan, see de Bary, "A Reappraisal," pp. 88–93; James T. C. Liu, *Ou-yang Hsiu*, pp. 88–89, and *Ouyang Xiu*, pp. 20–22; and D. K. Gardner, p. 11.

9. See de Bary, "A Reappraisal," pp. 100–106. Wang Anshi included a commentary on the *Odes*, now lost, in his *Sanjing (xin) yii* ([New] significance of three classics). Because of his political notoriety, and because he attempted to make his interpretations of the classics standard during the 1070's, Wang Anshi's role in the history of classical studies has been exaggerated. (For a typical account, see Honda, pp. 307–8.) In fact, Wang's influence on classical studies was minimal. He should be seen as part of, not the initiator of, the iconoclastic movement in Song scholarship. See Pi, *Jingxue lishi*, p. 221, where this point is made; see also Zhou Yutong's note 7 on p. 222 of the same work regarding the *Sanjing (xin) yi*.

10. On the eclectic sources drawn upon by these thinkers, see Henderson, pp. 120–26.

11. The *Spring and Autumn Annals* was particularly vulnerable to a type of interpretation that can be described only as a covert commentary on current events. This "misuse" of the classic became flagrant in certain works of the Southern Song; a famous example was the *Chunqiu zhuan* (Commentary on the *Spring and Autumn Annals*) of Hu Anguo (1074–1138). See Honda, pp. 311–12; or Pi, *Jingxue lishi*, pp. 250, 254 n6, for this work.

12. Wang Yinglin, *Kunxue jiwen*, 8.22a; quoted in Pi, *Jingxue lishi*, p. 220. The commentary on the *Documents* attributed to Kong Anguo (fl. 126–117 B.C.E.) is generally agreed by modern scholars to be a forgery, probably of the Jin dynasty (265–419); see Hung, pp. 102–3, but it still had defenders like Lu You in the Song. According to Pi Xirui, Lu You had Ouyang Xiu in mind when he referred to critics of the *Commentary on the Appended Words*; Ouyang, Su Shi (1037–1101), and Su Che (1039–1112) when he mentioned the *Institutes of Zhou*; Li Gou (1009–59) and Sima Guang (1019–86) when he mentioned the *Mencius*; Su Shi when he mentioned the *Documents*; and

Chao Yuezhi (1059–1129) when he mentioned the *Odes*. See Zhou Yutong's notes 19–23 on pp. 225–28 of Pi's *Jingxue lishi* for discussions of each of these works.

13. On the Song criticism of the *Preface*, see Chapter 8. On Ouyang Xiu's criticisms of the *Commentary on the Appended Words*, see Shchutskii, pp. 65–71. In scholarship on the Odes, Cao Cuizhong (fl. 1124) and Zheng Qiao (1104–62) developed sophisticated accounts of the institutional background to the exegetical tradition; Cao also pioneered the use of Han Three Schools materials. On their work, see Chapter 8. Wang Yinglin (1223–96) also produced a work of Three Schools scholarship, the *Verification of the Odes* (*Shikao*), as well as a *Geographical Verification of the Odes* (*Shi dili kao*). Cai Bian (1058–1117) produced a collection of glosses on the names of "birds, beasts, plants, and trees," the *Maoshi mingwu jie*. The *Shijing xieyun kaoyi* of Fu Guang (fl. 1210) is perhaps the best-known work of Song phonological scholarship on the Odes.

14. The idea of a "Song transition," first proposed by the Japanese cultural historian Naitō Torajirō, has been enormously influential in Chinese studies in Japan, in the West, and, to a somewhat lesser extent, in China. See James T. C. Liu and Golas for a collection of representative essays. The paradigm of a major reorganization in the late Tang and early Song has been fruitfully applied to literary history, particularly the history of Song poetry; see Yoshikawa, esp. pp. 14–19. Song landscape painting demonstrates a new power of realistic observation and depiction; Max Loehr (p. 192) speaks of its "almost scientific character." This same empiricist temper seems reflected in the remarkable achievements of the Song in the natural and mathematical sciences; see Elvin, pp. 179–99.

15. Pi, *Jingxue lishi*, p. 280; Twitchett, pp. 31–32. The Buddhist and Daoist canons were soon also printed (Twitchett, pp. 35–38).

16. See the discussion in Kasoff, pp. 4–5. According to some Song authors, the ready availability of printed texts resulted in a decline in the memorization of the classics and a shift from reading aloud to an internalized, silent reading. See Chapter 8.

17. Privately printed editions of the Confucian classics were banned until 1064 (Twitchett, p. 32).

18. The subcommentries on the *Analects*, *Classic of Filiality*, and *Erya* prepared by Xing Bing (932–1010) were in the manner of the *Correct Significance* commentaries. On the commentaries of Xing Bing and his near contemporary Sun Shi (962–1033), and on early Song classics study generally, see Ma, pp. 109–10.

19. Translation adapted from James T. C. Liu, *Ou-yang Hsiu*, p. 86. See also the story about Wang Dan as an examiner given in Pi, *Jingxue lishi*, p. 220. Liu, *Ou-yang Hsiu*, pp. 86–87, gives other examples of the literalism of the early Song classicists.

20. Pi Xirui (*Jingxue lishi*, p. 250) says that Sun Fu's comments on the

Spring and Autumn Annals were influenced by those of Dan Zhu, Zhao Kuang, and Lu Chun.

21. James T. C. Liu, "An Early Sung Reformer," pp. 109–10.

22. As in the accounts of Wang Yinglin and Lu You quoted in Pi, *Jingxue lishi*, p. 220; see also James T. C. Liu, *Ou-yang Hsiu*, p. 88. Hu and Sun's influence in the capital persisted even after the fall of Fan Zhongyan, thanks in part to the patronage of Ouyang Xiu (Liu, *Ou-yang Hsiu*, pp. 88–89).

23. For Liu Chang as one of the first figures of Song iconoclastic and speculative scholarship, see, e.g., Wang Yinglin as quoted in Pi, *Jingxue lishi*, p. 220, and Zhou Yutong's note 6 on p. 221 of the same work; or the quotes from Chao Gongwu and Chen Zhensun in Honda, p. 307. Liu Chang's *Qi-jing xiaozhuan* can be found in the *Tongzhi tang jingjie*.

24. Mei's work, the *Maoshi xiaozhuan* (Short commentary on Mao's Odes) in 20 *juan*, is listed as "lost" by Zhu Yizun (104.4a–b).

25. Qiu, p. 15; quoted in Jiang Shanguo, p. 119.

26. Cheng Yuanmin, p. 34.

27. See Cheng Yuanmin for an account of Wang's scholarship, as well as an account of earlier Song skeptical scholarship on the *Odes*.

28. On the establishment in the Yuan dynasty of Zhu Xi's commentaries as the orthodox exposition of the *Odes* and other classics and the relationship of this development to the triumph of Neoconfucianism as a state orthodoxy, see de Bary, *Neo-Confucian Orthodoxy*, pp. 1–66, esp. p. 56; James T. C. Liu, "A Neo-Confucian School"; and Pi, *Jingxue lishi*, pp. 281–82 (see also Pi, pp. 283–90, on Zhu Xi's Yuan and Ming epigones).

29. One particular refinement of the Qing foundationalist movement was the attention it paid to the Han New Text interpretations of the classics in opposition to the relatively later Old Text readings; on this, see Elman, pp. 22–26. Pi Xirui, the greatest historian of the classical tradition, was a product of this school, and its particular concerns and agenda color all his work. See his account (*Jingxue lishi*, pp. 341–42) of the Qing foundationalist progress back through the exegetical tradition; see also the similar account in Liang Ch'i-ch'ao (Liang Qichao), pp. 21–27.

30. On the sectarian piety of the Qing generally, and on the commentaries of Chen Huan and Chen Qiaocong in particular, see Pi, *Jingxue lishi*, pp. 320–21; and also Karlgren, "Glosses on the Kuo-feng Odes," pp. 73–74.

31. The *Fundamental Significance* (hereafter the *FS*) was composed in 1059, when Ouyang was 53 *sui* (He Zeheng, p. 66). (In traditional China, an individual was credited with one *sui* for each calendar year in which he or she lived.) All the editions of the *Shi benyii* available to me seem to derive from a common ancestor. I have used the *Sibu congkan* ed.

32. On whom, see Chapter 8.

33. The contrast between *yi* and *yii* appears in Wang Bi's hermeneutic, where, however, it did not serve quite the same function or have the importance it assumed for the Song scholars. See Fung, 2: 186; and Tang Junyi, 2: 343.

34. As, e.g., in the *Shuowen jiezi* (Explaining script and explicating graphs), where *yi* is glossed by *zhi*. See *Shuowen jiezi zhu*, p. 506.

35. But not "idea" in the realist or conceptualist sense; see Graham, *Later Mohist Logic*, pp. 213–14, and also his review of Hansen, pp. 697–98.

36. See Graham, *Later Mohist Logic*, pp. 21, 35–36.

37. See Fung, 2: 184–86. Generally speaking, those who, like the Mohist dialecticians and Wang Bi, thought of *yi* as mental images were optimistic about the possibility of their adequate representation in language.

38. *Xici zhuan* A.12. I alluded in Chapter 5 to the controversy that raged during the early Northern and Southern Dynasties period over this claim.

39. *Zhuangzi*, chap. 26 ("Waiwu"); trans. adapted from Watson, *Complete Works of Chuang Tzu*, p. 302.

40. *FS* 14.6b, 2.1b, 1.9b–10a.

41. *Wenyii* was, on the whole, relatively more common. For examples of *wenyi*, see, e.g., *FS* 1.3b, 2.6b–7a. The evidence suggests that during the eleventh and twelfth centuries the two words, originally phonetically distinct, were becoming the homophonous pair they are today. In Stimson's reconstruction of Old Mandarin (i.e., the langauge of the late Song and Yuan), both terms are rendered (in Stimson's romanization) as "ii5." (For the approximate phonetic values of this phonemic representation, see Stimson, pp. 14–24. On the periodization of the historical phonology of Chinese, see Norman, p. 23.) According to Stimson, however, in the Middle Chinese pronunciations represented by the *Qieyun* rhyme book the two terms were phonetically distinct. Stimson renders the character for "intention" as "qi 5," and that for "significance" as "nj." At what point between the sixth century (the period whose pronunciation the *Qieyun* represents; Stimson, p. 10) and the first part of the fourteenth century (the date of the composition of the *Zhongyuan yinyun*; Stimson, p. 6) was the phonetic distinction between *yi* "intention" and *yii* "significance" lost?

It is a problematical business to rely upon works like the *Qieyun* or *Zhongyuan* to date phonological change. Such works may have served to provide the speakers of nonstandard dialects with information about the pronunciation of some other area, usually the capital. (Stimson [pp. 5–6] believes this to have been the case with the *Zhongyuan yinyun*.) On the other hand, they may also have served to preserve canonical phonetic distinctions that had fallen out of the living language (see Norman, p. 24, on the *Qieyun*). If the Middle Chinese pronunciations preserved in the *Qieyun* served this function, it seems possible that the distinction of concern here had become obsolete before the eleventh century, or even before 600, the approximate date of the composition of the *Qieyun*.

Nevertheless, I believe that Cheng Yi and his contemporaries in the eleventh century—although perhaps not his successors in the twelfth—did make this distinction, not only in their writings but also in the conversations that, recorded by their disciples, are our primary sources for the teachings of most of these thinkers. I am convinced that the two terms formed a contrasting pair by the apparent consistency with which Cheng Yi and others used them and by passages like the following, which relates an incident that would seem to depend upon the two terms being aurally distinguishable: "The Master [i.e., Liu Anshi (1048–1125)] was talking with me about the Odes, and when we touched upon the Airs of the States, the Master said: 'Those who read the Odes ought to seek their intentions [*yi*]; they ought not to seek their significances [*yii*]' " (quoted in Cheng Yuanmin, p. 37).

It is my impression that the careful distinction of these two terms did not long survive the eleventh century; thereafter they tended to be used more or less interchangeably in a variety of contexts and compounds. That the relatively few anomalous uses of *yi* and *yii* in eleventh-century texts are the results of textual corruption, perhaps fostered by the phonological and semantic blurring of these two terms in later centuries, is suggested by the fact that variant readings in different editions can often be located for such anomalies. For instance, one anecdote in the *Tuoba chan congke* ed. of Liu Anshi's *Yuancheng yulu* has *yii* in a context where one expects *yi* (2.2.26a), but the *Yuancheng yulu jie* version of the same passage has *yi* (65.2.7b).

42. In such contexts, the term was often written with the addition of the "word" or "speech" radical (number 149 in the traditional numbering).

43. *FS*, "Linzhizhi" Ode (Mao #11), 1.10a. The Music Master was supposed to have edited and arranged the Odes into the collection we have today. For more on this passage, see below.

44. Waley, *Book of Songs* #89 (p. 83).

45. Ibid.

46. The first eight of the Zhounan Odes are referred by the *Preface* to "the Consort" (*houfei*); the "Quechao" and the three Odes that follow it are associated with "the wife" (*furen*) or "the wife of a great officer" (*daifu qi*). None of them is explicitly identified with Taisi, the famous consort of King Wen. In a number of cases, King Wen is referred to in the Lower Preface (e.g., those to Odes #9 and #22) but no mention is made in the Upper Preface to either the *houfei* or to the *furen*. Only the Preface to the "Gaoyang" Ode (Mao #18) seems to link the *furen* of the "Quechao" Ode with King Wen. The *Correct Significance*, on the other hand, systematically associates both the *furen* and the *houfei* with Taisi (see, e.g., the *Correct Significance* comment on the Preface to this Ode; *Maoshi zhushu* 1.77).

47. Ibid., 1.76.

48. *FS* 2.1b–2a.

49. As the water radical of its graph suggests, *yin* implies a situation where people's behavior overflows and obscures its proper boundaries; hence its translation by such terms as "abandoned," "excessive," "dissolute," or "debauched."

50. See Cheng Yuanmin for a thorough discussion of the history of the idea of the "debauched Odes" and its ascendance in the Song.

51. Waley, *Book of Songs* #22.
52. See the Prefaces to the "Xiongzhi" (Mao #33) and "Pao you kuye" (Mao #34) Odes.
53. See, e.g., Cheng Yuanmin, p. 34.
54. Zhu Xi, *Shi jizhuan* 1.2.24a.
55. Ouyang's experiences as an author and reader of *ci* "songs" perhaps disposed him to make the distinction between the persona of the poem's speaker and the personality of the author, since *ci* writers often adopted the persona of a neglected wife or concubine. These personae were read as related in a complex but essentially indeterminate way with the personality of the poem's author. The distinction of persona and authorial personality is quite common in the *FS*. See Ouyang's comments on it and other possible relations at the "Ye you sijun" Ode (Mao #23; *FS* 2.6b).
56. In other of his writings, however, he was less cautious. The possibility that the Odes expressed morally debauched intentions was perhaps suggested in an occasional poem of Ouyang's written to an importunate admirer, "Replying to the Monk Weiwu, Who is Studying Poetry" ("Chou xue shi seng Weiwu") (*Ouyang Wenzhong gong ji* 4.2a–b; *Ouyang Yongshu ji* 2.2). On the other hand, much of the poem's language derives from the medieval tradition of exegesis that emphatically affirmed the paradigmatically normative character of the Odes.
57. Zhu Xi, *Shizhuan yishuo* 13a–b. On this passage, see Chapter 8.
58. See Cheng Yuanmin.
59. This was an old strategy, one that, as I suggested in Chapter 1, may have been involved with the Odes from the beginning. Ouyang was perfectly capable of appreciating such pleasures and authored a number of erotic *ci* songs. (Ronald Egan has shown that there is no reason to reject the authenticity of these songs; see *The Literary Works*, pp. 161–95, esp. pp. 192–95.) Part of the pleasure of the song genre was that it allowed the exploration of erotic feelings and the suspension of the presumption of autobiographical historicity that characterized the *shi* lyric.
60. *FS* 14.5a–7b.   61. *FS* 14.6b.
62. *FS* 1.10a.   63. *FS* 14.6a–6b.
64. This is just the opposite formulation of the hermeneutical problematic from that of the *Correct Significance* discussed in Chapter 5. There, the ostensive reference of the Odes was plain, but the dispositions of their authors were obscure; here, those dispositions are apparent, but the historical reference of the Odes must be supplied by the exegetical tradition.
65. *FS* 14.6b–7a.
66. *FS* 14.7b.
67. *FS* 14.11b. On the authorship of the *Preface*, see Chapter 4.
68. *FS* 14.11b.   69. *FS* 14.12a.
70. *FS* 14.12a.   71. *FS* 2.2a, 1.4b.
72. *FS* 1.9b.   73. *FS* 14.7a.
74. *FS* 6.7b.   75. *FS* 1.1b.

76. Ouyang, *Ouyang Yongshu ji* 3.36.
77. *FS* 3.2a, 14.1b, 1.10a, 2.9b–10a, 2.2a, 3.2a.
78. *FS* 1.1b, 2b–3a, 7b–8a; 2.2a; 4.1a. See He Zeheng, p. 50.
79. The question for Ouyang was not whether an unprejudiced reading of the Ode bore out the *Preface* or Mao and Zheng—whether it could be demonstrated that the *Preface* or Mao and Zheng had interpreted the Ode accurately—but whether the Ode could reasonably be understood on the basis of those authorities' interpretation.
80. This essay is printed after Ouyang's edition of the *Supplement to the Chronological Table of the Odes* in an unnumbered chapter appended to the *FS*.
81. *FS*, "Postface" 15a.
82. Ibid.
83. The theme that the efforts of many minds have a validity and authority that the efforts of a single intelligence must lack also appeared when, in another context, Ouyang imagined the conditions under which his more iconoclastic insights might be validated: "Let scholars individually exhaust to the limits their insights, and let those who have understanding choose among them. . . . If the best [ideas] of a host of men are gathered together to repair and reconstitute [the tradition], we will not go far wrong" (*Ouyang Yongshu ji* 6.10).
84. *FS*, "Postface" 15b.
85. Moreover, living more closely to the age of Confucius than the men of the Song, the Han interpreters like Mao and Zheng presumably had access to relatively uncorrupted traditions concerning the classics. Thus in another context Ouyang said of an interpretation of Sima Qian's: "Sima Qian . . . was not yet distant from the Zhou. His teachings must reflect the traditions handed down by teachers and Confucians" (*FS* 14.3b–4a).
86. *FS*, "Postface" 15a.
87. Ouyang often leveled the charge of "self-contradiction" (*zixiang diwu*) against the Mao-Zheng interpretations of the Odes. For example, the Zheng *Annotations* claimed that the "Qiyue" Ode (Mao #154) was composed of sections written in each of the Three Forms, i.e., Air, Elegantia, and Laud. But as Ouyang pointed out, such a claim was contradicted by Zheng's own definitions of the Elegantia and Laud forms (*FS* 14.8a–b). (The definitions are actually those of Pericopes 15–17 of the Preface to the "Guanju," but Ouyang assumes that Zheng Xuan would have accepted these as correct.) Again, the *Preface*'s assumption that King Wen's moral-transformative influence extended only to the six regions (*zhou*) that he actually ruled before the fall of Yin was contradicted by other of the Prefaces in the Zhounan and Shaonan sections that spoke of King Wen's influence extending throughout the empire (*FS* 2.5b–6b).
88. Ouyang's interpretation of the "Guanju," for instance, was based on such a teaching, Confucius's famous comment at *Analects* 3.20 concerning the "Guanju." That comment, says Ouyang, refers to the fact that the Ode

"first urges duty and then is joyful" (and thus is "joyful but not excessive")
and that it "recalls the past to goad the present and yet is not importunate"
(and thus is "sorrowful but not harmful") (*FS* 1.2b). Ouyang thus claimed
that the "Guanju" was a product not of the heyday of the Zhou but of its
decline: the poet recalls King Wen and Taisi in order to "goad the present"
(*ci jin*). Ouyang also cites Sima Qian's comment that "when the House of
Zhou declined, the 'Guan ju' was produced" (*Shiji*, p. 3115).

89. For "leaving a blank," see *Analects* 2.18. A possible example of this kind
of restraint may be found in Ouyang's readings of the "Lu ming" Ode (Mao
#161). In his "Essay on Dating" ("Shishi lun"), Ouyang suggests that this
and several others of the Elegantiae and Lauds must be later than their traditional dates (*FS* 14.4a). But in the *FS* proper, the Ode is associated with
King Wen (*FS* 6.1a–1b). Ouyang believed that the failure of the Han scholars to exercise self-discipline led to the corruption and confusion of the exegetical tradition. Had they only left blank what they did not understand
instead of fabricating explanations, then those elements of the exegetical
tradition securely founded on the teachings of Confucius would not have
been confused and obscured.

90. This is not the only possible reading of this passage. It might be supposed that the two conditions of self-contradiction in the traditional interpretation and of the positive guidance of a Confucian teaching should be
understood to be linked by an "or" rather than with an "and." That these
conditions were cumulative rather than alternative is suggested by another
passage found in the "Discussion on Dating" ("Shishi lun"; *FS* 14.5a). After
discussing some incongruities in Zheng Xuan's dating of the Elegantiae and
Lauds, Ouyang says:

In the case of the Zhounan and Shaonan sections, I showed [*bian*] the inconsistencies; and in the case of the "Guanju," I selected [the interpretation]
closest to being correct. This was because that interpretation was consistent
with the words of Confucius. As for the Elegantiae and Lauds, I discuss
[*bian*] them, but I do not dare to be dogmatic, and rather hold them in suspension [*you dai yan*].

Now Mao and Zheng erred by believing too strongly in their own scholarship and by distorting their interpretations accordingly. If I were also to
be self-confident, then this would be like laughing at a speeding chariot's
overturning while careening along behind it. Nevertheless, seeing their errors, I cannot but refute them; but although I refute them, I would not dare
to be dogmatic [in asserting my own interpretation]. It will be enough if my
interpretations can stand together with Mao and Zheng's in future generations to await the choice of those who understand. (*FS* 14.5a)

91. Gadamer, pp. 268–69. The following quote applies to Ouyang's situation: "This, precisely, is the power of history over finite human conscious-
ness, namely that it prevails even where faith in method leads one to deny
one's own historicality" (p. 268). Although horizons are thus defined by his-

tory, for Gadamer they are not hermetically closed, but changeable and movable (pp. 270–74).

92. He Zeheng, p. 68.

93. James T. C. Liu, *Ou-yang Hsiu*, pp. 70–71. Moreover in 1070, when the "Postface" was written, the struggles over the institutionalization of Wang Anshi's classical commentaries were raging; orthodoxy and conservatism may have seemed like bulwarks against Wang's innovations.

94. *Song ren yishi huibian* 8.356, quoted in He Zeheng, p. 66.

CHAPTER SEVEN

EPIGRAPH: quoted in Hacking, p. 5.

1. The teachings of Cheng Yi and Cheng Hao are collected in the *Er Cheng ji* (Collected works of the two Chengs). This collection contains a number of separate titles (see Graham, *Two Chinese Philosophers*, pp. 141–51; and Ts'ai, pp. 29–61, for descriptions). The materials in the *Er Cheng ji* are very heterogeneous; it is often a problem to decide whether to attribute a particular saying to Cheng Yi or to Cheng Hao. See on this Graham, *Two Chinese Philosophers*, p. 142. The *Shi jie* (Explanation of the Odes; *Er Cheng ji* 4.1046–85) contains comments by Cheng Yi on the Odes; like most of the titles in the *Er Cheng ji*, it is not an integral work authored by Cheng Yi but a collection of his sayings as recorded by his disciples. Comments on the Odes and on reading and interpretation are also scattered throughout the *Er Cheng ji*. The best, most convenient, and (as I believe, based on my reading of the *Er Cheng ji*) representative source for comments by the Chengs on hermeneutics is the *Jinsilu* (Recorded reflections on what is near) compiled by Zhu Xi and Lü Zuqian (1137–81) in the 1170's, especially the third chapter, "The Investigation of Things and the Investigation of Principle to the Utmost." Most of the comments on which this chapter centers can be found there, and I cite such comments by their order in that chapter. Thus a reference of the form "3.39" directs the reader to the thirty-ninth section or comment in chap. 3 of the *Jinsilu*. In reading the *Jinsilu*, I have found the translation of Wing-tsit Chan (*Reflections on Things at Hand*) invaluable. I sometimes differ, however, with Chan on the translation of passages touching on the terminology or technical points of Song hermeneutics.

The hermeneutic of Zhang Zai resembled that of Cheng Yi in its emphases upon the reading process and upon the subjective disposition of the reader. At the same time, he differed from Cheng in his insistence upon the necessity of voiding the mind of all its prejudices (*xuxin*), in his view of the relation between language and intention, and in several other interesting respects. While I refer to Zhang's views throughout this chapter by way of contrast and explication, his hermeneutic deserves a fuller treatment. For a good general discussion of his thought touching on many of these issues, see Kasoff.

2. On Wang Anshi and Liu Chang, see Chapter 6. On Su Shi's commentary on the *Shujing*, see George Hatch's comments in Hervouet, pp. 13–19. Su was often speculative and highly subjective in his commentaries, but he took them seriously. For Su Che, see below in the text.

3. *Shi jizhuan* 1.6b. Su was followed in his division of the *Preface* by such important Song commentators on the Odes as Yan Can (fl. 1250) and Cheng Dachang (1123–95).

4. Ibid., 1.6a.

5. Ibid.

6. Su is quoting the fifth chapter of the "Commentary on the Appended Words" (*Xici zhuan*) to the *Yijing*. See Sung, p. 280. Su Che quotes the same passage while expressing similar opinions concerning the *Preface* at *Shi jizhuan* 1.5a–6b.

7. "Shang liangzhi zhugong shu" (Letter to the gentlemen of the two drafting groups), *Su Ziyou Luancheng ji* 21.3–6.

8. Thus the quotation contrasting "the humane" with "the wise," which recalls *Analects* 6.21.

9. Insofar as Cheng Yi was interested in the problems of the exegetical tradition, his views contained both innovative and traditional elements. He adopted the stratified picture of the *Preface* first broached by Cheng Boyu (*Er Cheng ji*, p. 1047). But he also insisted that those elements of the *Preface* he thought genuine provided indispensable guidance for the understanding of the Odes:

> Now the Master [i.e., Confucius] reflected that later ages might not understand the Odes, and so he made a "Preface" for the "Guanju" [i.e., the "Great Preface"] to demonstrate to them [the meaning of the Odes]. To study the Odes without seeking [the help of] the "Preface" is like trying to enter a house without going through the door. (*Er Cheng ji*, p. 1046)

10. *Jinsilu* 3.28.

11. Ouyang Xiu, "Shishi lun" (*FS* 14.1b).

12. *Mencius* 5.A.4.

13. Ibid., 4.B.21.

14. Following Karlgren, *Book of Odes*, p. 225.

15. *Jinsilu* 3.46.

16. *FS* 4.1a.

17. This is one of the important differences between Ouyang Xiu and Cheng Yi, a difference not attributable to chronology. As we shall see below, the specification of meaning interested Cheng Yi as little as questions concerning the criticism and reform of the exegetical tradition; his interest in the intentions behind the text came from a different source.

18. Quoted in Honda, p. 293.

19. *Er Cheng ji*, p. 378. The statement seems to me to be more in keeping with Cheng Hao's hermeneutic than with that of Cheng Yi.

20. It must be borne in mind, however, that statements like the above were

made in response to the very real and present threat of a kind of reading which focused so closely upon the literal meaning or significance of the text that it seemed to Cheng Yi and his contemporaries to block all possibility of an authentic engagement with the classics and their commentaries. That reading was of course associated with the *Correct Significance* orthodoxy.

21. *Jinsilu* 3.23.

22. It is clear that the negative model of reading whose characteristic failing was to be *ni* was closely connected with the traditional hermeneutic of the orthodox scholarship of the day, both in its reliance upon authoritative exegesis and in its pedagogical practice and explication of texts: "One reads in order to exhaust principle, and in order to make use [of what he has read]; it is useless to stick [*zhini*] as some do to the chapter-and-verse commentaries." This passage is quoted as coming from the *Chengzi yishu* under the *Cihai* entry for *zhini*.

23. *Jinsilu* 3.27; trans. adapted from Chan, *Reflections*, pp. 98–99. The saying quoted comes from *Mencius* 7.B.25.

24. The quotation that prefaces this chapter both parallels and contrasts with this passage. Bacon shares in common with the eleventh-century Neoconfucian writers the view that language represents a possible snare to the understanding. But Bacon proposes to deal with this danger by fully and definitively defining the meanings of the words he uses, whereas Cheng Yi rather sees difficulty as arising from precisely that desire for a unified, unambiguous vocabulary. For Cheng Yi, language cannot be purified, but only transcended.

25. *Jinsilu*, 3.26; trans. adapted from Chan, *Reflections*, p. 98.

26. Compare the story of Yingong Tuo and Yugong Chai at *Zuo* Xiang 14.

27. Ware, pp. 109–10; Lau, *Mencius*, pp. 132–33.

28. On the problem of the mobilization of the emotions, see Chapter 3. On the later history of this problem, see Nivison.

29. The passage also draws on *Analects* 6.20.

30. Xu, p. 44.

31. The passage translated here is collected in the "Du *Shi* fa" of Duan Changwu prefaced to his *Maoshi jijie*. It closely parallels, but is not identical with, a passage given in both Zhang Zai, *Zhangzi quanshu* (4.90); and the *Jinsilu* (3.72).

32. This passage is also collected in Duan Changwu, "Du *Shi* fa" (see preceding note). It can also be found as a note to *Jinsilu* 3.72. The similarity of the language of this passage to the one above leads me to think that Zhang Boxing was correct to attribute this passage to Zhang Zai. Chan (*Reflections*, p. 121n156) disagrees.

33. *Xici zhuan* A. 2.10.

34. As given in Sung, p. 275.

35. Petersen, p. 96. The parenthetical expansion is Petersen's.

36. In most of Cheng Yi's hermeneutic theory, the deferred level of mean-

ing is understood in personal terms—as some trace or inscription of the person whose utterance we are concerned to understand, most typically the intention that originally informed the utterance. *Wei*, however, seems to be a property of the language itself. As such, it suggests *wenyii* "literal significance." But *wei* as it is being used here is above all the product of a type of reading. It is thus perhaps not so different from intention; it might be thought of as intention considered from the perspective of the reader's experience of the text.

37. *Jinsilu* 3.33.

38. Ibid., 3.49.

39. For Xie, see Chan, *Reflections*, p. 52n85.

40. That is, he never indulged in *zhangju* "chapter and sentence"–style exegesis.

41. This passage is subject to a variety of readings. For a somewhat different translation, see Chan, *Reflections*, pp. 105–6.

42. See, e.g., *Jinsilu* 3.39: "Recite it and savor [*wei*] it in the daytime; think it over in the nighttime."

43. Ibid., 3.33.

44. *Zhang Zai ji*, p. 276. I suspect that some of the vehemence of Zhang Zai's statement derives from a fear that the proliferation of printed texts about this time would have the effect of discouraging memorization. On this, see the next chapter.

CHAPTER EIGHT

EPIGRAPH: Zhu Xi, *Zhuzi yulei* 10.225.

1. See de Bary, *Neo-Confucian Orthodoxy*, pp. 1–66, for an account of this process.

2. "*Shi zhi xu* lun," #1–4, can be found in Chao's collected works, *Songshan wenji* (6.11.30b–37a).

3. Ibid., 6.11.38a–b.

4. Zuo Qiuming (a disciple of Confucius) was traditionally supposed to be the author of the *Zuo Tradition*, a view modern scholarship rejects. Jia Yi (200–168 B.C.E.) was a scholar and poet in the early years of the Western Han. Liu Xiang (77–6 B.C.E.) edited and promoted the Old Text classics and commentaries.

5. Chao Yuezhi, 6.11.38b–39a.

6. Chao Buzhi, 8.36.9a–b.

7. See Chapter 6, note 56.

8. Huang Zongxi, 20.53.

9. *Song shi*, p. 5048. This work survives only in quotations and in traditions concerning it; these are collected in the *Cao Fangzhai shishuo*, edited by Zhang Shouyong.

10. Cao, 1.1a. Li Guang's teacher, Liu Anshi, was also interested in the

other Han traditions concerning the Odes. See his *Yuancheng yulu* 2.33b–34b.

11. Cao, 4.8a–b. This passage is also quoted in Zhu Yicun, 99.5b–6a.

12. See preceding note; trans. adapted from Karlgren, *Book of Odes*, p. 10.

13. Qiu is quoted in Zhu Yizun, 99.2a–b.

14. Gu Jiegang believes that although this text was added to and revised by later scholars, it does contain some of Zheng Qiao's own writing. See Gu's note at the head of his selection from the *Liujing aolun* in his edition of the *Shi bian wang*, pp. 79–84. This volume brings together Gu's reconstruction of Zheng's *Shi bian wang*, along with pertinent passages from the *Tong zhi* as well as the selections from the *Liujing aolun* mentioned above. All page references to the *Shi bian wang* in this section are to this work. A bibliography of works on Zheng Qiao can be found appended to S. Y. Teng's article on Zheng Qiao in Franke, 1: 155–56.

15. *Shi bian wang*, p. 3.

16. At the "Huashu" Ode (between the Odes #169 and #170 in the Mao arrangement).

17. *Shi bian wang*, p. 3.

18. Ibid., pp. 3, 7.

19. *Liujing aolun*, in ibid., pp. 96–97.

20. *Shi bian wang*, p. 4.

21. Ibid., p. 13. See also *Liujing aolun*, in ibid., p. 84.

22. *Shi bian wang*, p. 4.

23. *Tong zhi*, quoted in ibid., p. 71.

24. *Shi bian wang*, p. 6. The *Preface* referred this Ode to the famous story of the conflict between Duke Zhuang and his younger brother Shu Duan, for which, see Legge, *Ch'un Ts'ew*, pp. 5–6.

25. These essays originally formed part of Cheng's *Kao gu bian* and circulated separately under the title *Shi lun*.

26. Lin, 6.10.2b–3a; quoted in Cheng Yuanmin, p. 39.

27. For a remark by Zhu Xi on the popularity of Lü's work, see *Shizhuan yishuo* (hereafter *YS*) 75–513. This work, compiled by Zhu Xi's grandson Zhu Jian (1190–1258), conveniently brings together most of the comments in the *Yulei* on the Odes. In subsequent references to this work, I give the *juan* number followed by the number of the passage within that *juan*; thus the passage just mentioned would be cited as *YS* 1.67.

28. Concerning these interpretations, which were made while he still accepted the authority of the *Preface*, Zhu Xi said in his "Postface to *Notes on Reading the Odes in a Family School*" ("*Lüshi jiashu du Shu ji* houxu") (*Hui'an xiansheng Zhu Wengong wenji* 76.7b) that "what this book ascribes to 'Zhu' are in fact the ignorant and unenlightened opinions of my youth, but [Lü Zuqian] mistakenly made use of them."

29. *YS* 2.5. For a good discussion of the chronology of the change in Zhu Xi's thinking, see Qian, *Zhuzi xin xue'an*, 4: 53–80.

30. The *Shi jizhuan*, of which I have used the *Sibu congkan* edition, was

probably composed sometime after 1182 (Qian, *Zhuzi xin xue'an,* 4: 57). Zhu Xi criticized the Minor Prefaces in detail in his *Refutation of the "Preface to the Odes" (Shixu bian).*

31. *"Shi jizhuan* xu" (Preface to the *Collected Traditions on the Odes),* p. 2. This short essay is prefaced to some but not all editions of the *Shi jizhuan.* It does not appear, e.g., in the *Sibu congkan* edition, but does in the Hong Kong Zhonghua (1961) edition. The piece is dated 1177, and in the opinion of Qian Mu it was composed for one of the earlier versions of the *Shi jizhuan (Zhuzi xin xue'an,* 4: 54). It is translated in its entirety in Lynn, pp. 344–46. Zhu Xi is drawing here on the accounts of the collection of the Odes given in the "Wangzhi" ("Ordinances of the Kings") chapter of the *Liji (Liji xunzuan* 5.6b) and in the *Hanshu* (p. 1708).

32. *YS* 3.32.

33. *YS* 1.32. Zhu Xi typically urged his students to read the Odes slowly and carefully; see below.

34. For a brief description of this work, see Wing-tsit Chan's bibliographic note in Hervouet, pp. 225–26.

35. Sometimes Zhu Xi presented the teaching in a slightly different, somewhat expanded version, as at 10.36. This expanded version was also phrased in rhythmic, balanced phrases meant for easy memorization. See also 11.121 for an altogether different formulation of the same ideas.

36. See Chaffee (pp. 4, 189–91) for the requirements of the various imperial exams in the Song.

37. See Zhu Xi's advice for those no longer young at 10.64. On the promotion of the Four Books (the *Analects, Mencius, Great Learning,* and *Doctrine of the Mean*) as a Confucian core curriculum, see D. K. Gardner, pp. 5–16.

38. The thirteen classics were the *Changes,* the *Odes,* the *Documents,* the *Record of Ritual,* the *Yi Ritual,* the *Institutes of Zhou,* the *Spring and Autumn Annals,* the *Zuo Tradition,* the *Gongyang* and *Guliang* commentaries, the *Analects,* the *Mencius,* the *Classic of Filial Piety,* and the *Erya* dictionary. See 11.195 for strictures against those who would scamp the *Record of Ritual* or the *Zuo Tradition.* At 11.191, Zhu Xi complains that "scholars today mostly delight in concision [*yue*] and do not seek its confirmation in broad learning [*bo*]." At 11.138 he cautions that one cannot *de shao wei zu* "take the obtaining of a little as a sufficiency."

39. Compare 11.159, where Zhu Xi insists that the student must read not only the important places (*jinyao chu*) but also the less important places (*xianman chu*), and 11.91, where the importance of *bo* (extensive learning) is affirmed.

40. See, e.g., 10.42, where a student proposes reading all the Confucian texts "one after the other" (*xunhuan kan*), and 10.39, where Zhu Xi objects to the practice of reading several new books at once (*jiankan weiduzhe*).

41. *YS* 1.35.

42. See, e.g., 10.46.

43. "The words of the Sages have one layer and then another layer. You must enter deeply in to read them. If you settle for the skin, then you will go wrong. You must sink deep in" (10.11). See also 10.12–13, 10.22.

44. "The way to read books is simply to read them until you have mastered them and to soak yourself in them; then the harmonious energies [*heqi*] will naturally come flowing out from your breast" (*YS* 1.34). For the idea of a "godlike flow of moral power" as the ultimate goal of Neoconfucianism, see Metzger, p. 49.

45. "Someone who is greedy to read a lot will end up by not having read anything" (10.43).

46. See, e.g., 10.8, 10.49.

47. "It is as if two people meet and, having just met, part without having exchanged a word. What is the use in this? Thus the text does not generate any interest and does not penetrate; it is just dry. This is all because people are greedy" (*YS* 1.35).

48. Zhu Xi sometimes spoke of deep engagement with the text as a "natural" process that needed only to be allowed to happen; the function of a hermeneutic was thus to facilitate or allow such understanding. See, e.g., 11.130, quoted in the next section.

49. Ibid.

50. The contrast here is not only between reading aloud and reading silently to oneself, but also between reading aloud and reflecting or speculating on the text. See 10.65, where the contrast between "reading aloud" (*du*) and "thinking" (*siliang*) is explicitly related to the contrast at *Analects* 2.15 between *si* and *xue* "study." See also *Analects* 15.31 for another version of this contrast.

51. For example, 11.245: "Yang Zhizhi was distressed that he had no memory when it came to the histories." See also 10.39.

52. *Mencius* 6.A.11. For Chen Lie, see *Song shi* 458.

53. There are exceptions. Zhu Xi advocated the memorization of certain passages in the histories (11.244), and he sometimes spoke of the "ancients" as having memorized texts (10.67).

54. For example, 11.117: " . . . If you just go along memorizing like this [*rensheng jiqu*], then the principle [*daoli*] [of the text] will die."

55. See 10.55.

56. Note in this connection the anecdote at 11.245 of a man who memorized the *Institutes of Zhou* by burning each page after reading it.

57. Compare *zixi wanwei fanlai fanqu* "to carefully reflect upon its savor, turning it this way and that" (10.48); and *fanfu kanlai kanqu* "turn it over, looking at it this way and that" (10.49).

58. *YS* 1.22.

59. See esp. pp. 103–4.

60. Tu, "Inner Experience," p. 103.

61. Compare 10.142, where experiential understanding and studying to pass the examinations are opposed.

62. Compare *ying chuanzuo zhi shi he* "rigidly and obstinately bore and chisel to make it agree" (11.164) and the modern Chinese expression *zuan niujiao jian* "to worm oneself into the horn's point" (Liang Shiqiu, p. 1159).

63. Compare *li jianjie* (11.205), *xian li ji yi* (11.123); *xian li ge yi* (11.205); *ying chuanzao zhi* (11.164).

64. It is possible that the *ru* "enter" (in my translation, "subscribe") of *xianru zhi shuo* is a corruption of *ren* "human"; in which case the phrase would mean "the teachings of earlier men [i.e., authoritative teachers]."

65. See, e.g., *YS* 1.38.

66. See 11.205, where this failing is associated with a desire for "novelty" (*xinqi*), this desire for novelty in turn associated with an interest in writing (*zhuan yao zuo wenzi*). The *yi* (elsewhere "intentions") against which Zhu Xi cautions in passages of this type are the predetermined views that *Analects* 9.4 tells us Confucius did not have. Waley (*Analects*, p. 139n4) follows Zheng Xuan in reading *yi* as if it had the "man" radical, in which case it would mean "to make conjectures." See also *Analects* 14.31 (cited by Lau, *Analects*, p. 96n1), where this term means "to expect (something)." This meaning is not incompatible with and is probably connected with the more ordinary sense of *yi* as a thought determined upon a goal.

67. Kasoff, pp. 88–89.

68. Dubs, *Hsüntze*, p. 92; *Xunzi*, 15.5a. It is noteworthy that the other two elements of the hermeneutic Xunzi enunciates in this passage, unity of mind (*yi*) and calmness (*jing*), also find correlates in Zhu Xi's "Dushu fa." See Dubs, *Hsüntze*, pp. 91–98.

69. Dubs, *Hsüntze*, p. 92, quoting *Laozi*, chap. 3.

70. *Zhuangxi yinde*, p. 9; trans. adapted from Graham, *Chuang-tzŭ*, p. 68.

71. Graham, *Chuang-tzŭ*, p. 69.

72. *Zhuangzi yinde*, p. 86; Graham, *Chuang-tzŭ*, p. 249.

73. The *Mencius* passage appears at 5.A.4.ii. See 11.172–73 for other occurrences of *tuibu*.

74. See the series at 11.108–19 for passages stressing the importance of the *xin* for reading.

75. For example, the *zouzuo di xin* mentioned at 11.115–18 and at *YS* 1.35. *Zouzuo* literally means "to have left the tracks."

76. *YS* 1.20 (cf. 2.5), 1.41.

77. So said Zhu Xi: "Now that the Odes have been glossed like this, they are clear and easy to understand"; and, "I, Xi, have glossed the Odes so that each and every character is clear" (*YS* 1.29, 1.43).

78. The reference is to the anecdote about Butcher Ding in *Zhuangzi* (*Zhuangzi yinde*, p. 7). See also 10.50, 10.62, 10.63, and 11.185 for the idea that the mastery of a relatively small amount of text will enable one to read more easily.

79. See, e.g., 11.130 and 11.164, quoted above.

80. This teaching of Zhang Zai's appears at *Zhang Zai ji*, p. 275, and is quoted at *Jinsilu*, 3.74. See also Kasoff, pp. 85–88, on "this mind" and reading in Zhang Zai's thought; and Yu Ying-shih, pp. 235–36, on Zhu Xi and *weichi cixin*. In some early texts, *shi* "Ode" was paronomastically defined by *chi* "support." See Xu, p. 2, for examples. For other examples of the importance of reading for the *xin*, see 11.104–5.

81. Wang Fuzhi, pp. 4–5. See Siu-kit Wong, pp. 141–44, for a discussion of this passage.

82. So Dai Zhen (1724–77). See, e.g., Dai Zhen, p. 146; cited and trans. in Elman, p. 29.

83. Elman, p. 73.

84. See, e.g., the persistence of the vocabulary and categories of the traditional hermeneutic in the passages from Wang Fuzhi and Dai Zhen cited in notes 81 and 82 above.

85. On these, see Chap. 4.

86. See, e.g., the suggestive remarks on the provenance of Daoist texts in Seidel; and Lopez for Buddhist hermeneutics.

Works Cited

The following abbreviations are used in the Works Cited:

CSJC   *Congshu jicheng* 叢書集成
GXJB   *Guoxue jiben congshu* 國學基本叢書
SBBY   *Sibu beiyao* 四部備要
SBCK   *Sibu congkan* 四部叢刊
SQZB   *Siku quanshu zhenben* 四庫全書珍本
TTJJ   *Tongzhi tang jingjie* 通志堂經解

Austin, J. L. *How to Do Things with Words*. Ed. J. O. Urmson and Marina Sbisà. Cambridge: Harvard University Press, 1962.

Bainton, Roland H. "The Bible in the Reformation." In *The Cambridge History of the Bible*, vol. 3, *The West from the Reformation to the Present Day*, ed. S. L. Greensladde, pp. 1–37. Cambridge: Cambridge University Press, 1963.

Balazs, Etienne. *Chinese Civilization and Bureaucracy: Variations on a Theme*. Trans. H. M. Wright. Ed. Arthur F. Wright. New Haven: Yale University Press, 1964.

———. "Nihilistic Revolt or Mystical Escapism." In idem, *Chinese Civilization and Bureaucracy*, pp. 227–54.

———. "Political Philosophy and Social Crisis at the End of the Han Dynasty." In idem, *Chinese Civilization and Bureaucracy*, pp. 186–225.

Beishi 北史. Comp. Li Yanshou 李延壽. Beijing: Zhonghua, 1974.

Berman, Harold J. *Law and Revolution: The Formation of the Western Legal Tradition*. Cambridge: Harvard University Press, 1983.

Bernstein, Richard J. *Beyond Objectivism and Relativism: Science, Hermeneutics, and Praxis*. Philadelphia: University of Pennsylvania Press, 1983.

Birch, Cyril, ed. *Studies in Chinese Literary Genres*. Berkeley: University of California Press, 1974.

Bishop, Elizabeth. *The Collected Prose*. Ed. Robert Giroux. New York: Farrar, Straus & Giroux. 1984.

Bleicher, Josef. *Contemporary Hermeneutics: Hermeneutics and Method, Philosophy and Critique*. London: Routledge & Kegan Paul, 1980.

Breech, James. *The Silence of Jesus*. Philadelphia: Fortress Press, 1983.

Bultmann, Rudolf. *History of the Synoptic Tradition*. New York: Harper & Row, 1963.

Cahill, James F. "Some Confucian Elements in the Theory of Painting." In *The Confucian Persuasion*, ed. Arthur F. Wright, pp. 114–40.

Cai Bian 蔡卞. *Maoshi mingwu jie* 毛詩名物解. *TTJJ*.

Cao Cuizhong 曹粹中. *Cao Fangzhai shishuo* 曹放齋詩說. *Yueyuan ji yishu* 約園輯佚書.

Chaffee, John W. *The Thorny Gates of Learning: A Social History of Examinations*. Cambridge: Cambridge University Press, 1986.

Chan, Wing-tsit, trans. *Reflections on Things at Hand: The Neo-Confucian Anthology Compiled by Chu Hsi and Lü Tsu-ch'ien*. New York: Columbia University Press, 1967.

———, trans. and comp. *Source Book in Chinese Philosophy*. Princeton: Princeton University Press, 1963.

Chao Buzhi 晁補之. *Jile ji* 雞肋集. *SBCK*.

Chao, Yuen Ren. "Tone, Intonation, Singsong, Chanting, Recitative, Tonal Composition, and Atonal Composition in Chinese." In *For Roman Jakobson*, comp. Morris Halle et al., pp. 52–59. The Hague: Mouton, 1956.

Chao Yuezhi 晁說之. *Songshan wenji* 嵩山文集. *SBCK*.

Chen Huan 陳奐, annotator. *Shi Maoshi zhuan shu* 詩毛氏傳疏. Taibei: Taiwan xuesheng shuju, 1981.

Chen Qiaocong 陳喬樅. *Sanjia shi yishuo kao* 三家詩遺說考. *Huang Qing jingjie xubian* 皇清經解續編.

Chen, Shih-Hsiang. "The *Shih-ching*: Its Generic Significance." In *Studies in Chinese Literary Genres*, ed. Cyril Birch, pp. 8–41.

Chen Zhensun 陳振孫. *Zhizhai shulu jieti* 直齋書錄解題. N.p.: Jiangsu shuju, 1883.

Cheng Dachang 程大昌. *Kao gu bian* 考古辨. *CSJC*, 1st series, vol. 292.

———. *Shi lun* 詩論. *CSJC*.

Cheng Yuanmin 程元敏. *Wang Bo zhi Shijingxue* 王柏之詩經學. Taibei: Jiaxin shuini gongsi, 1968.

Chow Tse-tsung. "The Early History of the Chinese Word *Shih* (Poetry)." In *Wen-lin: Studies in the Chinese Humanities*, ed. Chow Tse-tsung, pp. 151–209. Madison: University of Wisconsin Press, 1968.

Cikoski, John S. "On Standards of Analogical Reasoning in the Late Chou." *Journal of Chinese Philosophy* 2, no. 3 (June 1975): 325–57.

Creel, Herrlee G. *Confucius and the Chinese Way*. New York: Harper & Row, 1960.

———. *The Origins of Statecraft in China*, vol. 1, *The Western Chou Empire*. Chicago: University of Chicago Press, 1970.

Cui Shu 崔述. *Lunyu yushuo* 論語餘說. In *Cui Dongbi yishu* 崔東壁遺書, vol. 5. Ed. Gu Jiegang 顧頡剛. Shanghai: Dongya, 1936.

Culler, Jonathan. *On Deconstruction: Theory and Criticism After Structuralism.* Ithaca, N.Y.: Cornell University Press, 1982.

Dai Junren 戴君仁. "Jingshu de yancheng" 經書的衍成. *Kong Meng xuebao* 孔孟學報 19 (Apr. 1970): 77–95.

Dai Zhen 戴震. *Dai Zhen wenji* 戴震文集, annotated by Zhao Yuxin 趙玉新. Hong Kong: Zhonghua, 1974.

de Bary, Wm. Theodore. *Neo-Confucian Orthodoxy and the Learning of the Mind-and-Heart.* New York: Columbia University Press, 1981.

———. "A Reappraisal of Neo-Confucianism." In *Studies in Chinese Thought*, ed. Arthur F. Wright, pp. 81–111. Chicago: University of Chicago Press, 1953.

DeWoskin, Kenneth J. *A Song for One or Two: Music and the Concept of Art in Early China.* Ann Arbor: University of Michigan, Center for Chinese Studies, 1982.

Dibelius, Martin. *From Tradition to Gospel.* New York: Charles Scribner's Sons, 1935.

Dien, Albert E. "Yen Chih-t'ui (531–591+): A Buddho-Confucian." In *Confucian Personalities*, ed. Arthur F. Wright and Denis Twitchett, pp. 43–64. Stanford: Stanford University Press, 1962.

Ding Chuanjing 丁傳經, ed. *Song ren yishi huibian* 宋人軼事彙編. Beijing: Shangwu, 1935.

Dobson, W. A. C. H. *Late Han Chinese: A Study of the Archaic-Han Shift.* Toronto: University of Toronto Press, 1964.

———. "Linguistic Evidence and the Dating of the *Book of Songs*." *T'oung Pao* 51 (1964): 322–43.

Dong Zhongshu 董仲舒. *Chunqiu fanlu* 春秋繁露. *SBCK.*

Duan Changwu 段昌武, comp. *Maoshi jijie* 毛詩集解. *Wenyuan ge* 文淵閣. Reprinted—Taibei: Shangwu, 1972.

Dubs, Homer H. "Did Confucius Study the Book of Changes?" *T'oung Pao* 24 (1927): 82–90.

———. *Hsüntze: The Moulder of Ancient Confucianism.* London: Arthur Probsthain, 1927.

———, trans. *The Works of Hsüntze.* London: Arthur Probsthain, 1928.

Eberhard, Wolfram. Review of Bernhard Karlgren, "Legends and Cults in Ancient China." *Artibus Asiae* 9, no. 4 (1946): 355–64.

Egan, Ronald C. *The Literary Works of Ou-yang Hsiu (1007–72).* Cambridge: Cambridge University Press, 1984.

———. "Narratives in *Tso Chuan*." *Harvard Journal of Asiatic Studies* 37, no. 2 (1977): 323–52.

Elman, Benjamin A. *From Philosophy to Philology: Intellectual and Social Aspects of Change in Late Imperial China.* Cambridge: Harvard University, Council on East Asian Studies, 1984.

Elvin, Mark. *The Pattern of the Chinese Past: A Social and Economic Interpretation.* Stanford: Stanford University Press, 1973.

Er Cheng ji 二程集. Beijing: Zhonghua, 1981.

Fan Wenlan 范文瀾. *Qunjing gailun* 群經概論. Beijing: Pushe, 1933.

Forke, A., trans. *Lun-Hêng*. 2 vols. 2nd ed. 1907. Reprinted—New York: Paragon, 1962.

Franke, Herbert, ed. *Sung Biographies*. 4 vols. Wiesbaden: Steiner, 1976.

Frankel, Hans. *The Flowering Plum and the Palace Lady: Interpretations of Chinese Poetry*. New Haven: Yale University Press, 1976.

Fu Guang 輔廣. *Shijing xieyun kaoyi* 詩經協韻考異. *CSJC*.

Fung Yu-lan (Feng Youlan). *History of Chinese Philosophy*. 2 vols. Trans. Derk Bodde. 1952, 1953. Reprinted—Princeton: Princeton University Press, 1973.

Gadamer, Hans-Georg. *Truth and Method*. Trans. Garret Barden and William G. Doerpel. New York: Seabury, 1975.

Gao Baoguang 高葆光. "*Maoshi xu zai jiantao*" 毛詩序再檢討. *Donghai xuebao* 東海學報 7, no. 1 (June 1965): 15–26.

———. "San lun *Maoshi xu*" 三論毛詩序. *Donghai xuebao* 東海學報 8, no. 1 (Jan. 1967): 83–94.

Gardner, Charles S. *Chinese Traditional Historiography*. Cambridge: Harvard University Press, 1961.

Gardner, Daniel K. *Chu Hsi and the Ta-hsueh: Neo-Confucian Reflection on the Confucian Canon*. Cambridge: Harvard University, Council on East Asian Studies, 1986.

Gerhardsson, Birger. *Memory and Manuscript: Oral Tradition and Written Transmission in Rabbinic Judaism and Early Christianity*. Uppsala, Sweden: Alsmquist & Wiksells Boktryckeri, 1961.

Graham, A. C. *Later Mohist Logic, Ethics and Science*. Hong Kong: Chinese University of Hong Kong Press; London: University of London, School of Oriental and African Studies, 1978.

———. Review of Chad Hansen, *Language and Logic in Ancient China*. *Harvard Journal of Asiatic Studies* 45 (1985): 692–703.

———. *Two Chinese Philosophers: Ch'êng Ming-tao and Ch'êng Yi-ch'uan*. London: Lund Humphries, 1958.

———, trans. *Chuang-tzŭ: The Inner Chapters*. London: Unwin, 1987.

Grant, Robert M. *An Historical Introduction to the New Testament*. New York: Harper Row, 1963.

———. *The Letter and the Spirit*. London: S.P.C.K., 1957.

Gu Jiegang 顧頡剛. "Lun *Shijing* suolu quanwei yuege" 論詩經所錄全為樂歌. In idem, *Gushi bian* 古史辨, 3: 608–57.

———. "*Maoshi xu* zhi beijing yu zhiqu" 毛詩序之背景與旨趣. *Zhongshan daxue yuyan lishi xue yanjiu suo zhoukan* 中山大學語言歷史學研究所週刊 10, no. 120 (Feb. 1930): 18–19.

———, ed. *Gushi bian* 古史辨. 7 vols. 1926–41. Reprinted—Shanghai: Guji, 1982.

Gunkel, Hermann. *The Legends of Genesis*. New York: Shocken Books, 1966.

Guo Shaoyu 郭紹虞, comp. *Zhongguo lidai wenlun xuan* 中國歷代文論選. 2 vols. Shanghai: Guji, 1979.

Hacking, Ian. *Why Does Language Matter to Philosophy?* Cambridge: Cambridge University Press, 1975.

Han Feizi 韓非子. *SBCK*.

Han Yu 韓愈. (*Yinzhu*) *Han Wengong wenji* (音註)韓文公文集. N.p.: Wenlu tang, 1934.

Hansen, Chad. *Language and Logic in Ancient China.* Ann Arbor: University of Michigan Press, 1983.

Hanshu 漢書. Comp. Ban Gu 班固. Beijing: Zhonghua, 1962.

Havelock, Eric A. *Preface to Plato.* Cambridge: Harvard University Press, 1963.

Hawkes, David. Review of Jean-Pierre Diény, *Aux origines de la poésie classique en Chine* . . . . *T'oung Pao* 55 (1969): 151–57.

————, trans. *Ch'u Tz'ŭ: The Songs of the South. An Ancient Chinese Anthology.* 1959. Reprinted—Boston: Beacon Press, 1962.

He Dingsheng 何定生. "Cong yanjiao dao jianshu kan *Shijing* de mianmao" 從言教到諫書看詩經的面貌. *Kong Meng xuebao* 孔孟學報 11 (1966): 101–48.

He Zeheng 何澤恆. *Ouyang Xiu zhi jingshi xue* 歐陽修之經史學. Taibei: Guoli Taiwan daxue wenxueyuan, 1980.

Heidegger, Martin. *Being and Time.* Trans. John Macquarrie and Edward Robinson. New York: Harper & Row, 1962.

Henderson, John B. *The Development and Decline of Chinese Cosmology.* New York: Columbia University Press, 1984.

Henricks, Robert G. "On the Chapter Divisions in the *Lao-tzu*." *Bulletin of the School of Oriental and African Studies* 65 (1982): 502–24.

Hervouet, Yves, ed. *A Sung Bibliography (Bibliographie des Sung).* Hong Kong: Chinese University Press, 1978.

Hightower, James Robert. "The *Han-shih wai-chuan* and the *San chia shih.*" *Harvard Journal of Asiatic Studies* 11 (1948): 241–310.

————. *Han Shih Wai Chuan: Han Ying's Illustrations of the Didactic Application of the Classic of Songs.* Cambridge: Harvard University Press, 1952.

Holzman, Donald. "Confucius and Ancient Chinese Literary Criticism." In *Chinese Approaches to Literature from Confucius to Liang Ch'i-ch'ao,* ed. Adele Austin Rickett, pp. 21–41. Princeton: Princeton University Press, 1978.

Honda Shigeyuki 本田成之. *Shina keigaku shiron* 支那經學史論. Kyoto: Kōbundō, 1932.

Hou Han shu 後漢書. Comp. Fan Ye 范曄. Beijing: Zhonghua, 1965.

Hsiao, Kung-chuan. *A History of Chinese Political Thought,* vol. 1, *From the Beginnings to the Sixth Century A.D.* Trans. Frederick W. Mote. Princeton: Princeton University Press, 1979.

Hsu, Cho-yun. *Ancient China in Transition.* Stanford: Stanford University Press, 1965.

Hu Nianyi 胡念貽. "*Shijing* zhong de fu bi xing" 詩經中的賦比興. *Wenxue yichan zengkan* 文學遺產增刊 1 (1957): 1–21.

Hu Pingsheng 胡平生 and Han Ziqiang 韓自強. "Fuyang Hanjian *Shijing* jianlun" 阜陽漢簡《詩經》簡論. *Wenwu* 文物 1984, no. 8: 13–21.

Huang Jie 黃節. "*Shixu fei Wei Hong suozuo shuo*" 詩序非衛宏所作說. *Qinghua Zhongguo wenxue hui yuekan* 清華中國文學會月刊 1, no. 2 (Apr. 1931): 5–17.

Huang Zongxi 黃宗羲. *Song Yuan xue'an* 宋元學案. *GXJB.*

Hung, William. "A Bibliographical Controversy at the T'ang Court, A.D. 719." *Harvard Journal of Asiatic Studies* 20 (1957): 74–134.

Ingarden, Roman. *The Cognition of the Literary Work of Art.* Evanston, Ill.: Northwestern University Press, 1973.

———. *The Literary Work of Art.* Evanston, Ill.: Northwestern University Press, 1973.

Iser, Wolfgang. *The Act of Reading: A Theory of Aesthetic Response.* Baltimore: Johns Hopkins University Press, 1978.

———. *The Implied Reader: Patterns of Communication in Prose Fiction from Bunyan to Beckett.* Baltimore: Johns Hopkins University Press, 1974.

Jauss, Hans Robert. *Toward an Aesthetic of Reception.* Trans. Timothy Bahti. Minneapolis: University of Minnesota Press, 1981.

Jian Boxian 簡博賢. *Jincun Nanbei chao jingxue yiji kao* 今存南北朝經學遺籍考. Taibei: Sanmin, 1986.

Jiang Boqian 將伯潛. *Jing yu jingxue* 經與經學. Shanghai: Shijie, 1948.

Jiang Shanguo 將善國. *Sanbai pian yanlun* 三百篇研論. Taibei: Shangwu, 1966.

Jinsilu 近思錄. Ed. Zhu Xi 朱熹 and Lü Zuqian 呂祖謙. *CSJC.*

Kageyama Seiichi 影山誠一. *Chūgoku keigaku shikō* 中國經學史綱. Tokyo: Daitōbunka-daigaku, Tōyō-kenkyūjo, 1970.

Karlgren, Bernhard. "The Authenticity and Nature of the *Tso Chuan.*" *Göteborg Högskolas Årsskrift*, 32, no. 3 (1926): 1–65.

———. "The Early History of the *Chou Li* and *Tso Chuan* Texts." *Bulletin of the Museum of Far Eastern Antiquities* 3 (1931): 1–59.

———. *Glosses on the Book of Documents.* Stockholm: Museum of Far Eastern Antiquities, 1970.

———. *Glosses on the Book of Odes.* Stockholm: Museum of Far Eastern Antiquities, 1964.

———. "Glosses on the Kuo-feng Odes." *Bulletin of the Museum of Far Eastern Antiquities* 14 (1942): 71–247.

———. *Grammata Serica Recensa.* Stockholm: Museum of Far Eastern Antiquities, 1972.

———. "Legends and Cults in Ancient China." *Bulletin of the Museum of Far Eastern Antiquities* 18 (1946): 199–366.

———, trans. "The Book of Documents." *Bulletin of the Museum of Far Eastern Antiquities* 22 (1950): 1–81.

———. *The Book of Odes.* Stockholm: Museum of Far Eastern Antiquities, 1950.

Kasoff, Ira E. *The Thought of Chang Tsai (1020–1077).* Cambridge: Cambridge University Press. 1984.

Katō Minoru 加藤實. "Kan Yu '*Shi no jo gi*' yakuchū" 韓愈詩之序議譯注. *Shikyō kenkyū* 詩經研究 1 (1975): 23–26.

Keightley, David N. *Sources of Shang History*. Berkeley: University of California Press, 1978.

Kelber, Werner H. *The Oral and the Written Gospel: The Hermeneutics of Speaking and Writing in the Synoptic Tradition, Mark, Paul, and Q*. Philadelphia: Fortress Press, 1983.

Kimura Eiichi 木村英一. *Kōshi to rongo* 孔子と論語. Tokyo: Sōbunsha, 1971.

Knechtges, David R. *The Han Rhapsody: A Study of the Fu of Yang Hsiung (53 B.C.–A.D. 18)*. Cambridge: Cambridge University Press, 1976.

Knoblock, John. *Xunzi: A Translation and Study of the Complete Works*. vol. 1, *Books 1–6*. Stanford: Stanford University Press, 1988.

Kunst, Richard Alan. "The Original *Yijing*: A Text, Phonetic Transcription, and Indexes, with Sample Glosses." Ph.D. dissertation, University of California, Berkeley, 1985.

Lau, D. C., trans. *Analects*. New York: Penguin Books, 1979.

———. *Mencius*. Harmondsworth, Eng.: Penguin, 1970.

———. *Tao Te Ching*. Harmondsworth, Eng.: Penguin, 1963.

Legge, James, trans. *The Ch'un Ts'ew with Tso Chuen*. *The Chinese Classics*, vol. 4, 1872. Reprinted—Hong Kong: Hong Kong University Press, 1960.

———. *The She King*. *The Chinese Classics*, vol. 4, 1871. Reprinted—Hong Kong: Hong Kong University Press, 1960.

———. *The Works of Mencius*. 3rd ed. *The Chinese Classics*, vol. 2, 1894. Reprinted—Hong Kong: Hong Kong University Press, 1960.

Liang, Ch'i-ch'ao (Liang Qichao). *Intellectual Trends in the Ch'ing Period (Ch'ing-tai hsüeh-shu kai-lun)*. Trans. Immanuel C. Y. Hsü. Cambridge: Harvard University Press, 1959.

Liang Shiqiu et al. *A New Practical Chinese-English Dictionary*. Taibei: Far East, 1973.

Liji xunzuan 禮記訓纂. Comp. Zhu Bin 朱彬. *SBBY*.

Lin Guangchao 林光朝. *Aixuan ji* 艾軒集. *SQZB*.

Lindbeck, George A. *The Nature of Doctrine: Religion and Theology in a Postliberal Age*. Philadelphia: Westminster Press, 1984.

Liu Anshi 劉安世. *Yuancheng yulu* 元誠語錄. Comp. Ma Yongqing 馬永卿. *Tuoba chan congke* 託跋廛叢刻.

———. *Yuancheng yulu jie* 元城語錄解. Annotated by Wang Chongqing 王崇慶. *Xiyin xuan congshu* 惜陰軒叢書.

Liu Chang 劉敞. *Qijing xiaozhuan* 七經小傳. *TTJJ*.

Liu, James J. Y. *Chinese Theories of Literature*. Chicago: University of Chicago Press, 1975.

———. *Language—Paradox—Poetics: A Chinese Perspective*. Ed. Richard John Lynn. Princeton: Princeton University Press, 1988.

Liu, James T. C. (Liu Zijian 劉子健). "An Early Sung Reformer: Fan Chung-yen." In *Chinese Thought and Institutions*, ed. John K. Fairbank, pp. 105–31. Chicago: University of Chicago Press, 1957.

———. "How Did a Neo-Confucian School Become the State Orthodoxy?" *Philosophy East and West* 23 (1973): 484–505.

———. *Ou-yang Hsiu: An Eleventh Century Neo-Confucianist.* Stanford: Stanford University Press, 1967.

———. *Ouyang Xiu di zhixue yu congzheng* 歐陽修的治學與從政. Hong Kong: Xinya yanjiusuo, 1963.

Liu, James T. C., and Peter J. Golas, eds. *Change in Sung China: Innovation or Renovation.* Lexington, Mass.: D.C. Heath & Co., 1969.

Liu Yiqing 劉義慶. *Shishuo xinyu jiaojian* 世說新語校箋. Ed. Yang Yong 楊勇. Taibei: Hongshi, 1976.

Loehr, Max. "Some Fundamental Issues in the History of Chinese Painting." *Journal of Asian Studies* 23, no. 2 (Feb. 1964): 183–93.

Loewe, Michael. "The Office of Music, c. 114 to 7 B.C." *Bulletin of the School of Oriental and African Studies* 36 (1973): 340–51.

Lopez, Donald S., Jr. *Buddhist Hermeneutics.* Honolulu: University of Hawaii Press, 1988.

Lynn, Richard John. "Chu Hsi as Literary Critic." In *Chu Hsi and Neo-Confucianism,* ed. Wing-tsit Chan, pp. 337–54. Honolulu: University of Hawaii Press, 1986.

Ma Zonghuo 馬宗霍. *Zhongguo jingxue shi* 中國經學史. Taibei: Shangwu, 1976.

Maoshi yinde 毛詩引得. Harvard-Yenching Sinological Index Series, Supplement no. 9. Beijing: Hafo Yenjing xueshe, 1934.

Maoshi zhushu 毛詩注疏. Comp. Ruan Yuan 阮元. *GXJB.*

Maspero, Henri. "La Composition et la date du *Tso tchouan.*" In *Mélanges chinois et bouddhiques,* 1: 137–215. Brussels: Institut Belge des Hautes Etudes Chinoises, 1931–32.

Mather, Richard B. *Shih-shuo Hsin-yü: A New Account of Tales of the World.* Minneapolis: University of Minnesota Press, 1976.

Mawangdui Hanmu boshu 馬王堆漢墓帛書. Vol. 1. Beijing: Wenwu, 1980.

McMullen, David. *State and Scholars in T'ang China.* Cambridge: Cambridge University Press, 1988.

Metzger, Thomas A. *Escape from Predicament.* New York: Columbia University Press, 1977.

Mou Runsun 牟潤孫. "Lun ru shi liangjia zhi jiangjing yu yishu" 論儒釋兩家之講經與義疏. *Xin Ya xuebao* 新亞學報 4, no. 2 (Feb. 1960): 353–415.

Morohashi Tetsuji 諸橋轍次. *Keigaku kenkyū josetsu* 經學研究序說. Tokyo: Meguro shoten, 1936.

———. *Shikyō kenkyū* 詩經研究. Tokyo: Meguro shoten, 1912.

Mozi 墨子. Harvard Yenching Sinological Index Series, Supplement no. 21. Beijing: Hafo Yanjing xueshe, 1948.

Mueller-Vollmer, Kurt, ed. *The Hermeneutics Reader: Texts of the German Tradition from the Enlightenment to the Present.* New York: Continuum, 1985.

Murayama Yoshihiro 村山吉廣. "Kaidai Kan Yu '*Shi no jo gi*'" 解題韓愈詩之序議. *Shikyō kenkyū* 詩經研究 1 (1975): 21–22.

Nivison, David S. "The Problem of 'Knowledge' and Action' in Chinese Thought Since Wang Yang-ming." In *Studies in Chinese Thought,* ed. Arthur F. Wright, pp. 112–45. 1953. Reprinted—Chicago: University of Chicago Press, 1967.

Norman, Jerry. *Chinese.* Cambridge: Cambridge University Press, 1988.

Noth, Martin. *A History of the Pentateuchal Traditions.* Englewood Cliffs, N.J.: Prentice Hall, 1971.

Ōkawa Tokitaka 大川節尚. *Tei Gen no shikyō gaku* 鄭玄の詩經學. Tokyo: Seki shoin, 1937.

Ouyang Xiu 歐陽修. *Ouyang Wenzhong gong ji* 歐陽文忠公集. *SBCK.*

—————. *Ouyang Yongshu ji* 歐陽永叔集. *GXJB.*

—————. *Shi benyii* 詩本義. *SBCK.*

Owen, Stephen. "The Self's Perfect Mirror: Poetry as Autobiography." In *The Vitality of the Lyric Voice: Shih Poetry from the Late Han to the T'ang,* ed. Shuen-fu Lin and Stephen Owen, pp. 71–102. Princeton: Princeton University Press, 1986.

—————. *Traditional Chinese Poetry and Poetics: Omen of the World.* Madison: University of Wisconsin Press, 1985.

Pan Zhonggui 潘重規. "*Shixu* mingbian" 詩序明辨. *Xueshu jikan* 學術季刊 4, no. 4 (June 1956): 20–25.

—————. "*Wujing zhengyi* tanyuan" 五經正義探源. *Huagang xuebao* 華岡學報 1 (June 1965): 13–22.

Perrin, Norman. *The New Testament: An Introduction.* 2nd ed. New York: Harcourt Brace Jovanovich, 1982.

Petersen, Willard J. "Making Connections: 'Commentary on the Attached Verbalizations' of the *Book of Change.*" *Harvard Journal of Asiatic Studies* 42 (1982): 67–116.

Pi Xirui 皮錫瑞. *Jingxue lishi* 經學歷史. Ed. and annotated by Zhou Yutong 周予同. Beijing: Zhonghua, 1959.

—————. *Jingxue tonglun* 經學通論. Beijing: Zhonghua, 1954.

Picken, Laurence E. R. "The Shapes of the *Shi Jing* Song-texts and Their Musical Implications." *Musica Asiatica* 1 (1977): 85–109.

—————. "Twelve Ritual Melodies of the T'ang Dynasty." In *Studia Memoriae Bela Bartok Sacra,* 2nd ed., pp. 147–73. Budapest: Aedes Academiae Scientiarum Hungariae, 1957.

Pope, Marvin H. *Song of Songs: A New Translation with Introduction and Commentary.* The Anchor Bible, vol. 7. Garden City, N.Y.: Doubleday, 1977.

Pound, Ezra, trans. *Shih-ching: The Classic Anthology as Defined by Confucius.* Cambridge: Harvard University Press, 1954.

Pulleyblank, E. G. "Chinese Historical Criticism: Liu Chih-chi and Ssu-ma Kuang." In *Historians of China and Japan,* ed. W. G. Beasley and E. G. Pulleyblank, pp. 135–66. London: Oxford University Press, 1961.

—————. "Neo-Confucianism and Neo-Legalism in T'ang Intellectual Life, 775–805." *The Confucian Persuasion,* ed. Arthur F. Wright, pp. 77–114.

Qian Mu 錢穆. *Liang Han jingxue jin gu wen pingyi* 兩漢經學今古文平議. Hong Kong: Xinya yanjiusuo [1958].

———. *Zhuzi xin xue'an* 朱子新學案. 5 vols. Taibei: Sanmin, 1971.

Qiu Guangting 邱光庭. *Jianming shu* 兼明書. *CSJC*.

Ricouer, Paul. *Hermeneutics and the Human Sciences*. Cambridge: Cambridge University Press; Paris: Editions de la Maison des Sciences de l'Homme, 1981.

Riegel, Jeffrey K. "Poetry and the Legend of Confucius's Exile." *Journal of the American Oriental Society* 106, no. 1 (Jan.–Mar. 1986): 13–22.

———. "Reflections on an Unmoved Mind: An Analysis of *Mencius* 2A2." *Journal of the American Academy of Religion* 47, no. 3, Thematic Issue 5 (Sept. 1980): 433–57.

Schneider, Laurence A. *Ku Chieh-kang and China's New History*. Berkeley: University of California Press, 1971.

Schwartz, Benjamin I. *The World of Thought in Ancient China*. Cambridge: Harvard University Press, 1985.

Seidel, Anna. "Imperial Treasures and Taoist Sacraments—Taoist Roots in the Aprocrypha." In *Tantric and Taoist Studies in Honour of R. A. Stein*, vol. 2, ed. Michel Strickmann, pp. 291–371. Brussels: Institute Belge des Hautes Etudes Chinoises, 1983.

Shchutskii, Iulian K. *Researches on the I Ching*. Trans. William L. MacDonald and Tsuyoshi Hasegawa with Hellmut Wilhelm. Princeton: Princeton University Press, 1979.

Shiji 史記. Comp. Sima Qian 司馬遷. Beijing: Zhonghua, 1962.

Shirakawa Shizuka 白川靜. *Shikyō kenkyū* 詩經研究. Kyoto: Hōyū shoten, 1981.

Shuowen jiezi zhu 說文解字注. Comp. Xu Shen 許慎. Annotated by Duan Yucai 段玉裁. Jingyun lou 經韻樓 ed. Reprinted—Taibei: Yiwen, 1974.

Siku quanshu zongmu tiyao 四庫全書總目提要. *Wanyou wenku* 萬有文庫.

Skinner, Quentin. "Motives, Intentions and the Interpretation of Texts." *New Literary History* 3, no. 2 (Winter 1972): 393–408.

Song shi 宋史. Comp. Tuo Tuo 托托 et al. Beijing: Zhonghua, 1977.

Soulen, Richard N. *Handbook of Biblical Criticism*, 2nd rev. ed. Atlanta: John Knox Press, 1981.

Stevens, Wallace. *Collected Poems of Wallace Stevens*. New York: Alfred A. Knopf, 1968.

Stimson, Hugh M. *The Jongyuan in yunn*. New Haven: Yale University, Far Eastern Publications, 1966.

Su Che 蘇轍. *Shi jizhuan* 詩集傳. *SQZB*.

———. *Su Ziyou Luancheng ji* 蘇子由欒城集. Shanghai: Dadong shuju, 1936.

Su Weiyue 蘇維嶽. "Lun *Shixu*" 論詩序. *Guofeng* 國風 7, no. 4 (Nov. 1935): 22–29.

Sung, Z. D. *The Text of Yi King*. New York: Paragon, 1969.

Takeuchi Yoshio 武內義雄. *Rongo no kenkyū* 論語の研究. Tokyo: Iwanami, 1940.

Taki Kumanosuke 瀧熊之助. *Shina keigaku shi gairon* 支那經學史概論. Tokyo: Taimeidō, 1934.

Tam, Koo-yin. "The Use of Poetry in *Tso Chuan*." Ph.D. dissertation, University of Washington, 1975.

Tang Junyi 唐君毅. *Zhongguo zhexue yuanlun* 中國哲學原論, vol. 2, *Yuandao lun* 原道論. Taibei: Xinya, 1976.

T'ang, Yung-t'ung (Tang Yongtong) 湯用彤. "Wang Pi's New Interpretation of the *I-ching* and *Lun-yü*." Trans. Walter Liebenthal. *Harvard Journal of Asiatic Studies* 10 (1947): 124–61.

―――. *Wei Jin xuanxue lungao* 魏晉玄學論稿. Beijing: Renmin, 1957.

―――. "Yan yi zhi bian" 言意之辨. In idem, *Wei Jin xuanxue lungao*, pp. 26–47.

Tillman, Hoyt Cleveland. *Utilitarian Confucianism: Ch'en Liang's Challenge to Chu Hsi*. Cambridge: Harvard University, Council on East Asian Studies, 1982.

Tjan, Tjoe Som. *Po Hu T'ung: The Comprehensive Discussions in the White Tiger Hall*. 2 vols. Leiden: E. J. Brill, 1949, 1952.

Trilling, Lionel. *Sincerity and Authenticity*. Cambridge: Harvard University Press, 1972.

Ts'ai Yung-ch'un. "The Philosophy of Ch'eng I." Ph.D. dissertation, Columbia University, 1950.

Tsuda Sōkichi 津田左右吉. *Rongo to Kōshi no shisō* 論語と孔子の思想. Tokyo: Iwanami, 1946.

Tu Wei-ming. "'Inner Experience': The Basis of Creativity in Neo-Confucian Thinking." In idem, *Humanity and Self-Cultivation: Essays in Confucian Thought*, pp. 102–10. Berkeley, Calif.: Asian Humanities Press, 1979.

―――. "The 'Thought of Huang-Lao': A Reflection on the *Lao Tzu* and Huang Ti Texts in the Silk Manuscripts of Ma-wang-tui." *Journal of Asian Studies* 39 (Nov. 1979): 95–110.

Twitchett, Denis. *Printing and Publishing in Medieval China*. London: Wynkyn de Worde Society, 1983.

Waley, Arthur, trans. *The Analects of Confucius*. 1938. Reprinted—New York: Vintage Books, n.d.

―――. *The Book of Songs*. London: George Allen & Unwin, 1937.

―――. *The Way and Its Power: A Study of the Tao Tê Ching and Its Place in Chinese Thought*. New York: Grove Press, 1958.

Wang, C. H. *The Bell and the Drum: Shih Ching as Formulaic Poetry in an Oral Tradition*. Berkeley: University of California Press, 1974.

Wang Fuzhi 王夫之. *Jiangzhai shihua jianzhu* 薑齋詩話箋注. Annotated by Dai Hongsen 戴鴻森. Taibei: Muduo, 1982.

Wang Guowei 王國維. *Hanwei boshi kao* 漢魏博士考. *Xueshu congshu* 學術叢書.

Wang Li 王力. *Hanyu shilü xue* 漢語詩律學. Shanghai: Jiaoyu chubanshe, 1962.

Wang Xianqian 王先謙. *Shi sanjia yi jishu* 詩三家義集疏. In *Shisi jing xinshu*

十四經新疏, 2nd series, comp. Yang Jialuo 楊家駱. Taibei: Shijie, 1956–61.

Wang Yinglin 王應麟. *Kunxue jiwen* 困學記聞. *GXJB.*

———. *Shi dili kao* 詩地理考. *CSJC.*

———. *Shikao* 詩考. *CSJC.*

Wang Zhi 王質. *Shi zong wen* 詩總聞. *CSJC,* 1st series, vols. 1712–15.

Ware, James R., trans. *The Sayings of Mencius.* New York: Mentor Books, 1960.

Watson, Burton. *Early Chinese Literature.* New York: Columbia University Press, 1962.

———, trans. *Complete Works of Chuang Tzu.* New York: Columbia University Press, 1968.

Wechsler, Howard J. *Offerings of Jade and Silk: Ritual and Symbol in the Legitimation of the T'ang Dynasty.* New Haven: Yale University Press, 1985.

Wei Peilan 魏佩蘭. "*Maoshi xu zhuan* weiyi kao" 毛詩序傳違異考. *Dalu zazhi* 大陸雜誌 33, no. 8 (Oct. 1966): 15–21.

Wenxuan 文選. Comp. Xiao Tong 蕭統. *SBCK.*

Wheatley, Paul. *The Pivot of the Four Quarters: A Preliminary Enquiry into the Origin and Character of the Ancient Chinese City.* Chicago: Aldine, 1971.

Wong, Siu-kit. "*Ch'ing* and *Ching* in the Critical Writings of Wang Fu-chih." In *Chinese Approaches to Literature from Confucius to Liang Ch'i-ch'ao,* ed. Adele Austin Rickett, pp. 121–50. Princeton: Princeton University Press, 1978.

Wright, Arthur F., ed. *The Confucian Persuasion.* Stanford: Stanford University Press, 1960.

———. "T'ang T'ai-tsung and Buddhism." In *Perspectives on the T'ang,* ed. Arthur F. Wright and Denis Twitchett, pp. 239–63. New Haven: Yale University Press, 1973.

Wu Jing 吳兢. *Zhenguan zhengyao* 貞觀政要. Shanghai: Guji, 1978.

Wu qiu bei zhai Lunyu jicheng 無求備齋論語集成. Comp. Yan Lingfeng 嚴靈峰. Taibei: Yiwen, 1966.

Xu Chengyu 徐澄宇 (Xu Ying 徐英). *Shijingxue zuanyao* 詩經學纂要. Shanghai: Zhonghua, 1936.

Xunzi 荀子. *SBBY.*

Yang Bojun 楊伯俊. *Lunyu yizhu* 論語譯注. Beijing: Zhonghua, 1958.

Yen Chih-tui (Yan Zhitui 顏之推). *Family Instructions for the Yen Clan.* Trans. Teng Ssu-yü. Leiden: E. J. Brill, 1969.

Yili 儀禮. *SBCK.*

Yoshikawa, Kōjirō. *An Introduction to Sung Poetry.* Trans. Burton Watson. Cambridge: Harvard University Press, 1967.

Yu, Pauline, "Allegory, Allegoresis, and the *Classic of Poetry.*" *Harvard Journal of Asiatic Studies* 43, no. 2 (Dec. 1983): 377–412.

———. *The Reading of Imagery in the Chinese Poetic Tradition.* Princeton: Princeton University Press, 1987.

Yu Ying-shih, "Morality and Knowledge in Chu Hsi's Philosophical System." In *Chu Hsi and Neo-Confucianism*, ed. Wing-tsit Chan, pp. 228–54. Honolulu: University of Hawaii Press, 1986.

Yu Zhengxie 俞正燮. *"Wujing zhengyi"* 五經正義. In idem, *Guisi cungao* 癸巳存稿, pp. 57–58. Shanghai: Shangwu, 1937.

Zhang Xitang 張西堂. *Shijing liulun* 詩經六論. Shanghai: Shangwu, 1957.

Zhang Zai 張載. *Zhang Zai ji* 張載集. Beijing: Zhonghua, 1978.

———. *Zhangzi quanshu* 張子全書. *GXJB*.

Zheng Qiao 鄭樵. *Shi bian wang* 詩辨妄. Ed. Gu Jiegang 顧頡剛. Beijing: Pushe, 1933.

Zheng Xuan 鄭玄. *Zhengshi yishu* 鄭氏遺書. *Qingdai gaoben baizhong huikan* 清代稿本百種彙刊.

Zheng Zhenduo 鄭振鐸. "Du *Maoshi xu*" 讀毛詩序. In *Gushi bian*, ed. Gu Jiegang, 3: 382–401.

Zhou Yutong 周予同. *Jing jin gu wen xue* 經今古文學. Taibei: Shangwu, 1966.

Zhouli 周禮. *SBCK*.

Zhouyi 周易. *SBCK*.

Zhu Guanhua 朱冠華. "Guanyu *Maoshi xu* de zuozhe wenti" 關於毛詩序的作者問題. *Wen shi* 文史 16 (Nov. 1982): 177–87.

Zhu Xi 朱熹. *Hui'an xiansheng Zhu Wengong wenji* 晦庵先生朱文公文集. *SBCK*.

———. *Shi jizhuan* 詩集傳. Hong Kong: Zhonghua, 1961.

———. *Shi jizhuan* 詩集傳. *SBCK*.

———. *Shixu bian* 詩序辨. *Zhuzi yishu* 朱子遺書.

———. *Shizhuan yishuo* 詩傳遺說. Comp. Zhu Jian 朱鑑. *SQZB*.

———. *Zhuzi yishu* 朱子遺書. Taibei: Yiwen, 1969.

———. *Zhuzi yulei* 朱子語類. Taibei: Zhengzhong, n.d.

Zhu Yizun 朱彝尊. *Jingyi kao* 經義考. N.p.: Zhejiang shuju, 1897.

Zhu Ziqing 朱自清. *Shi yan zhi bian* 詩言志辨. Shanghai: Kaiming, 1947.

Zhuangzi yinde 莊子引得. Harvard-Yenching Sinological Index Series, no. 20. Cambridge: Harvard University Press, 1956.

Chinese Character List

The entries are ordered alphabetically, word by word.

Anhui 安徽
ansong 暗誦
bei 背
"Beishan" 北山
beixue 北學
ben 本
"Benmo lun" 本末論
benqing 本情
benyi 本意
benyii 本義
bi 比
bian ("changed," "changing") 變
bian ("disputation," "show") 辨
bianfeng 變風
bo ("broad learning") 博
bo ("pressing on") 迫
Bo You 伯有
Bochun 伯淳
boshi 博士
Boyu 伯魚
bubi xiangxiang jihuo 不必想像計獲
bushu 不恕
buyao zuanyan lishuo 不要鑽研立說
Cai Bian 蔡卞
Cao Cuizhong 曹粹中
Chang 長
Chao Buzhi 晁補之
Chao Gongwu 晁公武

Chao Yuezhi 晁說之
chen 陳
Chen 陳
Chen Gang 陳亢
Chen Huan 陳奐
Chen Lie 陳烈
Chen Qiaocong 陳喬樅
Chen Zhensun 陳振孫
cheng 誠
Cheng, King of Zhou 周成王
Cheng Boyu 成伯瑜
Cheng Dachang 程大昌
Cheng Hao 程顥
Cheng Mingdao 程明道
cheng wen 成文
Cheng Yi 程頤
Cheng Yichuan 程伊川
chengu 陳古
chi 持
Chonger 重耳
"Chuanshou" 傳受
"Chuci" 楚茨
Chuilong 垂隴
"Chun zhi benben" 鶉之奔奔
Chunqiu 春秋
Chunqiu zhuan 春秋傳
ci ("satire," "satirize," "jab") 刺
ci ("song") 詞

ci ("words") 辭
ci jin 刺今
congrong wanwei 從容玩味
Cui Shu 崔述
Da Mao gong 大毛公
Da Tang yayue 大唐雅樂
daifu qi 大夫妻
"Daju" 大車
Dan Zhu 啖助
dang 黨
dao ("guide," "way," "the Way")
  道
dao zhi 道之
daodi 到底
daoli 道理
daosha 倒殺
"Datian" 大田
"Daxia" 大夏
"Daxu" 大序
Daxu 大序
Daxue 大學
"Daya" 大雅
daya 大雅
dayi 大意
dayuezhe 達樂者
de 德
de qi suo 得其所
de shao wei zu 得少為足
di 禘
dier shi 第二事
dier yi 第二義
dingben 定本
dong 動
Dong Zhongshu 董仲舒
"Dongfang zhi ri" 東方之日
du 讀
"Du Shi fa" 讀詩法
dushu 讀書
"Dushu fa" 讀書法
Du Yu 杜預
Du Yuankai 杜元凱
duanzhang 斷章
dujiang 都講
dushu fa 讀書法
Erya 爾雅
Fan Chi 樊遲
Fan Ye 范曄

Fan Zhongyan 范仲淹
fanfanran 泛泛然
fanfu 反覆
fanfu kanlai kanqu 反覆看來看去
fanfu tiyan 反覆體驗
fanfu wanwei 反覆玩味
Fangzhai shishuo 放齋詩說
fei shi wei 非是謂
"Fei shier zi" 非十二子
fei yiren zhi zuo 非一人之作
feng ("indirect criticism") 諷
feng ("wind," "sway," "Air") 風
feng zhi shi 風之始
fenghua 風化
fengjiao 風教
fengsu 風俗
fu ("recite," "recitation";
  "rhapsody"; "direct
  presentation") 賦
fu ("repeat") 復
Fu Bi 富弼
Fu Guang 輔廣
Fu Qian 服虔
Fu Zishen 服子慎
furen 夫人
fushi 賦詩
Fuyang 阜陽
"Fuyou" 蜉蝣
fuzi 夫子
gandong ren zhi shanxin 感動人之
  善心
"Gaoyang" 羔羊
Gaozong, Emperor of Tang 唐高宗
Gaozu, Emperor of Han 漢高祖
Gaozu, Emperor of Tang 唐高祖
ge yu qi dang 各於其黨
gong 宮
Gong, Duke of Cao 曹共公
"Gongmeng" 公孟
Gongxi Hua 公西華
Gongyang Commentary 公羊傳
gu 故
Gu Jiegang 顧頡剛
"Gu ming" 顧命
Gu Sou 瞽瞍
guan ("head," "beginning") 冠
guan ("observe") 觀

guan guan 關關
"Guanju" 關雎
"Gufeng" 谷風
Guliang Commentary 穀梁傳
guo 國
Guo Xiang 郭象
"Guofeng" 國風
guofeng 國風
guoren 國人
guoshi 國史
Guoyu 國語
guwen 古文
guxu 古序
Han 韓
Han Qi 韓琦
Han Ying 韓嬰
Han Yu 韓愈
Hanshi waizhuan 韓詩外傳
Hanshu 漢書
hao se 好色
he 河
He Yan 何晏
Heng 亨
heqi 和氣
"Heshui" 河水
houfei 后妃
housheng 後生
houxu 後序
Hu Anguo 胡安國
Hu Yuan 胡瑗
hua 化
Hua Ding 華定
Huan, Duke of Qi 齊桓公
Huang-Lao 黃老
Huang Kan 皇侃
"Huangniao" 黃鳥
"Huangyi" 皇矣
huanle 歡樂
"Huashu" 華黍
Hubei 湖北
Huilin 慧林
huyan 互言
ji 記
Jia Puyao 賈普曜
Jia Yi 賈誼
jiafa 家法
jian ("annotations") 箋

jian ("remonstrate," "remon-
   strance") 諫
jiande ci yi zhang chele) 見得此一章
   徹了
"Jiang Zhongzi" 將仲子
jiangjing 講經
jianjie 見解
jiankan weiduzhe 兼看未讀者
jiao 教
jiaojiao ran 嘐嘐然
jiaoqing 矯情
jiaren xishi 家人細事
jide 記得
Jie 桀
jie 解
"Jie bi" 解蔽
jie zhi 節之
"Jieshuo" 解說
jieyu 接余
jiezhi 節制
Jigu lu 集古錄
jihuo 計獲
Jin 晉
jing ("calm," "peaceful") 靜
jing ("classic") 經
Jing, Emperor of Han 漢景帝
Jingnü 靜女
jingshi zhi ye 經士之業
jingshu 精熟
jingsi 精思
jingxue 經學
"Jingxue fenli shidai" 經學分立時代
jingyii 經義
jinren 今人
jinri 今日
jinshi 進士
Jinsilu 近思錄
jinwen 今文
jinyao chu 緊要處
"Jiong" 駉
Jisun 季孫
jiu 鳩
Jixia 稷下
jiyi 己意
ju wen qiu yii 據文求義
juan 卷
"Kai feng" 凱風

Kaiyuan 開元
kan 看
kao 考
Kao gu bian 考古編
kaozheng 考證
Kong Anguo 孔安國
Kong Qiu 孔丘
Kong Yingda 孔穎達
"Kongzi shijia" 孔子世家
kouzhong du 口中讀
kuangzhe 狂者
kuanxin 寬心
le 樂
lei 類
li (measure of distance) 里
li ("principle") 理
li ("rites," "ritual," "ceremony") 禮
Li Gou 李覯
Li Guang 李光
li jianjie 立見解
Liang Qichao 梁啓超
Liji 禮記
lile 立了
lile yi 立了意
lin 麟
Lin Guangchao 林光朝
"Linzhi" 麟趾
"Linzhizhi" 麟之趾
Liu Anshi 劉安世
Liu Chang 劉敞
Liu De 劉德
Liu Xiang 劉向
Liu Xuan 劉炫
Liu Zhiji 劉知幾
Liu Zhuo 劉焯
Liujing aolun 六經奧論
"Liuyue" 六月
Lo 洛
Lu 魯
Lu Chun 陸淳
Lu Deming 陸德明
Lu Ji 陸機
Lu You 陸游
lun ("arrange") 綸
lun ("discuss," "discussion") 論
lun ("relate") 倫
lun ("wheel") 輪

Lunheng 論衡
Lunyu 論語
Lunyu jijie 論語集解
Lunyu yiishu 論語義疏
Lunyu zhengyii 論語正義
Lupu Gui 盧蒲癸
Lü Zuqian 呂祖謙
"*Lüshi jiashu du Shi ji* houxu")
　呂氏家塾讀詩記後序
Ma Jiayun 馬嘉運
Ma Rong 馬融
maitou lihui, buyao qiuxiao 埋頭裡會
　不要求效
Mao 毛 school
Mao gong 毛公
Maoshi 毛詩
"*Maoshi daxu*" 毛詩大序
Maoshi guxun zhuan 毛詩詁訓傳
Maoshi jian 毛詩箋
Maoshi mingwu jie 毛詩名物解
Maoshi xiaozhuan 毛詩小傳
Maoshi xu 毛詩序
Maoshi zhengyii 毛詩正義
Maoshi zhishuo 毛詩指說
Maoshi zhuan 毛詩傳
Master Gao 高子
Mawangdui 馬王堆
mei 美
mei renqing 沒人情
Mei Yaochen 梅堯臣
Meng Ke 孟軻
Mengzi 孟子
Mengzi zhangju 孟子章句
mian 沔
"Mianshui" 沔水
ming 名
ming hu 明乎
"Minlao" 民勞
mo 末
Mozi 墨子
Mu, Duke of Shao 召穆公
Mu Shu 穆叔
Nan Rong 南容
nan yi yi fa tui zhi 難以一法推之
nanxue 南學
nei 內
neiji 內集

ni ("meet") 逆
ni ("mire," "enmired") 泥
ni wenyii 泥文義
nigu 泥古
nüshi 女史
Ouyang Xiu 歐陽修
"Pan Geng" 盤庚
"Pao you kuye" 匏有苦葉
Peng Meng 逢蒙
pian 篇
po 迫
qi 氣
Qi 齊
Qi Wei 齊威
qi zhi shuai 氣之帥
qianjiu 遷就
qianshuai 牽率
qianxu 前序
Qieyun 切韻
Qijing xiaozhuan 七經小傳
Qin 秦
Qin Guan 秦觀
qing 情
Qing Feng 慶封
qing fu 輕浮
Qingli 慶曆
qingtan 清談
Qiu Guangting 丘光庭
"Qiyue" 七月
qu 取
quan 勸
Quan Zuwang 全祖望
quanshixue 詮釋學
"Quanxue" 勸學
que ("blank") 闕
que ("magpie") 鵲
"Quechao" 鵲巢
qun 群
"Qusheyii" 取捨義
Ran You 冉有
ren ("human") 人
ren ("humane," "humaneness") 仁
"Renjian shi" 人間世
renli 人理
renqing 人情
rensheng jiqu 恁生記去
Rong 戎

ru 入
Ru 儒
Ruan Yuan 阮元
"Rufen" 汝墳
san ti 三體
"Sangzhong" 桑中
sanjia 三家
Sanjing (xin) yi 三經(新)義
shang 商
"Shang liangzhi zhugong shu"
　　上兩制諸公書
"Shangshang zhe hua" 裳裳者華
Shao 韶
Shao, Duke of 召公
Shao Yong 邵雍
shaokan 少看
Shaonan 召南
shen 神
Shen Pei 申培
Shen Zhong 沈重
sheng ("sage") 聖
sheng ("sound," "voice") 聲
shengde 盛德
shengren 聖人
shengren suoyi yongxin 聖人所以用心
shengren yezhe, dao zhi guan ye
　　聖人也者, 道之管也
shengren zhi zhi 聖人之志
shenqiu wanwei 深求玩味
shi ("affairs") 事
shi ("beginning") 始
shi ("history," "historian") 史
shi ("Ode," "lyric") 詩
Shi 詩
Shi bian wang 詩辨妄
Shi dili kao 詩地理考
Shi jie 詩解
Shi kao 詩考
Shi lun 詩論
shi shou 詩首
Shi wei fan li shu 詩緯氾歷樞
shi yan shi qi zhi ye 詩言是其志也
shi yan zhi 詩言志
shi yi yan zhi 詩以言志
"Shi zhi xu lun" 詩之序論
"Shi zhi xu yi" 詩之序議
Shi zong wen 詩總聞

shifa 師法
Shiji 史記
Shijie tongxu 詩解通序
Shijing 詩經
Shijing xieyun kaoyi 詩經協韻考異
Shipu 詩譜
"*Shipu buwang* houxu" 詩普補亡
　後序
Shisan jing zhushu 十三經注疏
"Shishi lun" 時世論
Shishuo xinyu 世說新語
shiwen 詩文
shiyii 詩義
shou 首
Shu 書
shu 熟
Shu Duan 叔段
Shu jing 書經
shu wanwei 熟玩味
Shu Xiang 叔向
"Shu yu tian" 叔于田
shudu 熟讀
Shui jing zhu 水經注
Shun 舜
shunü 淑女
shuo 說
Shuowen jiezi 說文解字
Shusun 叔孫
si 思
si shi 四始
si wu xie 思無邪
Sibu beiyao 四部備要
Siku quanshu 四庫全書
siliang 思量
Sima Guang 司馬光
Sima Qian 司馬遷
Sima Xiangru 司馬相如
"Siyi" 絲衣
siyi 私意
"Song" 頌
Song 宋
song ("Laud") 頌
song ("poem"; "recite aloud";
　"repeat") 誦
Songren yishi huibian 宋人軼事彙編
Songshi yiwenzhi 宋史藝文志
Songshu 宋書

Su Che 蘇轍
Su Dongpo 蘇東坡
Su Shi 蘇軾
sui 歲
Sun Chuo 孫綽
Sun Fu 孫復
Sun Shi 孫奭
suoyi yongxin 所以用心
suoyi yun zhi yi 所以云之意
tai 胎
Taigong bingfa 太公兵法
taishi 太士
Taisi 太姒
Taizong 太宗
tanduo 貪多
Tao Qian 陶潛
ti 體
tian 天
Tiandao 天道
tianxia 天下
tianyi 天意
tianzhi 天志
ticha 體察
tihui 體會
tiren 體認
tiyan 體驗
tong guan 彤管
Tong zhi 通志
Tongguan yifan 彤管懿範
tuanzhuan 彖傳
tui zai xia 退在下
tuibu 退步
tuishi 退食
waiji 外集
waishu 外書
"Waiwu" 外物
wan 玩
Wan Zhang 萬章
Wang Anshi 王安石
Wang Bi 王弼
Wang Bo 王柏
Wang Chong 王充
Wang Dan 王旦
Wang Deshao 王德韶
Wang Fusi 王輔嗣
Wang Yinglin 王應麟
Wang Zhi 王質

"Wangzhi" 王制
wanwei 玩味
Wanyu wenku 萬有文庫
Wei 衛
wei ("do," "study") 為
wei ("savor," "taste") 味
wei ("subtle") 微
Wei Hong 衛宏
wei ren 為人
wei wen 為文
Wei Xiaowendi 魏孝文帝
Wei Zhao 韋昭
Wei Zheng 魏徵
weichi cixin 維持此心
wen ("cultivation," "literature,"
    "literary patterning or form")
    文
wen ("questions") 問
Wen, Duke of Jin 晉文公
Wen, Emperor of Han 漢文帝
Wen, King of Zhou 周文王
Wen, Marquis of Wei 魏文侯
wen ci 文辭
wenli 文理
"Wenti" 文體
Wenxuan 文選
wenyi 文意
wenyii 文義
wenzi 文字
Wu 吳
wu ("impose upon") 誣
wu ("non-being," "nothing") 無
Wu, Emperor of Han 漢武帝
Wu, Emperor of Liang 梁武帝
Wu, Emperor of Zhou 周武帝
wu jixing 無記性
wu xie 無邪
Wujing zhengyii 五經正義
xi ("bound up with," "tied to") 繫
xi ("small," "trivial," "intricacy")
    細
Xi, Duke of Lu 魯僖公
Xia 夏
Xian, Prince of Hejian 河間獻王
xian li ge yi 先立箇意
xian li ji yi 先立己意
xian zexiao 先責效

Xiang, Duke of Lu 魯襄公
xiangqian 向前
xiangshou 相授
xiangzhuan 象傳
xianman chu 閑慢處
Xianqiu Meng 咸丘蒙
xianru zhi shuo 先入之說
xiansheng 先生
"Xianxue" 顯學
Xianyun 玁狁
Xiao jing 孝經
Xiao Mao gong 小毛公
Xiao Tong 蕭統
xiao zuo kecheng 小作課程
Xiaoxu 小序
"Xiaoya" 小雅
xiaoya 小雅
xiaxu 下序
Xici zhuan 繫辭傳
xie 寫
Xie Liangzuo 謝良左
Xie Xiandao 謝顯道
xin 心
Xin Tang shu 新唐書
Xin Wudai shi 新五代史
xinfu 心腹
xing ("nature") 性
xing ("stimulate," "stimulus,"
    "inspire") 興
Xing Bing 邢昺
"Xing shu" 興述
xing yu ren 興於仁
xing yu shi 興於詩
"Xinglu" 行露
xinong 戲弄
xinqi 新奇
"Xiongzhi" 雄雉
"Xisang" 隰桑
xishi 細事
Xu 序
xu ("empty," "tenuous," "void") 虛
xu ("order"; "preface") 序
"*Xu Chuci xu*" 續楚辭序
Xu Xing 許行
Xu Yu 徐寓
Xuan, Duke of Wei 衛宣公
Xuan, King of Zhou 周宣王

xuanxue 玄學
xue 學
Xue Shilong 薛士龍
Xun Qing 荀卿
xunhuan kan 循環看
Xunzi 荀子
xuxin 虛心
ya ("crow") 鴉
ya ("elegant"; "Elegantia") 雅
ya yan 雅言
yan 言
yan bu jin yi 言不盡意
Yan Can 嚴粲
yan er zhi 言爾志
Yan Hui 顏回
Yan Shigu 顏師古
Yan Yuan 顏淵
yan zhi 言志
Yan Zhitui 顏之推
Yang 陽
Yang Liang 楊倞
Yang Zhizhi 楊志之
Yang Zhu 楊朱
yanxi 研習
Yao 堯
yayue 雅樂
ye 也
"Ye you mancao" 野有蔓草
"Ye you sijun" 野有死麕
Yi 易
yi ("conjecture") 億
yi ("discussion") 議
yi ("easy") 易
yi ("intention"; "opinion") 意
yi ("unity [of mind]") 壹
Yi, Marquis of Zeng 曾侯乙
Yi Feng 翼奉
yi guan qi zi zhi zhi 以觀七子之志
yi qi xin 易其心
yichu 疑處
yiguo 一國
yii 義
yiili 義理
yiishu 義疏
Yijing 易經
Yili 儀禮
Yili jingzhuan tongjie 儀禮經傳通解

yin ("debauched") 淫
yin (the feminine principle) 陰
yin ("tone") 音
"Yin zheng" 胤征
ying 應
ying chuanzao zhi 硬穿鑿之
ying chuanzuo zhi shi he 硬穿鑿之使合
Yingong Tuo 尹公佗
yinshi 淫詩
yinyangjia 陰陽家
yisi 意思
yiwei chang 意味長
yiyii 意義
"Yiyiijie" 一義解
"Yong" 雍
you dai yan 有待焉
yu ("farfetched") 迂
yu ("stand for") 喻
yu gao ru yu nan ru shezhe you zhi 予告汝于難如射者有志
yuan 怨
Yuan Gu 轅固
Yuanhe 元和
yue ("concision") 約
yue ("music") 樂
yuefu 樂府
"Yueji" 樂記
"Yuelun" 樂論
"Yuezhi" 樂志
Yugong Chai 庾公差
Yugong Zhisi 庾公之斯
"Yunhan" 雲漢
za 雜
zai xia 在下
ze 澤
Zeng Xi 曾皙
Zengzi 曾子
Zha, Duke of Wu 吳公子札
zhang 章
Zhang Boxing 張伯行
Zhang Liang 張良
Zhang Zai 張載
zhangju 章句
Zhangsun Wuji 張孫無忌
Zhao 趙
Zhao, Duke of Cao 曹昭公
Zhao, Duke of Lu 魯昭公

Zhao Cui 趙衰

Zhao Hongzhi 趙弘智

Zhao Kuang 趙匡

Zhao Meng 趙孟

Zhao Qi 趙歧

Zhao Qianxie 趙乾叶

Zheng 鄭

Zheng Kangcheng 鄭康成

Zheng Qiao 鄭樵

Zheng Xuan 鄭玄

Zhenyuan 貞元

zhi ("aim," "intention,"
  "project") 志

zhi ("go") 之

zhi ("point") 旨

zhi shi 志士

zhi yu 志於

zhi yu dao 志於道

zhini 滯泥

zhini er bu tong 滯泥而不通

zhiyi 志意

zhong 重

Zhongsun 仲孫

Zhou (legendary tyrant) 紂

Zhou, Duke of 周公

Zhou Dunyi 周敦頤

Zhouli 周禮

Zhounan 周南

zhu 逐

Zhu Xi 朱熹

zhuan 傳

zhuan yao zuo wenzi 傳要作文字

Zhuang, Duke of Zheng 鄭莊公

zhuanyi 傳一

zhuo 著

Zi Chan 子產

Zi Dashu 子大叔

Zi Zhan 子展

Zifan 子犯

Zigong 子貢

Zigong[a] 子弓

Zilu 子路

ziran kejian 自然可見

Zishi 子石

Zisi 子思

zixi 子細

zixi wanwei fanlai fanqu 子細玩味
  反來反去

Zixia 子夏

zixin 自信

Ziyou 子游

Zizhang 子張

Zizhuo Ruzi 子濯孺子

zizuo yisi 自作意思

"Zouyu" 騶虞

zouzuo 走作

zouzuo di xin 走作底心

zu 足

zuan niujiao jian 鑽牛角尖

zuanyan lishuo 鑽研立說

Zuo Qiuming 左丘明

zuoshi 作詩

Zuo zhuan 左傳

zuoyi 作意

Index

In this index an "f" after a number indicates a separate reference on the next page, and an "ff" indicates separate references on the next two pages. A continuous discussion over two or more pages is indicated by a span of page numbers, e.g., "57–59." *Passim* is used for a cluster of references in close but not consecutive sequence.

Library of Congress Cataloging-in-Publication Data

Van Zoeren, Steven Jay
  Poetry and personality : reading, exegesis, and hermeneutics in
traditional China / Steven Van Zoeren.
    p.   cm.
  Includes bibliographical references and index.
  ISBN 0-8047-1854-7 (cloth : acid-free paper) :
    1. Shih ching. I. Title.
PL2466.Z7V36 1991   90-38044
895.1'1—dc20   CIP
                                             Rev.

∞ This book is printed on acid-free paper

DATE DUE

DEMCO 38-297

MAR 1 7 1992